THE EXPERIENCE

BY

BRANDON WADE ALCOCER

This book is dedicated to my amazing parents, Steve and Joyce. Two people who have always supported my journey of self-discovery.

Chapter 1

Please...just tell me that you love me.

Professor Reid Bradley should be hustling into class, but he can't get himself to move; he's frozen stiff with a sharp pain in his chest. He steps away from the entrance to the lecture hall, gripping a briefcase in one hand and his cell phone in the other. The lecture is set to start in two minutes. He usually stands tall before entering; now he's hunched forward, struggling to steady his hand as he reads and re-reads the text message from Jasmine, his girlfriend of two years, his soon-to-be fiancée, his everything. She's texted to inform him that she can't make it to his birthday dinner this evening, due to a work deadline. A seemingly innocent text, yet he can't shake the heavy feeling in his gut, a feeling that he's all too familiar with.

His face burns as he continues to stare at the text, hoping she'll follow up with the magical three words that always make him feel better. Nothing. As much as he tries, he can't shake the sense that Jasmine isn't being herself. She's become increasingly distant since returning home from her friend's bachelorette party in Las Vegas a week ago. Something is happening that's pulling her away from him. And it's not her work.

He glances at the clock near the top of the screen; one minute before he must start the lecture. *Shit.* He's got one minute to figure out how to not be a jealous wreck in front of a hundred students, because today's lecture is supposed to include *how to never be a jealous wreck.* He stares at his shoes, aching to discover some form of relief. He could cancel class due to illness, but he knows the students are excited about today's lecture. He knows they're eager to learn from their social psychology professor, *the expert on relationships,* about how to manage jealousy and prevent infidelity.

Reid takes several deep breaths, hoping to calm himself. He glances at Jasmine's text one last time, forcing a smile. *My little angel works so hard.* He slides his phone back into his pocket and puts on a serene look for any students who may walk past.

He's in the middle of his first semester as a professor. Thus far, his class has caused a buzz throughout campus. The students take well to his modern, non-traditional teaching style. He rejects the option to teach like other professors who regurgitate facts from a textbook, showing up for their pay check while not giving two shits if the students connect with the material. His unique sense of empathy disallows such an approach. He doesn't judge his abilities by the amount of A's earned or F's given. He judges by the number of students waiting in line, desperately wanting to talk to him about relationship challenges during office hours. His answer to colleagues as to why his class maintains a high attendance rate: *students learn best through storytelling, not textbook lectures.* Today's lecture is set to include his story, the most uncomfortable truths about his story — except prior to this week he thought he'd mastered the mistakes of his past.

Reid enters the hall, absorbing the eager murmurs of dedicated undergrads. He strolls down the dividing row, continuing to force his smile, then sets his briefcase on the tall desk off to the side of the lecture stage. He centers himself in front of the white marker board, pops the cap off a dry-erase pen, then freezes again, feeling that sharp pain return to his chest. *I can't be a hypocrite in front of these students. Come on, Jasmine loves you. You know she loves you more than anything.*

He places the felt-tip marker on the board, but his hand goes weak and he drops the pen to the floor. He quickly scoops it up and, flushing, returns the pen to the board. He only needs to write one specific word. But this word represents the source of his suffering, his arch nemesis, something that's affected him since adolescence. Up until this past Sunday, he believed he had put that fire-spitting dragon to rest. *For good.*

An image of Jasmine's smile creeps into his mind, except her expression is not one of puppy love, but more like the conniving smile of a con-artist who got away with a crime. He struggles to steady his shaking hand as he writes the first letter on the board, I. The letter looks more like a serrated knife than a vowel. He erases the letter. *Get yourself together, man. Jasmine promised she would never hurt you. You have a hundred students watching.* He places the marker on the shelf below and grabs a different one, hoping the students assume his struggle is with a dulled dry-erase marker, not his cowardly thoughts. Reid steadies his wrist and writes the word:

INFIDELITY

The room goes silent. Reid stares at the written word, feeling blood drain from his head. Jasmine promised to never hurt him, swearing to never break his heart like the other women in his past.

He sets the pen on the shelf, straightens his spine, then turns to face the class. His gaze settles on several wide-eyed students, pens pressed on their notebooks, ready to fill the pages with words of wisdom. He walks to the center of the stage and takes a deep breath. *Focus on serving the students. They'll benefit from hearing about my truth.*

"Every girlfriend I've had in my life," says Reid, "has cheated on me."

Several students gasp, while others look befuddled.

"I'm embarrassed. As someone who teaches this stuff, I shouldn't have had so many negative experiences in relationships. I was a fool in the past, but the pain from my mistakes fuels the driving force within me. I'm determined to master the prevention of infidelity and share it with you. I'm being honest about my past, because I believe today's lecture will positively affect you more than any other lecture you will have throughout your life."

"All of your girlfriends cheated?" says Katie, an enthusiastic student who sits in the front row. "But you've said your current relationship is going well."

"I was referring to the three girlfriends prior. Jasmine and I are doing great." Reid grins, but feels a quiver inside his cheeks. "She's never cheated on me."

That's right, she's never cheated on me. It's silly of me to worry. She's just having a tough time with work. I'm sure missing my birthday dinner is the last thing she wants to do.

"Did you find out why those girlfriends were unfaithful?" asks a male student named Derek. "My girlfriend cheated on me when she found out I went to a strip club."

"It was my fault those girlfriends chose to be unfaithful," says

Reid. "I didn't give them enough attention. I became lazy. I only cooked for them three or four times a week, I only bought them gifts a few times a month. I never watched their favorite shows with them. I ignored their needs. However, I was lucky to be in college when it happened, because I went to my psychology professors for guidance, which helped immensely. Their suggestions mimic what's written in your textbook about unfaithfulness in relationships. Your assignment from last class was to read Chapter Seven. What did the book suggest are the main points of emphasis for preventing infidelity?"

"Don't go to strip clubs," says Derek. The class chuckles. And so does Reid.

"I've never been to one of those places — not really my thing." Reid wants to express that strip clubs are probably filled with disease-laden, slutty women who have daddy issues. But he holds his tongue, just in case there might be students who work such jobs in the class.

"If my man were to go to a strip club," says a woman in the back, "then he'd better be fine with me going to one as well. I've got no problem paying Mr. Muscles to shake his ding-a-ling in front of me."

The class erupts with laughter. Many students cover their mouths, turn to look at the woman, then look back at Reid.

Reid grins, pretending to laugh along, but tenses inside. Perhaps Jasmine went to a "Mr. Muscles" strip club in Vegas, considering she was part of a bachelorette party. Reid walks towards the chest-high desk. *She'd never do such a thing.* He turns on the projector, then pulls his laptop out of his briefcase and connects the projector cord to the laptop portal.

As the projector illuminates on the screen above the whiteboard, he locates the PowerPoint slides in the computer. He clicks on the slide labeled *Chapter 7 Infidelity.* Seeing that word again sparks a visualization of Jasmine having sex with another man. The sting in his heart intensifies. He shakes his head to scramble the image, but the resistance expands his agony, adding clarity to the picture in his mind's eye. Jasmine is being thrust into by a muscle-bound male stripper. She beams a vicious smile, as if she's happy to see Reid suffer from the sight of her bliss. His knees go weak. He bends over as if to tie his shoe, hiding behind the tall desk, panting with a heavy heart. He rises and glances at the students, then up at the screen. Warmth spreads along the back of his neck, as if they can somehow see his jealous visions projected on the screen as an X-rated movie.

"Are you okay, Professor?" says Katie.

Reid looks at Katie, nods, and looks at the screen, then back at the students. "Sorry, my brain got off track a bit." He clears his throat and reads the first slide. "Infidelity most often occurs because one partner gets lazy in the relationship. They stop taking into consideration the importance of fulfilling the needs of their partner. Clear communication is key. Each must be willing to listen to what the other desires and do their best to fulfill that request. Relationships are like the dinner plates that spin on sticks at the circus, constantly needing attention or they'll fall off." *I don't know why I'm so worried. I've certainly been on top of everything I just shared.*

"Can you call my boyfriend right now? He needs to hear this lecture," says a female student. "He's got no problem ignoring my needs."

"I'm willing to help any student who seeks guidance. Anyone can visit me during office hours," says Reid.

A student named John, who recently visited Reid for guidance, speaks out. "I've been giving my girlfriend a small bouquet of flowers every single day, just like you do for Jasmine. It's amazing — my girlfriend is always smiling and telling her friends how great a man I am."

"Well done," says Reid. "Those actions show how much you care. Don't stop — you are minimizing the chances of her becoming unfaithful."

"What do you do when you feel jealous?" says Katie. "I bet you never get jealous, since you teach this stuff for a living."

The mention of jealousy stirs the uneasy sensation inside Reid.

"I experience jealousy from time to time. Granted, this is my first semester teaching these topics since completing graduate school. I'm still a work in progress."

He stares at the floor for a moment, then returns his gaze to the students. "To be honest, I felt a bit of jealousy last weekend. Jasmine went to Las Vegas for her friend's bachelorette party and hardly communicated with me. I almost acted out of line and sent Jasmine a rude text. I kept envisioning her having a fling with some guy who was muscular and larger than me."

"No way," says Derek. "You're the superstar of relationships. I can't see you ever slipping up."

"I appreciate the compliment, but I'm far from being perfect. I had a moment of weakness. The thing to remember is that jealousy is emotional energy released due to an imagined threat. If you feel jealous, try to channel that energy into acts of love towards your partner. Work on your insecurities by giving more love."

As the class hums with responses, Reid silently thanks the class for reminding him that he's a great boyfriend and his fears are overblown.

"My brain was filled with jealous thoughts, but deep down I knew the thoughts were a protection mechanism which came from past experiences with women. We eventually talked on the phone while she was in Vegas. She claimed she was doing nothing wrong. It took some work, but I convinced myself to believe her. I then focused my jealous energy into doing acts of love. I cleaned our house, organized her closet, cooked our food for the week, and washed her car. I also had a bouquet of flowers waiting for her when she arrived home."

He hears several female students coo throughout the room. They always coo when he mentions flowers for Jasmine.

"Each of those actions helped ease the jealous thoughts in the moment. She had a warm smile when she walked in the house."

Although he had anticipated Jasmine being more appreciative and affectionate. He figured she was hungover.

He narrows his eyes. *She just doesn't seem to be as loving since she got home.* Again, Reid's mind conjures images of Jasmine with a male stripper; he sees her tiny hands grip the man's large biceps, hears her moan louder than she'd ever do with him.

He wiggles his head. *Stop it, man. Nothing happened.*

Reid continues the lecture, educating the students on how to better serve their partners, and finds as he does, his worries subside. The session nears its dismissal time. The students pack their belongings.

"I won't be having my office hours today," says Reid. "I apologize. You know that I'm always eager to help in any way I can. But today, I'm visiting my mom. She lives an hour away and I need to leave now to beat the traffic. And remember, next week we're off for Spring Break."

The students cheer, then shuffle out of the lecture hall. He pops open his briefcase, then sneaks a glance at a female student in the third row as she gathers her things. Although he maintains a strictly professional relationship with his students, he can't help his attraction to this particular student. Her name is Micah; she's stunning. He's secretly observed how Micah doesn't talk to anyone, and nor does she raise her hand to participate during the lecture. However, her shyness is in stark contrast to her choice of outfits: skin-tight leggings tucked into knee-high boots, and a tank top squeezed over C-cup breasts. *Today, a white tank top and white bra — excellent choice.* She stands, then bends over to pick up her bag. Reid catches a glimpse of a white G-string. *A matching set.* His eyes fixate on the curves of her backside, then scan towards her face.

Their eyes meet. He darts his gaze to the briefcase. Flushed, he packs away his laptop. *Even if I was single, I'd never be able to attract a woman like her. She looks just like the girls who teased me in high school and college. And she probably prefers to date tattooed biker-douche-bags who treat her like crap.*

"Any special occasion to visit your mom?" says a female voice.

Reid's throat tightens. *Micah?* He cocks his head upward, then sighs at the sight of Katie. He looks over Katie's shoulder, catching a last glimpse of Micah as she exits the room. He returns his attention to Katie, who appears perplexed by his ignoring of her question.

"Sorry, I thought I saw a student forget something in the back of the room. Umm, you asked about ... oh, visiting my mother. Yes, the special occasion is that tomorrow is my twenty-ninth birthday. My mom is cooking a birthday dinner tonight. Then tomorrow, Jasmine and I will drive to Las Vegas for a night of fun. I can't wait. I love Vegas."

"Awe, sounds fun," says Katie. "It seems like you and Jasmine are a match made in heaven. I hope to have a relationship like the two of you someday. You handled your jealousy really well."

"I'm sure your Mr. Wonderful is on his way to you," says Reid. "Stay focused on doing the right thing and I promise you'll always be rewarded. At times it can be exhausting, but I never miss a day being the best man I can be for Jasmine. I'm sure you'll be an amazing woman for your man as well."

Katie grins and walks away.

Reid sets his laptop in the briefcase, relieved that the students didn't seem to notice his internal struggle. Then his mind flips back to hearing breathless gasps from Jasmine and her mystery lover. Reid presses his fingers onto his temples and closes his eyes. *Stop torturing yourself. Everything is fine. You get to enjoy Mom's cooking tonight and Las Vegas tomorrow. Life can't get any better. Well, life would be better if Jasmine would come to dinner, but everything can't always be perfect.*

Chapter 2

Reid plans to stay overnight at his mom's house and pick Jasmine up in the morning. Prior to bed, he calls Jasmine to wish her goodnight, but the call goes straight to her voicemail. Such an occurrence isn't just odd, its concerning. They haven't missed saying "goodnight," in person or on the phone, since the day they met.

He explores the reasons why her phone might be turned off. She wouldn't let the phone battery die; there are battery chargers all over the house. He calls again, and it goes straight to her voicemail. Her phone is clearly turned off. The unsettling sensation in his core tightens. *Jasmine's phone is never turned off.*

After that, Reid can't continue fighting the jealous visions in his mind. He speeds home from his mom's and parks his car in his driveway. *This can't be happening ... not again.* Reid steadies his shaking wrist to examine his watch as the hands tick to midnight. He exits his car and walks towards the home that he and Jasmine rent.

Reid slides the key into the front door lock, searching for excuses to ease his fear. Maybe she dropped her phone in the toilet? Maybe she turned it off to avoid her boss. *She wouldn't think to fool around on me. I'm probably just overreacting.*

He pushes the door open and enters. His nose is hit with an unfamiliar scent. And it's not from food or candles. It's the scent of someone else being there. Reid hears faint moaning in the distance. Thoughts of fleeing race through his mind, but a rolling sensation in his gut nudges him towards facing reality. He moves down the hallway, fury building with each step. He's read every book on relationships, and been mentored by highly regarded professors — *this wasn't supposed to happen to me anymore.* As he steps closer, the sounds of bodies thumping together become louder. *After all I've done for you, Jasmine.*

He grips the door handle, but hesitates to turn it further. Something inside him senses that the moment he enters this room, his life will never be the same. He considers leaving and dealing with her later, but the vengeful curiosity in his gut overpowers all reasonable thoughts. He turns the handle and peeps through the cracked-open door. Jasmine is naked and lying on her back with someone thrusting into her. *You bitch.*

He explodes into the room. "What the hell is going on?"

The mystery lover steps away from Jasmine. Reid's testosterone-clouded eyes adjust to the reality of what he was witnessing. Jasmine was being penetrated by a penis, but it wasn't from a man. It was strapped onto a woman.

Jasmine scuffles off the bed and covers herself with a pillow. "What are you doing here? You don't live here anymore."

"What the hell are you talking about?" says Reid.

Jasmine winks while walking towards him. "Why are you here? Did you come by to get more of your stuff?" Jasmine winks a few more times.

"What the hell are you talking about? I live here. Why are you winking? I'm not playing along."

The woman rolls her eyes, then unhooks the strap-on. She gathers her clothes, and goes into the bathroom.

Jasmine lowers her voice. "Daphne is a lesbian. I told her I was single and we broke up six months ago. Don't screw this up for me. If she finds out we're together, I'll have to pay her."

"What the hell?" Reid lifts his palm to his brow.

Daphne returns from the bathroom wearing a black leather dress with the strap-on dildo dangling over her shoulder.

Reid turns to Daphne. "I don't know what Jasmine told you, but I live here and we're in a committed relationship." He rips open the closet and throws his clothes onto the bed. "This is all mine — the shirts, shoes, belts. I live here."

Jasmine looks at her friend. "I'm sorry, Daphne, I should've told you. He doesn't live here, but I let him store his stuff in the closet."

"You're a lying bitch," says Daphne. "Somebody here owes me three hundred dollars."

"You said I wouldn't have to pay," cries Jasmine. "Plus, you said you only charge two hundred."

"You're a prostitute?" says Reid.

Daphne turns to Jasmine. "You lied. You know I charge straight bitches. The price is two hundred for lip service plus another hundred for strap-on action."

"You hired a fucking whore?" says Reid.

"She said you're the worst lay ever," says Daphne. "I'd better get paid or I'm calling Claudel. You don't want him involved, trust me."

"I'm the worst you've ever had?" Reid glares at Jasmine.

Jasmine crumbles to the floor, then crawls to the corner of the room. She wraps her arms around her shins and sobs.

"Who's gonna pay me?" says Daphne.

"I don't want any trouble," says Reid. "I don't have cash on me. Will you accept a personal check and leave?"

"Make it out to 'cash' and add fifty. You'd better not cancel it, or else you're gonna have big problems."

Reid pulls a check book from his dresser, then scribbles out a check. Daphne snatches it from his hand, then storms off. He turns to face Jasmine and sees her head buried between her legs.

"I can't believe I had plans to marry you. I've been nothing but amazing to you and this is what I get in return? You disgust me." He grabs a duffle bag and stuffs it with enough clothing for an overnight stay. "In case you forgot, it's my birthday. I'm driving to Vegas right now, alone."

He glares at Jasmine as she looks up at him. He hopes she'll say something, anything that resembles an apology. Her gaze is cold and empty, but he waits still. Jasmine remains silent.

Reid knows the look all too well. It's the same look his past girlfriends had when caught; no remorse or shame, more like relief.

He walks to his car and embarks on the four-hour drive to Las Vegas. He swears to himself that he will never feel like this again. But he's said that before. He's tried all logical paths to solve this problem. He doesn't know what to do about it, but for now he knows one thing: he's got to get away.

Chapter 3

"Hello, sir. Welcome to the Cleopatra Hotel. How may I help you this morning?" says the clerk, whose nametag reads "Jen."

"Do you know how to give good relationship advice?" asks Reid. "I don't trust psychologists."

"I'm sorry, sir. I'm only allowed to discuss hotel accommodations. Do you have a reservation with us?"

"Forgive my silly question. It's been a long night for me." Reid hands Jen his credit card and identification. "I booked a room using your hotel app. I know it's five in the morning, but I was hoping to check in."

"It appears you booked our basic room. What brings you to Vegas, sir?"

"Today is my birthday," says Reid. "A few hours ago I caught my girlfriend having sex with a hooker, a female hooker, who I ended up having to pay."

"Oh my." Jen lifts her hand towards her chest.

"The whore charged an extra hundred for strap-on service." He rolls his eyes. "Even prostitutes know how to upsell."

"I'm sorry to hear that, sir. I can't say that I have any good advice for you. But at least you're in Vegas. Perhaps you would benefit from going a bit wild during your visit." She examines his identification and types on the computer.

"Go wild?" He taps his fingers on the desk. As he considers her suggestion, he realizes he doesn't even know how to go wild. Would that mean going to a strip club? Snorting cocaine, then hiring a prostitute and gambling away the few hundred dollars left in his bank account?

Jen returns her attention to Reid. "I upgraded your basic room to one of our Jacuzzi suites with a view of the fountain show across the street. The room number is thirty-three, thirty-three. Many believe it's the luckiest room we have."

Reid smiles as he takes the room key-card. He throws his bag over his shoulder, then walks through the casino towards the elevator. *A suite upgrade is a good start. Maybe I'll have a wild Vegas party in my suite like I've seen in movies.* He begins to sense that this town might show him what he's been missing — what he's searching for. He's been conservative throughout his life, an approach which seemingly leads to poor results. Why not try the opposite?

A group of scantily dressed women stroll towards Reid as he nears the bank of elevators. Though his heart flutters with attraction, he stares at the floor while they walk past. He loves Vegas, knowing the city is filled with beauties seeking adventure, but he's always been afraid to approach women.

He takes the elevator to his floor and enters the suite with wide eyes. He peeks at the marble bathroom, then goes into the oversized main room. The living area consists of modern furniture and floor-to-ceiling windows which provide a central view of the fountain show across the street.

He marvels at the majestic view, but his excitement soon dissipates as he moves his gaze away from the pond to the street corner and sees people handing out flyers, the flyers that typically advertise call girls. His suppressed pain creeps up through his stomach and into his mind. He wonders how Jasmine could not only cheat, but cheat with a prostitute. Was there more he could have done? He gazes at the fluffy bed, feeling his body crash from exhaustion. *Maybe I'll send her flowers when I wake up. Flowers always seem to make her smile.* He closes the blackout shades, slides into the bedsheets, and feels a sense of calm permeate his body as he falls asleep.

He wakes in the early evening and quickly grabs his phone, hoping to see a series of apologetic texts from Jasmine. There are a few birthday wishes from friends, but nothing from Jasmine. He slumps on the side of the bed, drops his face into his hands, and sobs. *She was my little angel. She promised to never hurt me. Why did she do this to me?*

Minutes pass; the tears run dry. He opens the curtains, then sees bursts of water streams dancing to Frank Sinatra's "Fly Me to the

Moon." While mouthing the lyrics, he feels slightly uplifted. The song connects him to his passion for this city. He's always loved Las Vegas and views himself as an advanced-level tourist. He has a solid understanding of the city layout and tourist traps, and a proper strategy when playing blackjack. He enjoys gambling, but plays conservatively. His entry-level professor salary only allows him to risk a few hundred dollars each trip.

The fountain show ends, leaving him to feel like a coat of numbing cream has been applied to his wound. He races to his bag and puts on his favorite pair of jeans and a white dress shirt — his go-to outfit. It was the outfit he'd wear when going out on the town with friends before meeting Jasmine two years ago. Except he didn't meet Jasmine in this outfit. He never met any women when going out. He was terrible at picking up women. He met Jasmine through an acquaintance of his mom's. And a similar story could be told of his other three girlfriends.

Reid exits the suite, walks to his car, and drives down the famous Las Vegas Boulevard — the Strip.

While driving, a radio commercial captures his attention. *"Come to Mick's Cabaret, the classiest gentlemen's club in town. Free admission to those who drive their own cars to our Sahara Avenue location."*

Reid wipes his clammy hands on his jeans, realizing the event with Jasmine could be a great excuse to check out Mick's Cabaret. If she somehow found out, he could tell her he was upset and sought revenge. He glances at the street sign and sees he's passing Desert Inn Road; Sahara Ave is next. He taps a finger on the steering wheel, surprised by his growing urge to be risqué. Truth is, he's secretly wanted to know what it would be like to experience a stripper, but never given himself permission to explore the taboo. And now he's by himself in Las Vegas, nobody will ever know. He shrugs, then turns his car onto Sahara Avenue, heading towards Mick's Cabaret.

He parks in the back of the Mick's Cabaret lot, but doesn't unbuckle his seatbelt. *People like me don't go to places like this.* Yet he can't ignore the strange sensation rising from his core, urging him to get out of the car and dip his toe in a pool of naughty. He looks at his phone, hoping to see a text that will rescue him. Something that says,

Happy Birthday, baby. I was a fool. I'm catching the next flight to meet you in Vegas. All he sees is the cell phone clock. He rubs the middle of his forehead and closes his eyes. The image of Jasmine and that hooker instantly arrives. He slams his fist on the center console. *How could Jasmine be attracted to a hooker?* Several seconds pass, then he sits up and unbuckles the seatbelt. *Hell, I had to pay for her damn hooker, might as well pay for one myself.*

He exits the car, then walks with heavy feet towards the entrance. He hears police sirens faintly in the distance, adding horsepower to his already rapid pulse. He nears a large bouncer, who nods at Reid. He can't ignore the sirens; they're getting louder. If the strip club is about to face a police raid, he'll be caught in the middle of it. His feet itch to run away. He looks at the bouncer, then pats his front pockets while lifting his eyebrows, implying that he's forgotten his wallet — even though he has his wallet. He turns, then speed-walks towards his car, hearing the police cars buzz past Mick's Cabaret.

He slumps into the car seat, knowing he used the police sirens as an excuse to chicken out. He can't understand why everything inside him wants to go inside the club, but he can't get himself to go in. Water droplets develop in his eyes, and he glances at the sun visor, trying to force the tears back.

He notices a car pull into the neighboring spot. His mouth falls agape as he watches a woman with a goddess-like figure step out of the coupe. He snaps his head to face his steering wheel, feeling flushed. She looked familiar. *Micah from class?* He slowly turns his head for a second glance. Their eyes connect, then he hastily turns away, bending towards the passenger seat. She isn't Micah, but she's just as attractive.

He waits for fifteen seconds, then sits up, glances at the rear-view mirror, and catches her plump backside as she walks away. Her presence disappears from the reflection, leaving Reid to examine himself in the mirror. *I'm not meant to experience a woman like that. I'm ugly and shy, and I have this stupid-looking, oversized head.* He turns on the ignition, unable to fight back the tears that roll down his cheeks. *And I'm a goddamned cry baby.* He steers the car out of the spot, then speeds off the lot. He stops at a nearby gas station, grabs a six-pack of beer, then returns to his hotel room.

While slouching in the chair near the window of his suite, he sips beer and takes in the view of the fountain show. Something's pinging at him. He considers that it might be Jasmine, or being afraid to visit the strip club, but something inside senses the ping beyond the obvious — like a call to action. He can't isolate it, and tells himself he's just overwhelmed.

His phone vibrates in his pocket. He springs up and pulls out his phone, hoping to see Jasmine's name. Instead, it's a text from his mom.

The 29th year of life is a significant year of change for many historical figures. Siddhartha left his life of riches to go on his journey to become the Buddha. Jesus stopped being a winemaker and focused on performing miracles. Julia Childs stopped being a spy and devoted her life to cooking. Today, my meditation vision portrayed a new life waiting for you. Be careful, but be courageous, my son.

He smiles; it's as though he feels his mom has pulled him in for a loving hug. He loves how she can be a bit "woo-woo spiritual" at times, but moments like this, he often wonders what a father might say. Reid has never had a father figure in his life. His dad passed away before his birth. A car accident took the life of his father and his father's mistress. As sweet as Reid's mom could be, she would ignore questions about his father, leaving Reid to assume he was a cheating asshole.

The fountain show finishes. Reid stands, lightly buzzed as he downs the last sip of beer number three, and places his hand on the window as he further examines the Strip. Behind the pond rests the brand-new Largo Hotel. Like an eager puppy, he hops in place as he recalls how it opened a month ago. An article he read called it one of the classiest party hotels in the world, with a hot-spot called the Diamond Bar.

Reid hurries to the bathroom for a squirt of cologne. Thoughts of being rejected during his days as a single man begin to creep into his mind, but things could be different now that he's older and working as a college professor. He leaves the room and embarks on the short walk to the Largo Hotel.

In the Diamond Bar he slides onto a bar stool in the middle of a long wooden bar facing a wall of liquor bottles and two TVs. The article he read was spot on in its description of this place: sharply dressed people talking vibrantly, scattered in booths and at high-top tables and chairs.

"Hi there. What can I make for you?" says the bartender. His name, Ronald, is typed on his nametag. The man's friendly tone contrasts with his wide physique, shaved bald head, and tattoos covering his arms and neck.

"A screwdriver, please." Reid turns to observe several groups of women sipping colorful drinks, while the men suck down beers at the booths behind the bar.

"Here you go." Ronald sets the glass of orange juice and vodka in front of Reid. "What's been the most interesting thing about your week so far?"

Reid draws a long sip through the straw, feeling the vodka sting his throat. "Last night, I discovered that my girlfriend is a whore." He sucks in another gulp.

"I've been there, man," says Ronald. "I've had a few girlfriends who turned out to be prostitutes as well. Remember — to them it's just a job. Except it can be annoying when they get arrested."

Reid gags mid-sip. He covers his mouth with a napkin, coughing until he regains his breath.

"She's not actually a prostitute," says Reid. "I meant — I caught her cheating. I thought prostitution was legal in Las Vegas?"

"Prostitution is illegal in Las Vegas and all of Clark County. It's legal in the next county over, an hour's drive away. However, that doesn't stop the ladies of the night from working in Vegas. The amount of money a woman can earn from turning tricks here outweighs the risk of jail time. I see working girls all over this town."

"Maybe I should start paying women for sex. At least then they wouldn't break my heart."

"Many men prefer that simplicity. A gentlemen's club would be a good place to see if you'd get comfortable with the idea. Those places are legal."

Reid struggles to swallow his next gulp. "Really? I don't think I could ever pay a woman for attention. I've spent my life learning how to be the best partner for a woman. I just don't know why I always end up getting screwed."

"Is that why you order a screwdriver?"

Reid smirks, then finishes the remainder of his drink. Two attractive women approach the bar and sit three seats away. He glances at them, then stares at his straw. *Here comes that old feeling — the misery of being single.* His mind flashes to the memory of a tragic moment when he was twelve years old.

After months of contemplation, the young Reid finally mustered up the courage to ask his first crush to be his girlfriend. He expressed his desire through a handwritten note that he slid into her locker. She never responded to him directly; instead she told the entire school she thought he smelled, was ugly, and had a head that was too large for his body. The indirect message made its way into the boys' locker room, where the boys called him Fathead and pelted him with deodorant bars.

Ronald refreshes Reid's drink. "This one is on me."

The gesture pulls Reid out of the flashback and he nods with gratitude.

Ronald leans closer. "Most nights around this time, a man enters this bar who is a bit of a woman whisperer. He is a pimp."

Reid's eyes bulge.

"Relax," says Ronald. "He's not an evil smack-a-ho pimp. Everyone who meets him ends up feeling better about themselves. You may want to engage in a chat." Ronald looks past Reid. "In fact, he's walking in right now."

A cool breeze hits the back of Reid's neck. He turns to see a tall, slender, mocha-skinned African-American man with a sharp triangular face and pronounced cheekbones. He's wearing a slim-fitting black suit with a matching black fedora that sports a white feather on the brim. The once dimly lit bar appears two shades brighter with this man's presence. Reid looks about and notices that most people have paused their conversations to observe the man. The pimp stops in the middle of the room, glances left and right, then strolls to the women sitting near Reid.

Reid stares on as the man goes into action, appearing to charm the two women. Within seconds, the ladies' closed-off posture shifts into wide-shouldered openness. The pimp interacts with both women like a maestro leading an orchestra. They appear to hang on his every word, then burst into giggles like two teenage girls meeting a pop star. The man is demonstrating a skillset that Reid has always dreamed of having — and never believed was possible. He leans in their direction, hoping to hear the conversation, but the surrounding bar banter drowns them out.

He watches the pimp instruct one of women to write her number on a napkin, and she obliges gratefully. Before now Reid had only seen such ease when watching James Bond movies. Reid centers himself, contemplating how he can talk to this man to learn more. The women take their drinks and exit. The pimp then sits at the bar, a seat apart from Reid.

"Ronald, my friend, the usual. Mescal, chilled." The man's voice rings out deep and clear, like a news anchor's.

"You got it. Did you know those women?" Ronald shakes the liquor with ice, then pours it into a small glass.

"I know them now." The pimp lifts his drink to toast Ronald. "Those women are the type who understand that fulfillment in life occurs through experiences derived from taking risks. Sadly, such people are becoming a rarefied breed."

Reid bends slightly towards them, hoping to hear more. His mind fills with questions. Was this man born knowing how to interact with women? Or was it something he learned from life experience? And most importantly, *could it be taught?* He continues leaning sideways and almost slips off the stool, but catches himself. The slip helps him recognize he's buzzing from alcohol. Feeling slightly embarrassed, he questions if he's had too much to drink. *But it's my birthday. I can be drunk today.* He centers himself on the chair, grips his drink, and lifts it towards the pimp.

"Ch-cheers to my birthday."

The pimp quickly twists his neck and glares at Reid. Something about the man's piercing hazel eyes causes Reid's hand to shake. The juice nearly splashes over the edge of his glass, but Reid keeps the glass held high. The pimp cracks a half-smile, then lifts his drink, prompting Reid to steady his nerves.

"To a life of accepting all the gifts the world provides for us, the good and the bad," says the pimp.

They clink glasses. *Accepting good and bad? My girlfriend turned out to be a lying tramp who hires a prostitute. Who in their right mind could accept that?* Reid takes a sip, sets the glass on the bar, then lowers his head.

"You look like you have a lot on your mind, kid," says the pimp.

Reid nods.

"What's on your mind?"

Reid hesitates, figuring if he tells this guy the truth, he'll probably try to sell him one of his whores. "I'd rather not talk about it."

"I'm not one to pry, but you may want to share your problem with someone. Your eyes look to be filled with deep anger."

"Psychologists haven't helped me with my problem. And I'm sure if I saw another shrink, they'd just tell me to examine my childhood and work to heal the wounds, while being thoughtful of other people's struggles."

The pimp doesn't respond. He takes a long sip of his drink while keeping his eyes on Reid.

Reid wants to break eye contact with the man, but he can't. Something about the man's presence connects to Reid. It makes him want to open up. He takes a deep breath. "I walked in on my soon-to-be fiancée having sex with a female hooker."

The pimp remains stoic. "Okay. What else is on your mind?"

Reid narrows his eyes, befuddled by the neutral response. "She said I was the worst sex she's ever had."

The pimp's pearl-white teeth sparkle through his grin. "What else?"

"Our song is called 'Anything.' We'd listen to it often. We promised we'd do anything to make each other happy. We swore we'd never hurt each other. I did everything for her." He slams his fist on the bar. "That bitch didn't appreciate me."

The pimp's grin becomes tight-lipped. "What else?"

What else? Is that all you know how to say? You sound like another shitty psychologist. Reid reaches into his pocket for cash, plops twenty dollars on the bar, then stands to leave. His forearm suddenly stings from becoming tightly gripped. Just as Reid identifies that the pimp's grabbed him, he is yanked down into his seat. *What the —?*

"I'm not wired to do a disservice to society." The pimp sips his drink. "It would be a disservice to let you leave here without understanding that a mature man would never refer to the female goddess as anything less than perfection."

Reid exhales a long breath, knowing the man is correct. But treating women like goddesses still gets him screwed over.

"I brought her flowers every day. I took her to dinners and movies, and on vacations, and I sat through all of her shitty TV shows. I gave her what every woman would die for. Yet she still cheated on me."

The pimp nods while giving a friendly grin, then looks away towards the TVs. Reid sits up, further engaged.

"Oh good," says Reid. "You get where I'm coming from. Women don't respect a good man. It seems like all women want is assholes who treat them like crap."

The pimp slowly turns back to Reid. "I have an important question to ask you. It may help you with your problems."

"Yes, I'll take any advice at this point. As it turns out, the mentors from my past were clueless."

The pimp studies him, looking down at Reid's shoes, then slowly moving his gaze upward until their eyes meet. The man pauses to study Reid's face, then speaks. "How long have you been abusing women?"

"What?" Reid draws his head back. "I'd never harm a woman. Never in a million years."

"Based on what you've just shared, I should have you arrested for domestic abuse."

Reid's head becomes hot. He considers leaving, but fears he'll be thrown down again. "What makes you think I abuse women?"

"Every single second of every single day, every human behaves in a way that they believe will lead them towards their own unique version of happiness. You've been verbally assaulting her happiness quest since you got here. Frankly, it's no different than physically assaulting her. Buying her flowers or punching her in the face — both are attempts to manipulate and control another human being. Both are external actions that won't solve your internal problems — internal problems that have nothing to do with her."

The pimp nods towards the bartender. "Hey, Ronald, call the cops. We need to have this young man arrested for abusing women."

Ronald looks up while rinsing his shaker. "I'll call it in right now."

"No, wait, stop," blurts Reid. "I promise my intentions were good. I worked my ass off to make sure her needs were met. Maybe you misheard what I said — I did everything for her. From the moment I woke till the time I fell asleep, I focused on her needs. I cooked every meal. I cleaned our house and her car. I paid for everything. I gave up watching sports so we could watch her reality shows. I surrounded her with gifts. I fucking brought her flowers every day because I love her."

"My goodness, it's more extreme than I thought. You are shamelessly abusive," says the pimp. "If you haven't hit her yet, I'm sure it will happen soon. You're very upset that your attempts at manipulating her haven't worked."

"My intentions were always to make sure she was happy." *This guy is crazy. I don't need to defend myself. Maybe he's just as ignorant as Jasmine. Nobody seems to understand the meaning of true love.*

Reid sees the pimp's head turn upward, towards the ceiling. The man closes his eyes and mumbles quietly to himself. He then turns towards Reid and places a hand on his shoulder. Something about his touch floods Reid with a strange uplifting sensation, as if icy medication was shot into his bloodstream, calming him.

"Was she smiling when you saw her with the other woman?" asks the pimp.

"Yes." Reid stares at his glass. "The prostitute was ramming her with a strap-on penis."

"Do you see the irony? You claim that you want her to be happy, but then you get angry when she appears to be experiencing pleasure."

"But we were committed to each other. She's not allowed to do that."

"So you are her god? You want to control when she can be happy and when she can't. As if her happiness can only exist on your terms. Sounds like the definition of an abusive relationship."

"No, I'm obviously not her god," says Reid. "How would you respond if you were in my shoes?"

Their conversation is halted by the hand of a woman caressing the pimp's shoulder from behind. Both men turn to see a tall, forty-something blond glowing as if she's won the lottery.

"You absolutely gave me my wish," says the woman. "Your wife was amazing, the most potent sexual experience of my life." She draws her index finger down her neck towards her stomach. "My body is still pulsating all over. I'm forty-two years old and I finally feel alive. Namaste, my friend."

Reid's jaw drops. He watches the woman kiss the pimp on the cheek, then hand him an envelope stuffed with something in the shape of cash.

Reid narrows his eyes while observing her walk away, then turns to the pimp in shock. "Your wife is a ..."

The pimp chuckles and slides the envelope into his breast pocket. He then looks up to the ceiling, puts his hands together as if in prayer, and dips his forehead to his fingers.

"Synchronicity," says the pimp.

"Synchronicity?" says Reid. "I remember reading about that in college, but I don't remember exactly what it means."

"When a person is aligned with their life's mission, things happen with seemingly perfect timing." The pimp returns his focus to Reid. "Guiding messages arrive at the exact time the person is ready to listen. Those moments are called synchronicities."

"Are you going to get all woo-woo spiritual on me?" Reid huffs a short breath. "Based on everything I've been through, I think I'll only believe stuff that can be proved scientifically."

The pimp smiles. "Neuroscience can go a long way towards explaining why we have certain experiences, but the unexplainable must be observed through a spiritual lens. I'm willing to bet that you have secret desires hidden within that you aren't giving yourself permission to experience. Once you give yourself permission, the universe will open doors for you to go after your desires and help you discover who you really are. The key is recognizing when a door has been opened, and having the courage to step through it."

Reid continues to look at the man, shocked to hear such intellect from a street hustler. "Are you saying we're experiencing synchronicity right now?"

"You asked me how I would respond if I knew my wife was with another woman. It's not a coincidence that the woman who paid for sex with my wife entered our conversation."

"I can't believe you're so accepting of your wife with someone else. How do you do it?"

"I accept all of who she is. I do not own her, and nor do I attempt to play the role of knowing what makes her happy. I'm not her god. Any attempt to change someone always results in suffering. We're not on earth to make people happy, we are here to support each other on our unique quests for happiness."

The pimp scans the room, then returns to Reid. "Your fiancée enjoys hookers who wear a strap-on; accept that truth about her. You can support her happiness quest by staying with her, or you can support her from a distance while being broken up. Both will result in positive outcomes, but to judge her will only result in you suffering."

"On paper that makes sense. But most people, including myself, would find it unrealistic to live that truth."

"It's unrealistic to you because your brain is underdeveloped. You're a grown man navigating this world with an adolescent brain. Truth is, people who cannot accept the behavior of others do so because they aren't accepting of themselves. Neuroscience has proven that it's physically impossible for the brain to do such a thing. You hate yourself because you barely know who you are, so how can you accept what you don't fully understand? You have a repressed dark side that you have masked with actions like overwhelming women with flowers and gifts. I encourage you to explore your dark side, let it out. There's an entire other half of you that you must come to understand."

"A dark side?" Reid sits up. "I almost entered a strip club before coming to this bar. A voice inside was screaming at me to go. I parked in front of the club and walked to enter, then quickly returned to my car. I sat and cried. I just couldn't get myself to go inside."

"I'm not surprised. Tears can often be your dark side's last means of expression before it turns to violence. You, like many people, have a dark side that's filled with repressed sexuality. It's important that you listen to that voice."

The man removes his fedora and places his hand on Reid's shoulder. Again, the strange uplifting energy fills Reid's body.

The pimp continues: "When you're in line with your life's mission and have an understanding of your whole self, it will be easy for you to accept all of the gifts that life brings. Your fiancée just gave you an amazing gift. Soon you may see that last night was the best night of your life."

Reid glances up at the TVs, questioning how last night could ever be viewed as a gift.

He turns back to the pimp. "The Cleopatra Hotel gave me a cool birthday gift, upgrading me to their lucky suite, thirty-three, thirty-three."

Unamused, the pimp stands and scans the room once again. He adjusts the lapels of his suit and pulls his collar straight.

"What's your name, kid? What do you do for work?"

"Reid Bradley. I'm a college professor — psychology."

The pimp belts out a deep laugh. "I'm not surprised," he says. "Here's some advice: stop teaching the shit you learned in college and what's in your textbooks. Most of it won't help this generation. It was probably written by people who don't understand their severely repressed dark side as well."

Reid leans back, dumbfounded; yet he senses he should agree with the pimp.

"I gotta run," says the pimp.

"Wait, what's your name?" says Reid.

"It's safer for you not to know. Perhaps synchronicity will have us meet again."

"Thank you for the chat. Forgive me, but I thought you were just trying to sell me one of your ... well, you know."

"My employees only spend time with clients who understand how to use the experience to grow as human beings. You'd have to prove to me that you're worthy. Right now, because of your emotional state, sex would just be escapism. Neither you, nor my employee, nor society would benefit from such an experience. We have no interest in feeding addictions or escapism; only personal growth."

The man strolls away. Reid gazes at his drink. *That's a heck of a sales tactic, saying someone could benefit from sex with a prostitute. Jasmine chose to do that and it ruined my life.* Reid shakes his head, feeling the buzz of alcohol rattle his brain. *I'm drunk. I'm actually listening to life advice from a pimp.*

Reid places both hands around his drink and sighs. He can't deny that the advice makes sense. It seems he's learned more in a few minutes with this pimp than in all of his years in college. He wonders how many nuggets of wisdom the pimp might have. He sucks down the last of his beverage and stands, hoping he'll have the chance to speak to this man again.

A hand grips Reid's shoulder from behind, nudging him back to his seat. He turns his neck, excited to see the pimp return. Instead, he sees a police badge.

Chapter 4

"Name's Detective Youngblood. I'd like to ask you a few questions about the interaction you had with that man."

Reid feels a prickling on his scalp as he hears the man's slight southern drawl. He's never been questioned by law enforcement. The detective reaches into his back pocket, appearing to be searching for something. Reid studies the man's disheveled appearance: faded khakis, a wrinkled polo shirt, and a frazzled salt-and-pepper goatee. Youngblood's hand returns, holding a notepad and pen.

"Did that man attempt to sell you a prostitute?"

"No, sir. We just had a friendly bar conversation."

"A woman handed him an envelope during your conversation. Do you know why she did that?"

The question startles Reid. He knows damn well why she handed the pimp the envelope and that the act was against the law. He taps his toes on the bar stool, surprised to find he has an urge to protect the pimp. He wonders if the pimp forces his wife to be a prostitute, but recalls how the blond lady said the experience changed her life.

Youngblood shuffles his stance. "It's a simple question, young man."

Reid looks towards the floor. His life has always been by the book and that approach continues to fail him. *Maybe it's time I consider breaking a rule or two? Plus that pimp didn't seem like a bad person.*

He lifts his gaze. "There's a lot going on in my head, sir. I wasn't paying attention. I just caught my soon-to-be fiancée cheating on me. I wanted to have a drink and go to bed."

"I'm sorry to hear that." Youngblood sighs, then slips the notepad into his back pocket. "I've been there. My wife cheated on me last year and ran off with her lover. Nowadays people are running wild with their sexual liberties. Traditional marriage and faithfulness are dying. I recently transferred into this town for a fresh start, but Vegas seems like the breeding ground for the sexual problems in our country."

Youngblood puts his hand on Reid's shoulder. The touch causes Reid's body to tense, the opposite sensation to that caused by the touch of the pimp.

Youngblood continues: "I'm determined to change the sex problems in society. The man you were talking with is the scum of the earth. He's a pimp who profits from forcing women into prostitution. I'd advise you to stay away."

"Thank you, sir."

They shake hands and exit the bar in opposite directions.

Reid hurries to the restroom and locks himself in a stall. Fully clothed, he sits on the toilet and covers his face with his hands. *Good gracious, what am I doing?*

Minutes pass, then he leaves the stall and washes his hands. He catches a glimpse of himself in the mirror and sees something different, something mysterious. He's always wondered what it would be like to be bad, to break rules, or even the law. Something rises in him, a sensation that feels alien but strong; it's as if the pimp's words have unleashed his inner bad boy. He straightens his collar. *Maybe I'll see this through a bit more.*

Reid strides along Las Vegas Boulevard to his hotel. He enters the lobby, hearing the excitement of casino action while feeling the trickle of discomfort inside his new skin. His attention is drawn to an attractive woman playing video poker at an empty casino bar. Everything in his body yearns for him to talk to her, but he hesitates. His mind flashes to the moment the pimp went up to those women, knowing the perfect thing to say. He stands a few feet behind her, hoping a magical opening line comes to mind.

Nothing.

He sits two seats away, pressing the buttons of a video poker machine, smiling off his tension.

"I wouldn't sit there if I were you," says the attractive woman. "That machine is unlucky."

"Oh, really," says Reid. He turns to flee.

"You can sit next to me," she says. "I only let the cute boys come close."

Reid halts and lifts his hand to his chest, as if to say, *Are you sure you're talking about me?* She nods and he slides onto the chair next to her.

"My name is Amber. Where are you from? What brings you to Vegas?"

"Los Angeles. And I'm here because —" *Don't go into your pity story again, Reid.* "It's my birthday."

"Awe, Happy Birthday. Are you staying at this hotel?"

"Yeah, have you ever seen the suites here? They're fantastic."

"No, I haven't. I'd love to see your suite."

She draws her fingernail along his forearm. Her touch ignites a warm sensation that courses through his arm and up to his brain. He gazes at her with wide eyes. This is the first time he's been touched adoringly by another woman in two years.

She continues: "I believe humans learn the most about each other through physical touch. Do you agree?"

"Yes. Yes, I do."

Her fingers slide off his arm, then pitter-patter along his stomach, inching below his belly button. He wonders if he should let her continue. What if Jasmine found out? What if Jasmine chose to drive here and surprise him tonight?

Reid's hesitancy is quickly forgotten as her erotic touch escalates. She applies pressure-point massage to his inner thigh, seemingly knowing which spots are potent nerve centers, shooting beams of excitement into his core.

"You don't mind that I touch you, do you?" she says. "There's something about you … my hands just want to connect with your body."

Reid can't avoid thinking about worst-case scenarios. If he continues, he risks upsetting Jasmine and losing her forever; if he says "no," he'll spend his life wondering what could have been tonight. His entire body now crackles with sparks of euphoria. *Screw Jasmine. She's never made me feel like this.* He nods, signaling to Amber to continue.

Her fingers pet his hip bone in tiny circular motions, inching towards his member, then stop just short of contact. The pause allows him to feel the flow of erotically infused blood rush from the edges of his body into his core. She presses her fingers on the crevice where his thigh and groin meet. Reid notices her eyes are focused intently on the pattern created by her hands, as if she is performing some kind of touching ritual.

He glances at the ceiling. He's never had a one-night stand. But something inside is screaming for him to go all in with Amber.

His legs sprawl open, allowing her palm greater access. She applies deeper pressure with her hand, in a rhythmic fashion, nudging his erect shaft. He drops his chin towards his chest, closing his eyes, absorbing the warmth of her touch through his pants.

Amber stops her movements. He feels her pillowy lips graze his ear as she leans close. "What does your room number add up to? Let's see if it's a lucky suite."

He opens his eyes. His mind is fogged with an erotic haze. "Lucky suite?"

"If the room numbers total an even number, then it's lucky. Like one-two-two-five is one plus two plus two plus five, which equals ten. That's a lucky room number."

"My room number's simple, three-three-three-three. That equals twelve."

"Today is your lucky day, birthday boy. Show me your suite." Amber stands, then takes his hand. "Let's go."

They walk arm and arm towards the elevator and take it up to the thirty-third floor. All the while, Reid feels he's living in a surreal moment. He's always fantasized about a wild Vegas fling. Never has he given himself permission to admit to such a thought; nor did he think it was possible for a social imbecile like himself. As they near his room, he begins to question the ease with which this is occurring. But he figures Amber would have asked him for money downstairs if she was doing this as a job.

Reid slides the key-card into the lock and pushes the door open. As he enters, he suddenly feels a shove from behind, forcing him onto the wall beside the door. A nervous tingle crawls up his spine as the door slams shut. He cautiously turns to face Amber, then relaxes as he sees a playful grin on her face. He opens his mouth to speak, but is silenced by Amber's lips locking onto his. His mouth is tense at first, then settles into the sensual kiss. Her taste is different than Jasmine's, tangy and sweet like a raspberry.

Amber releases Reid, and he gazes at her, in a love-laced trance, seeing images of what their potential future could be. She steps back, extends her arms out straight, then launches forward with her hands extended, shoving Reid against the wall. She pins her legs against his, and unbuttons and takes off his shirt. Then she strips away his pants and underwear, tossing all the clothes near the bed. Now Reid stands before her, naked. He moves his hand to cover his privates. The cool air causes his skin to ripple with goosebumps, but his nerves quickly settle as he feels her warm kisses across his chest and stomach. He reaches down for her breast, but she quickly swats away his hand. His brow furrows.

Amber extends a finger towards his face. "We play by my rules, birthday boy. Whatever I say, respond with, 'Yes, ma'am.' Am I clear?"

"Yes, ma'am." Reid smiles, fascinated by her taboo behavior. He's never experienced such sexual expression. He should've had the courage to explore his dark side a long time ago.

Amber removes a set of pink-fur handcuffs from her purse and signals to Reid to turn and face the wall. He rotates around, heated with arousal, then feels the furry cuffs lock his wrists behind his back. *Jasmine would have never thought to use handcuffs.*

She leads him away from the wall to the edge of the bed. "Lie on your stomach and keep your feet together."

"Yes, ma'am."

Her light shove causes him to fall face first on the white duvet cover. Reid hears the sound of duct tape ripping from a roll. He feels the tape bind his ankles together. *She's so kinky.* Amber rolls the duct tape around his head three times to cover his eyes, and now he begins to worry to what extreme she intends to take the sexual act. He knows one thing is certain: the tape is gonna hurt like hell when it's removed.

"Stay put, birthday boy." Amber's voice deepens. "I'm taking your room key and getting some ice."

He hears the front door open, then slam shut. He remains on the bed, bound and blindfolded. In the silence, he develops a stronger sense that something seems off. Feeling a surge of fight or flight, he attempts to break free from the handcuffs, but it's no use. He takes a deep breath. *This is just part of a kinky act. Relax, man. You're breaking your rules and getting wild.*

He hears the sound of the front door rip open, followed by two voices mumbling. The door slams shut.

"Don't fucking move," commands a male voice.

Reid squirms into the fetal position. *Oh no. Fuck, fuck, fuck, fuck, fuck.*

He then hears someone riffling through a bag that sounds like his luggage.

"His wallet is in his jeans," says Amber.

Reid has never been a victim of a crime, but instantly he realizes he's being robbed. He curls in tighter. A large hand grips the hair on the rear of his head and yanks backward, exposing his neck. He feels a sharp sting just below his ear; it's from a knife poking his skin.

"This eight-inch blade is eager to slice a smile across your neck," says the male voice.

Reid's eyes water uncontrollably. His excessive shivering has caused the knife to slightly cut his skin, and he feels what seems to be a trickle of blood crawl down his neck to his chest.

"This prick only has forty dollars," says Amber. "Who gets a suite and only carries forty bucks? Let's hit his ATM."

The man speaks into Reid's ear. "What's the pin number for your ATM? My bitch is gonna go get your cash. If you lie, I'll slice your balls off."

"Twenty-two, twenty-four." Reid clenches his chattering teeth. He vaguely hears Amber's heels click along the marble entry towards the exit, followed by the sound of the door creaking open.

Reid anticipates the sound of the door slamming shut; instead he hears Amber screaming, then a loud thud. Someone is attacking her. Reid feels the knife lift away from his neck, then hears the assailant shuffle in the direction of the front door.

"You hit my girl. You're gonna die, mother fucker."

Reid jerks his body, hoping to break free, while hearing the sounds of a scuffle and Amber pleading for mercy. He rubs his face on the duvet, attempting to peel the blinding tape away from his eyes, but to no avail. He curls in tight, hearing the thud of bodies falling to the floor.

"You disgust me," says a dominant male voice that sounds familiar to Reid, then he hears Amber sobbing out apologies.

Reid feels the body heat of someone near him. That person's fingers grip the tape near the center of his forehead and rip it apart downward to his nose, freeing just his eyes, with the remainder of the tape stuck to his hair. Reid widens his eyes at the sight of his rescuer — the pimp.

He sees the pimp walk towards the front door, where the assailant is on the floor, either knocked out cold or dead. Amber is on the floor next to the assailant, trying to shake him awake as the pimp approaches her.

"Come on, wake up," says Amber. The pimp grabs her arm. "No, lemme go."

She tries to free herself, but can't overcome the pimp's strength as he drags her across the room and throws her on the couch.

"You are my greatest regret," the pimp says to Amber. She cowers near the edge of the couch, hands covering her face. "Using all that I have taught for evil. All that time in the cage, the lessons that helped you grow, you're more gifted than any of the Sexmysts."

The pimp lowers his head and continues: "You swore to be committed to our mission. You swore you were committed to saving the future of society." He steps closer to Amber and extends a finger toward her face. "I'd have you erased, but the god-damned *divine duality* requires that druggie fuck-ups like you must exist."

Reid narrows his eyes. *What the heck is he talking about? Time in a cage? A mission? Does he kill people?*

Amber doesn't move. The pimp grabs Reid's pants and shirt, sets them on the bed, then breaks away the handcuffs.

The pimp turns to Amber. "And you're using this cheap, furry, plastic shit."

Amber says nothing. Reid moves a finger across the knife wound near his ear, relieved to find it's only a small incision, as if he'd cut himself shaving. He starts to take the remaining tape off his head, but feels it pull the roots of his hair tightly. He leaves it, then tears off the tape around his ankles, wincing as his leg hairs rip out. As he quickly slides on his jeans, the pimp reaches into Amber's purse, takes a squeeze tube of something, and tosses it near to Reid.

"Cover your hand with the lip gloss and smush it into the hair that's stuck to the tape. Otherwise, the tape will rip chunks of hair off your head."

Reid follows the instructions, peeling the tape away from his hair with ease while becoming a gooey mess. A towel, tossed by the pimp, hits him in the face. Reid wipes his hands and hair. Then he dabs the towel on his neck to soak up the small amount of blood.

Reid hears groaning from the man on the floor, and he bolts to the rear corner of the room, his hands forming into fists.

"Don't worry, kid, you're safe now." The pimp walks towards the body of the assailant, who looks to still be out cold. The pimp picks up the long knife, folds it into its safety cover, then slides it into his pocket.

Reid feels nauseous from the sight of the gigantic knife. He knows a single swipe across his neck could have taken his life. Though he feels somewhat safe now, he remains alert, just in case this is all part of the same scam.

Reid sees Amber slide his wallet into her bra.

"You don't know when to quit, do you?" says the pimp to Amber.

The pimp walks to the bed and grabs the roll of duct tape. Amber leaps off the couch and sprints towards the door. The pimp intercepts her, wraps his large hand around her neck, lifts her up, and slams her to the floor. He flips her over to lie on her stomach, pinning her with his knee, then swiftly tapes her wrists together behind her back. He grabs the wallet and tosses it towards Reid, then throws Amber back on the couch. *Maybe this guy is on my side after all?*

The pimp grabs a chunk of Amber's hair and yanks her head back, exposing her neckline. He extends his free arm outward, prepping for a swift attack to her open neck. Amber's hips rise, attempting to close the exposed gap. Her shoulders shake vigorously as she tries to break free, but she can't overcome his strength. Reid moves his hands to cover his eyes, hoping not to witness a violent act. But he can't resist the urge to see vengeance taken on Amber. He peeks through a crack between fingers, seeing the pimp's hand explode towards her neck. Amber releases a deathly scream. The pimp halts his hand prior to connecting.

"It would do me no good to hurt you," says the pimp. Reid releases his hands to his sides. "I can't come close to causing the depth of pain you've mastered inflicting on yourself."

Amber stares at the pimp. Her eyes look like busted panes of glass. The male assailant groans on the floor. The pimp takes out the envelope that was gifted by the woman at the bar. He thumbs through the large amount cash within and takes out a few bills.

"Here's five hundred to get the fuck out of town." He stuffs the cash inside Amber's bra strap and returns the envelope to his pocket. "Don't let me see you around Vegas ever again."

Reid sees the male robber roll onto his side. The pimp yanks Amber off the couch and shoves her towards the goon. She stumbles and then falls on him.

"Fucking druggies," says the pimp.

The assailant stands, gathers Amber, and leaves. Reid stares at the pimp with fearful eyes, unable to put together a sentence.

"It's okay, young man, you're safe," says the pimp.

The words cause Reid to relax his fists. He leans back on the wall, then gazes downward as he processes all that has occurred. He feels safe, but also realizes he needs to report this crime. He rushes to grab the room's wireless phone.

The pimp extends his palm out towards Reid. "Stop. Don't call the police."

Reid clicks the phone on. "I just got robbed. I have to call nine-one-one."

The pimp explodes towards Reid, grips his neck, and shoves his body against the wall. The phone falls to the floor before Reid can dial the number. Reid's eyes bulge and he feels his throat seal so no air can enter. He looks at the man's gaze and sees concern, not a threat — like a parent who is upset he has to discipline his child.

The pimp's grip gradually lessens, then releases. Reid cowers forward, hands pressed onto his knees, and coughs. He sees the pimp grab the phone off the floor and return it to the console on the dresser. Reid slowly rises, rubbing his neck as he studies the mysterious man before him.

"I'll never hurt you," says the pimp. "I only use extreme force for protection. Even if it means protecting you from yourself."

Reid can't deny the strange connection he feels to this man. He's perplexed as to why the pimp's caring touch always seems to make him feel uplifted.

"Think about it, kid. Do you want to explain to the police that you brought a hooker to your room?" The pimp pulls a handkerchief from his breast pocket and hands it to Reid. "Things are handled differently in this town. The last thing this hotel wants is publicity about their customers being robbed. I'll handle those druggies."

The pimp nears the window. Reid moves to sit on the edge of the bed. He notices the pimp open a vintage cellular phone and press a button to connect a call.

"A flip phone?" Reid says. The pimp extends a middle finger towards Reid while his phone call connects. Reid chuckles while relaxing his shoulders.

The pimp paces in front of the window while talking to the person on the other end of the call. "There will be a man in a black leather jacket and a girl in a pink dress coming to Rex's within the hour — Amber and her boyfriend. They'll have five hundred cash in hand. You should be able to catch them buying enough dope to lock them up for a while." The pimp pauses to listen, then responds. "Thank you, Detective. It hurts to know I wasn't able to get through to Amber."

Reid lifts an eyebrow, wondering if the pimp just called Detective Youngblood. He considers telling the pimp about his interaction with Youngblood, but figures it's safest to stay aloof for now.

The pimp puts his cell phone in his pocket and picks up the hotel room phone. He shifts the tone of his voice to sound like a perky tourist. "Hi. I just called to say that I'm really happy with this suite. However, I noticed a blood stain on the entryway. Would it be possible to switch me to a different room? Blood makes me queasy."

The pimp hangs up the phone. "Pack your shit. Your new room key is at the front desk."

Reid gathers his things, then looks up at the pimp. "How did you know I was in trouble with that girl?"

"I didn't. But then another synchronicity occurred. A source told me that Amber started running the bob-and-rob scam recently, and that she was at this hotel tonight. I was walking through the casino and saw you enter the elevator with Amber. I would have arrived sooner, but it took me a few minutes to remember your room number. It was stupid of you to tell me your room number, but perhaps your instincts knew trouble was heading your way."

Reid extends a hand for a shake. "I don't know how to thank you. You saved my life."

"You courageously stepped into your dark side. Whenever a man crosses a threshold of a fear, he grows." Their hands grip, then release. "Don't let tonight stop you continuing to explore your dark self. Obstacles like this are not random during the journey, they are necessary. All obstacles exist so that a person develops the skills that their future self will most certainly require."

My future self? Reid suddenly senses he is about to embark on something that he can't quite define.

The pimp pulls a cigar from his breast pocket and puts it in his mouth, leaving it unlit. He stares out the window, appearing to be pondering something important. He turns back to Reid. "The strange thing is, your challenges appear significantly more potent than what most people face. You're a nice guy who's gone through a lot in forty-eight hours."

"Do you see some deeper reasoning for this?"

The pimp sucks on his cigar and brings his hands together in a prayer position. He closes his eyes momentarily, as if in deep thought.

The pimp pulls the cigar from his mouth. "Your inner truth, your inner spirit, is repressed and trying to break free. And it's likely been trying to break free for a while, but now your brain is developed enough to support your inner spirit. The potency of your recent obstacles means that inner spirit is not only seeking freedom but it's also ready to battle the external forces."

"Battle external forces?"

"I'm sensing there are forces in this universe which greatly fear you becoming a fully realized version of yourself. Specifically, these forces know they will lose their power over the world if you become self-actualized."

"But why would these forces care about me?"

"Throughout history, the people who changed societies for the better were always met with resistance from external forces wanting to maintain the status quo. Bottom line: I'm sensing you might have a special gift that will dramatically change the world."

The pimp hands Reid a business card. Reid examines the velvety black card with gold lettering. A phone number is printed on it, along with the word "Wish."

"Your name is Wish? You grant wishes?"

"I'm no fucking genie," responds the pimp — Wish. He heads towards the exit. "I gotta get back to work."

"Wait, you said you regretted teaching that girl. What did you teach her?"

Wish halts, takes a breath, then speaks over his shoulder.

"I taught her how to provide the most life-altering sexual experiences on the planet, freeing the client from their repression." Wish shakes his head and slows his speech. "She knows how to use sex to ignite the receiver towards liberation and self-actualization. Unfortunately, such powers can also be used to manipulate for evil gains."

Liberation through sex? Reid notices Wish drop his chin towards his expanding chest; he appears to be increasingly angry with each breath. Wish releases an earth-shattering grunt and launches his fist into the wall. Reid jumps up from the bed and takes a few steps back.

"She's using the powers for evil." Wish pants heavily and lifts his fists to his head. "I don't train women to be hos. I train goddesses to save lives from the repression of the Collective Shadow."

Reid returns to sitting on the edge of the bed. He suddenly feels a tingling sensation, seemingly left over from Amber's strange triangle-touch ritual.

"Amber and I didn't have sex, but she made me feel — something," says Reid. "I don't know how to describe it, but it's beyond what I thought I was capable of feeling inside my body. A sensory explosion.

Even after having that knife on my throat, my body is tingling from her touch."

"Other than my wife, Amber was my smartest disciple. At first, she was determined to continue our mission." Wish's voice cracks like a disappointed father's. "She got lost in the dark side. The Collective Shadow won in her battle, keeping her from fully knowing and loving herself, keeping her lost in the land of addiction. Without self-knowledge and, ultimately, self-love, the Collective Shadow will always have control over us."

"What's the Collective Shadow?" says Reid.

"It's best I don't share any more. I'm not certain you belong in our world. The universe has brought us together, but I'll need more proof that you're the one I've been searching for. You'll probably wake up tomorrow and run home. I can't control your choice to stay in your safe, vanilla life. I am not your god."

"But I now know what the experience that you teach feels like."

"Did she press her palm into your pelvic region?"

Reid nods. "She did some strange palm touch in the shape of a triangle."

"Fuck." Wish squeezes his hands into fists. "She used the Shadow Palm Technique." He moves to swing a fist at the wall again, but stops himself, and slowly returns his hands to the prayer position in front of his nose.

Reid narrows his eyes as the pimp goes through some kind of meditative process. Wish exhales several deep breaths.

"I apologize for my momentary lack of self-control. I'm not perfect." The pimp lowers his head and smiles. "Although it's always exciting to be reminded that there is still plenty of work to do on myself."

"Why did you get angry?"

"She used the Shadow Palm Technique on you. When done correctly, it will change the recipient's life for the better, but if done with ill will, very bad things can happen. A second ago, I feared the worst for you, because Amber's intentions were not to guide you towards liberation from your repression. But your journey is stronger than her ill will. She gave you a gift, just as your girlfriend's actions are a gift. You can't see it now, but life-changing gifts usually come in the ugliest packages."

Reid thinks about Wish's words. *I would tell a student the same thing about life experiences being a gift, but that wisdom doesn't make me feel any different.* "What's the Shadow Palm Technique?"

"She touched you in a way that unlocks the internal cage that contains your dark side, your shadow-self. Like water seeping through a crack in cement, your shadow-self now has the opportunity to become free. Your behavior during the next few months will either free it for good or permanently repress the other half of who you are, leaving you with a life of mediocrity. You'll be easily controlled by the leaders of the Collective Shadow. You'll settle for being a slave to what society dictates is best for you. You'll never know who the fuck you are. Instead, you'll always wonder, 'What if ...?'"

Reid shakes his head. He'd always wondered, what if Jasmine cheated on him?

Wish opens the hotel room door. "You're on your own, kid. But if the impulse to call me becomes undeniable, I may entertain a formal meeting." Wish walks off, letting the door slam shut.

Reid slides off the bed, then collapses to his knees. *Cheated on, scammed, assaulted, robbed, questioned by a detective, and now I'm listening to psychology from a pimp. I work so hard at being good and things just get worse.* He stares at the lights of the Strip, half-dreaming. Their sparkle looks different than before, as if the signs that usually flash advertisements for hotel buffets are now flashing his name across the displays. Reid shakes his head to get out of the dreamlike state. He can't help but feel Las Vegas is a place he needs to be in the near future. He mimics Wish's relaxation technique, lifting his hands to the prayer position, centered to his nose, while breathing deeply.

The calmness brings to mind an important question for Wish. Reid leaps to his feet, exits the room, and sprints down the hallway. He catches Wish entering the elevator.

"Wait," says Reid. "Why did you say the world needs screw-ups like Amber?"

The elevator doors start to close as Wish responds. "The human brain is a duality mechanism — evil people must exist in order for the brain to be able to recognize good people."

"Duality mechanism? Wait! What does that mean?"

The elevator doors close.

Chapter 5

Reid wakes with a pounding headache. He sees the clock flash to half past eight in the morning. He glances around the room, realizing he's in a different suite. Last night wasn't a dream; he's lucky to be alive.

He hurries to pack his stuff and saunters towards his car. His head continues to throb as he turns onto the I-15 freeway towards Los Angeles, eager to return home. The long stretch of road allows logic to creep back into his mind. He figures this has all been an overreaction to Jasmine's infidelity. At least she cheated on him with a woman, not a man. *It's really not that big of a deal. I can forgive her.* His mind locks onto how they can overcome this minor speed bump. *I'm a professor of psychology, for God's sake.*

As he cruises down the empty freeway, his mind wanders to loving thoughts of Jasmine — their first date, first kiss, and first slow dance. Yet he can't help but feel his body tingle with the sensations created by Amber's touch, followed by the unease of guilt. *That was a one-time thing. Jasmine will never find out. But if she did, she'd probably be happy to know I was robbed as a result.*

Reid sits up straight, knowing he needs to cleanse the "Amber" garbage out of his system. He programs his phone to play the song he and Jasmine claim represents their relationship, titled "Anything." His body fills with fluttery sensations of love as he listens to the song on repeat for the remainder of the drive. His mind conjures visions of Jasmine's sweet smile and loving embrace, which renews his commitment to do anything and everything for his woman.

While stopping for gas at a midway point, he sends a text to Jasmine.

I'll get over what happened. You're still my girl. I'll do whatever it takes to make this work. I'm coming home right now.

Let's make this right.

The song continues to repeat for the next two hours, until he arrives at a grocery store near their home. He examines his phone again and shrugs; Jasmine has yet to respond. *That's okay. I know flowers will bring a smile to her face.* He buys a bouquet of roses, and enjoys the high he gets from other women smiling at him as he carries the flowers to his car. His optimism increases by the second as he completes the short drive home. Knowing she'll arrive home from work any minute, he quickly places the flowers in a large vase in the center of the coffee table. *Jasmine will be ecstatic when she sees these.*

Reid goes to the bedroom and halts in the doorway, paralyzed by the sight before him: the room looks like it was hit by a tornado. He struggles to work out how it could have happened. His clothes are scattered everywhere. He wonders if Jasmine is physically okay, if something worse happened after he left. He calls Jasmine; the line rings but she doesn't answer. He goes into the bathroom and feels her toothbrush; it's damp. She used it after lunch as she always does. He sighs and returns to the bedroom.

He proceeds to tidy the bedroom, feeling as if he's piecing his life back together with each item he returns to the closet. Under the last article of misplaced clothing, he finds a leather tassel. His face burns as he figures it must have been left by that hooker. The sight triggers an onslaught of torturous images of Jasmine moaning blissfully while being penetrated by that woman. His breath becomes short; he wiggles his head to scramble the signal, but it doesn't help. He hurries to the kitchen and throws the tassel in their large trash bin, intending his memories to join the tassel in the trash.

He walks to the living room and takes a long whiff of the roses, hoping the beautiful plants will work their magic as they usually do. *Be strong. I know we can work through this.*

Reid hears her car pull into the driveway and hurries to open their front door. He stands tall under the doorway, feeling his immense love for her as she walks closer, as if she were walking down the aisle to him in a white dress. Except her gaze remains fixated on the ground as she nears.

His arms open wide, then wrap around her in a hug. "I'm sorry,

I'm sorry. I'm sorry I ran off to Vegas."

Jasmine doesn't reciprocate; her arms stay glued to her sides. He senses her discomfort, and quickly points to the roses as if to say, *You always love flowers.* He dips his head towards her face, eager to feel her soft lips.

Jasmine ducks his move, shuffles forward, and settles on the couch. "We need to talk."

Reid's bottom lip quivers as he moves to sit next to her. "Don't worry about anything that happened. We'll make it work. I've failed you to the point that you wanted to see someone else. I was not attentive enough. I'll do anything for you."

She crosses her legs away from him, then stares at the roses on the coffee table. He's hoping for a smile, but instead she exhales a long breath and looks at Reid with heavy eyes. "I'm in love with Daphne."

The loving aura coming from Reid's heart shifts to one of heated anger. He runs both of his hands through his hair, hoping to calm himself, but it only escalates his rage.

Jasmine extends her palms out towards him. "I want to see both of you. I don't want to lose you. But I've fallen for her too. We're still talking. She's not going to cash the check."

"Fuck you!"

He explodes off the couch and flips the wooden coffee table, launching the rose vase into the air. It flies across the room in a high arc, connects with the hardwood floor, and shatters. Roses are spread about, with the shrapnel of broken glass in-between.

"What the hell is wrong with you? She's a god-dammed whore who has a pimp. How the hell do you envision this working out? All four of us go on a double date, then come home and watch you two fuck? You're crazy, beyond crazy. You're an insane bitch."

Jasmine releases a piercing scream and lunges closer to Reid, pointing a finger at his face. "You might want to look at yourself, Professor. I'm not the one destroying our home because I can't accept the truth."

He and Jasmine now stand face to face. He feels a pounding in his ears, stronger than anything he's ever felt in his life. *Why don't you appreciate who I am?* His hands clench into fists. He swore to his mother that he would never hit a woman, but everything inside him craves a swing at her. He extends his right arm back.

"You want to hit me?" says Jasmine. "Go ahead. At least I'll feel something that's real from you."

His arm remains extended outward; he hopes that something will prevent him swinging it down on her. Reid's chest expands with heavy breaths. His mind flashes to Wish's words in their first conversation, and how flowers or punching her are both forms of abuse. He realizes that both are attempts to control her, and that he must get to a place of acceptance. Reid remains in this position for a few more breaths, until his body fills with just enough courage to follow Wish's guidance.

"I love you." He drops his hands to his sides, battling tears as he struggles to get the words out. "I ... support you on your quest for happiness." He sobs. "We can no longer be together. I'm forever grateful for all of our experiences and all that I have learned from you. We are done."

Jasmine falls onto the couch and begins to cry. Reid steps around the shards of broken glass, ambles to the bedroom, and packs a large suitcase with as much as he can. Several minutes pass. He returns to the living room with the suitcase, shaking his head at the sight of the scattered roses.

He then looks at the couch. Jasmine's face is buried in her phone, and she's laughing at what appears to be social media posts. He rolls his eyes, then explains he'll be staying at his mom's house and they'll sort out the lease and moving details later. Her eyes stay glued to her phone. She nods once, but doesn't acknowledge him any further.

Reid moves to leave, then hears a pop as he steps on broken glass. He sees that Jasmine is barefoot, sighs, then goes to the kitchen to grab a broom and dustpan. He brushes the flowers and broken glass into the dustpan, then returns to the kitchen. He feels pathetic. *I'm her god-damned slave. Never again will I feel like this.* He dumps the shards in the trash and sees the tassel he threw away earlier. *Disgusting. Why would I want someone who has all these psychological issues anyway? Someone with a healthy mind wouldn't need to use something like that during sex.*

He meanders towards the front door, pulls it open, then glances back for a final goodbye. Jasmine ignores his gaze. He exhales a conformational sigh. *Never again will I be in this position.* He drags the suitcase to his car, tosses it in the trunk, then embarks on the hour-long drive to his mom's home.

Although his heart stings while he drives, his mind wanders back to that strange pimp he met. He wonders if that fascination will pass, and if perhaps he should seek professional help. But professional help appears to have failed him.

He arrives at his mom's house and explains to her that he and Jasmine have mutually agreed to take a break.

His mother responds, lovingly as always, "I'm not surprised. It's your twenty-ninth year of life. The universe has created a path to get you away from the life you have and into the life that's waiting for you."

He knows he can't see the path yet, but he trusts his mom's words are an accurate description of what's to come.

Reid is off work for the remainder of the week due to Spring Break. He spends the next two days bedridden in the room he grew up in. His mind constantly explores what went wrong with Jasmine. He journals as an attempt to self-medicate, yet his confusion magnifies. He wants to analyze their relationship through his academic lens, searching for answers as to why she cheated and why she claims to have fallen in love with a female prostitute. But the pimp's wisdom about her happiness quest seemingly makes the most sense. Reid realizes he must accept how Jasmine is wired. Attempting to control her happiness — play her god — is creating his suffering. The words make sense on paper, but his strong emotions still cause pain.

Aside from thoughts of Jasmine, Reid tosses restlessly in bed each night with fantasies about Las Vegas. Deep down, he knows the Vegas itch has to be scratched. He senses that there is something there he's destined to discover. He can't put a finger on exactly what it is, but he knows he's got to meet with Wish again. In a moment of courage, he texts Wish.

Reid: **This is Reid Bradley. If it's okay with you, I would like to learn more. I can be in Vegas this weekend.**

Wish: **Describe what you would like to learn.**

Reid: **I don't want to feel this pain. I want to be the guy who gets the girl, any woman he chooses. I want to enter a room and have the women desire me, and know exactly what to do. Just like I noticed when I observed you that night at the Diamond Bar.**

Wish: **I will not teach boyish, approval-seeking behaviors. Try again.**

Reid feels an urge to defend himself, but then figures it's best he take some time to consider his answer.

Reid: **I'm done with feeling pathetic all of the time, unworthy. I want to know who I am, so I can then accept others for who they are.**

Wish: **This will require a great deal of courage, Professor. You must be willing to explore the depths of your dark self. Meet me at the Diamond Bar, Friday night, 9pm.**

Chapter 6

The thrill of a new beginning excites Reid as he strides through the Largo Casino and enters the Diamond Bar. Seeing Wish stand, he widens his eyes in awe. Wish is dressed immaculately in a slim-fitting navy-blue suit, a white shirt with a grey ascot tucked into the collar, and brown wingtip shoes. The tailoring is such that he can tell this man is dedicated to fitness. Reid feels his spare-tire-shaped belly fat wobble as he looks down at his oversized dress shirt and baggy jeans. He looks hideous compared to the sparkle of Wish's outfit.

The men shake hands and sit at the bar.

"Man, you dress amazingly," says Reid.

"You dress like shit," says Wish. "Assuming we end up working together, I'll be teaching you about how fashion ties with your sexuality at some point."

"I'm willing to do whatever it takes to learn from you."

"You'll have to pass some tests tonight. I need to see if you're meant for this." Wish sips his drink. "You'll need to prove to me how far you are willing to explore your shadow-self, also known as your dark side. I always have time for pussy, but I don't have time for pussies."

"I'm ready. How do I know what my dark side wants?"

"Start by listening to the voice within. As you connect with the source, you'll begin to operate at your animalistic level. Your instincts become your guiding system. The other night, you called your ex-girlfriend a whore. Is that an insult you commonly use towards women?"

"Yes," says Reid. "I've shunned all sexually open women since I was a teenager."

"The flaws we notice in others are often a reflection of our own characteristics — the characteristics we're ashamed to accept and repress into our shadow-self. Repression of those characteristics is highly dangerous to oneself and society."

"Projecting," says Reid.

"Precisely, Professor. And people who do not free their shadow-self are often weak-minded, leaving them vulnerable to being controlled by a higher power. We call this higher power the Collective Shadow, or CS. They are forces created by a culmination of shadows from the people who aren't willing to explore their repressed dark side. Because the members of the CS do not fully accept themselves, their brains are not capable of fully accepting other humans. We've seen examples of this from extremist groups, cults, gangs, and shady governments — all social groups who gain power by promoting unacceptance. The Collective Shadow fears self-actualized individuals, because it knows it cannot control them. Therefore, the CS will do its best to prevent you from gaining access to your personal powers. I'm sensing you have a gift the Collective Shadow greatly fears, a gift that it knows it can't overcome if you master yourself. There's a reason why you have faced many potent obstacles in a short amount of time: the Collective Shadow knows you are embarking on the journey of mastering that gift."

Reid sits silently, absorbing all that has been shared. He recalls how every time he's tried to step outside of his comfortable life, something has come along to keep him from growing.

"That's why I got robbed by Amber," Reid says.

"Exactly. The Collective Shadow has thrown bigger challenges at you than most people have to face. This means the Collective Shadow fears your potential more than the average person's. It's possible that you are wired to be the leader of a pivotal movement against the CS."

Reid taps his foot on the floor. "So, if I don't do this, I'll be contributing to the powers of the CS?"

"Yes. And there's a greater threat to society on the horizon. More extreme than the extremist groups I just mentioned."

"What could possibly be worse than those things?"

"It's better I don't tell you until you prove yourself worthy. For now, I'll need to see your capabilities."

"I'm ready. Where do I start?"

"You'll start by exploring your projections," says Wish. "Tonight you're going to pay for a sexual experience — with a woman you'd describe as a whore."

"What?" Reid shakes his head. "I'd never be with a prostitute. It's illegal, and the girl is probably messed up in more ways than I can count. I could get a disease."

Wish adjusts the lapels of his suit as he stands to leave.

"Wait." Reid rises. "I'm sorry, I'm sorry. I'm committed to learning from you." He struggles to swallow his next gulp. "I'll pay for sex. How much will it cost?"

"Three thousand dollars."

Reid snaps his head back.

"Relax, kid. I'll give you the money." Wish returns to sitting and Reid follows. "There's a small favor I'll ask for in return." Wish pulls a handful of purple casino chips from his breast pocket and hands them to Reid. "I'll need you to cash these out. Each chip is worth five hundred — six grand in total. Use three thousand for your experience. I'll tell you later where to give the rest to me."

"You want me to launder money? It's against the law. I have a career to protect. I don't think — never mind."

"Your brain is full of white-collar, higher-education bullshit. To enter my world, you must be committed to doing things my way. No more questioning my methods. You cannot understand your light side until you've gone to the depths of your dark side. Understood?"

Reid nods, but doesn't fully connect to Wish's words. Regardless, he's open to trying anything, since everything else has failed him.

Wish glances to his left, then to his right. "We always need to look out for a new detective. His name is Youngblood. He's slick, creeps out of corners I didn't know existed."

"He questioned me after we met the other night," says Reid.

"I'm not surprised. But that's a good thing. It's important he sees you with me. What did he say to you?"

"He said he's determined to fix the sex problems in Las Vegas. And he told me to stay away from you, because you're a scum-of-the-earth pimp."

Wish smirks. "Hopefully, he's watching us right now."

A chill crawls up Reid's spine. He scans the bar. "Why do you want him to see us together?"

"Youngblood works by himself. He can't follow both of us at the same time."

"I'm a decoy?" asks Reid.

Wish nods. "Youngblood has only been in town a few weeks. I've dealt with plenty of cops throughout the years. I don't know if it's his southern accent, but something seems off about him." Wish taps a finger on the bar. "His motivation is beyond the norm for a cop. He can't see the good that we do, which leads me to think he has some form of sexual shame. I wouldn't be surprised to learn that he engages in unsavory acts due to his repression."

Reid nods in agreement. "I remember hearing about a governor a few years back who was adamant about passing anti-gay laws in his state, then he got caught in a public restroom having sex with another male."

"You catch on quickly, Reid. Yes, that governor is a perfect example of a man who's running from his shadow-self. Luckily, he didn't harm anyone, but plenty of people in power have. The members of the Collective Shadow seek to create chaos in the world, simply because they don't understand or accept the chaos within themselves."

Wish sips his drink. "Detective Jones runs the vice department. He and I have been friends for many years. Jones supports our mission, but Jones is limited in how much he can control Youngblood's actions because he's retiring soon."

"Doesn't Jones put his job at risk by helping you?"

"We have an agreement. I often come across many low-life pimps and hookers with lost souls and assist Jones in capturing them. We keep these streets cleaner than Youngblood seems to understand. Jones is who I called to bust Amber the other day."

Reid breaks eye contact with Wish, relieved to hear that Jones was the man Wish called to handle Amber.

"Jones is retiring soon, and Youngblood is seeking a big bust so he'll be promoted to head of the department. Keep an eye out."

"Yes, sir." Reid looks about the bar, feeling a tightness in his chest. Youngblood could already be watching them.

"Your anxiety seems high," says Wish. "Remember, your journey of self-discovery could ultimately result in serving others in a way that will positively impact the world. Anytime the anxiety is high, use this mantra: *this is to serve others.*"

"This is to serve others," Reid states.

"Cash the chips at the Sahara Hotel. Then text me for further instructions about your prostitute. Be sure to keep an eye on the money. The casinos are filled with thieves who spot customers walking around with large amounts of cash."

"Yes, sir." Reid stands. "What do I do if I come across Youngblood?"

"Listen to the voice of your shadow."

Chapter 7

Minutes later, Reid hops into his car and drives out of the Largo Hotel garage and towards the north end of the Strip. Fearing that Youngblood may already be on his tail, he alternates his gaze between the rear-view mirror and the road going forward. Reid turns the car off Las Vegas Boulevard into the parking garage of the Sahara Hotel and parks. He pats his pockets while stepping out of the car to make sure he still has the chips, and sighs with relief when he feels the six grand in casino chips. He keeps his head elevated while striding towards the entrance, yet he can't avoid the secretion of sweat on his palms.

As Reid pulls open the casino door, he hears slot machines chiming, along with joyful screams from the excitable Friday night crowd. The Sahara is one of the original Vegas hotels. Though it's seen better days, it still makes enough money to look like a classy Vegas joint.

Reid moves towards the middle of the casino, feeling his shirt stick to his back from sweat. Wish instructed him to simply cash the chips, but Reid wonders if such action would bring heat. He considers playing a few hands to appear like a gambler. Reid pulls two of the chips out of his pockets, clinking them in his hand as he examines a few twenty-five dollar limit tables.

He pauses in front of a busy table to scan the action. He glances at the pit boss, only to receive an unwelcoming stare. Reid quickly turns around and walks towards a slot machine. *Wish said to just cash the chips. He didn't mention gambling. Do the deed and get the hell outta here.*

He eyes the cashier's desk in the distance and promptly moves in its direction. A middle-aged woman at the desk smiles at Reid. He places the twelve purple chips under the iron rods of the cage. The cashier studies the money, then shifts her smile into a suspicious frown. Though he reminds himself to maintain a cool appearance, Reid can't avoid the beads of sweat crawling down the back of his ear.

"I'll be right back," she says, pushing the chips towards Reid.

The uncertainty in her voice causes Reid to hunch forward. He catches himself, straightens his spine, and slows his breathing. He glances left, seeing only men in khakis. Every old fart in the casino looks like Youngblood. He returns his attention to the center of the cage, feeling his pulse skyrocket. He slides his hands into his pockets, then mumbles the words he must repeat when the anxiety is high: *This is all to serve others. This is all to serve others. I have no idea how, but this is all to serve others.*

He continues to repeat the mantra, not feeling any calmer. Instead, he wonders if the pimp has hustled him into doing some dirty work.

The cashier returns with a man in a suit following behind. Reid's career flashes before his eyes; he believes he is screwed. Reid doesn't move, keeping a tight-lipped grin, as the man in the suit looks him up and down. The man whispers something into the ear of the cashier, then looks back at him.

"ID please," says the suited man.

With a shaky hand, Reid slides the ID out of his wallet and onto the counter. The man scoops up the plastic card and examines it for what seems like an eternity.

"Happy belated birthday, Mr. Bradley." He returns the ID and turns to the cashier. "You did the right thing. This man has a young face, but he's twenty-nine years old. Cash his chips." The suit exits as the cashier places the fresh bills in an envelope, which she hands to Reid.

"Have a nice day," says the clerk.

Reid gleams a false *business-as-usual* smile and steps away, boneless with relief. He slides the envelope into his jeans and fishes out his phone. He notices a text message from Wish with instructions.

There's a room booked in your name. Get the key from the front desk.

What am I supposed to do about meeting a prostitute? Reid stuffs the phone into his front pocket and heads towards the front desk, speed-walking because every middle-aged man in sight resembles

Youngblood. He recalls that Wish said the shadow-self is more in touch with instincts, operating in raw animal form. Perhaps his instincts are sensing that Youngblood is nearby.

Reid checks in at the front desk. With his room key in his hand, he takes the elevator to his floor, and arrives in front of his room.

He unlocks the door, slowly pushes it open, and sees several lit candles across the room. He considers that he may have entered the wrong room. Before Reid has a chance to expand on his thought, the hand of woman appears from behind the door. Her warm fingers meet his cold, stiff palms and pull him forward. He's guided by a woman wearing a silky black robe. She stops him in front of a massage table at the foot of the bed. As his eyes adjust to the lighting, she turns towards him and undoes the belt of her robe. He swallows his gulp slowly, studying her black lace lingerie and the immaculate curves of her body.

A quiver vibrates through his lower lip. "H-hi, I'm ..."

The woman places her index finger on her glossy mouth, signaling silence. She guides Reid to sit on the edge of the massage table, his feet dangling. With both hands, she caresses his knees, appearing intently focused, as if she values every particle of skin covering his kneecaps. She draws circles lightly with her fingernails. His body lights up like a Christmas tree, shooting hits of electric pleasure into his brain. She gazes at Reid with a smile of admiration unlike any he has seen before; her smile graces his soul with approval. He realizes in this moment that this woman is different. *She's another woman who's been trained by Wish.*

She carefully removes one of his shoes, then massages the length of his ankle, somehow knowing which spot will sting, pleasurably, from a deep touch while she removes the sock. His brain is flooded with an unfamiliar masculine revelry at the sight of this woman kneeling below him, performing such a simple task. The woman continues on to the other foot, removing the sock and shoe while massaging similarly.

Kneeling on the floor, she glances up at Reid. He sees something in her eyes, a softness that suggests she cares, really cares, about him. Her gaze launches tingles in his bones. The woman rises, leans towards him, and applies moist kisses along his cheek, releasing euphoric chills into his body. She then steps away from him and stares into his eyes. His awestruck gaze connects with hers. No woman has made him feel anything close to this, and he's only been there a few minutes.

"I'm honored to be your guide tonight, Professor Bradley," she says. "I've learned that you're a man of service. You have many special gifts hidden inside. I am here to help you connect with your deepest self, so you can soon express those special gifts to the world."

Reid lowers his gaze to the floor, while remaining seated with his feet dangling off the massage table. She places a hand on each of his thighs and traces her index fingers up towards his stomach. There's something about how she touches him that fuels in him an unfamiliar yet positive feeling.

"My name is Tasha. I'm a Sexmyst. Tonight there will be zero focus on serving me. In order for you to grow from this experience, you must be selfish."

"Nice to meet you, Tasha. What's a Sexmyst?"

"Wish will explain when the time is right." She draws a finger down his chest. "Close your eyes, Professor, and focus on receiving. In order for you to get closer to yourself, you must receive this experience into your soul."

Reid shuts his eyes; his body erupts with sensory fireworks from her touch. Tasha unbuttons his shirt, applying tender kisses to his chest after each undone button. She removes the shirt completely, then steps back to examine Reid. The exposure triggers him to look down and cover his stomach with his hands, hoping she doesn't notice his body fat and lack of muscular definition.

"Show me all of you," she says, guiding Reid to stand.

He moves his hands to rest on his sides, anticipating her expression of disappointment. Instead, he sees her studying him with a look of admiration. His heart flutters.

She points at his zipper fly, then nods for him to remove his pants. The thought of exposing his erect penis causes him to freeze. He gazes at the ceiling, then unzips, but only partially. He looks at her with a nervy gaze.

"I accept all that you are," she says and steps closer. "When will you do the same for yourself?"

The word *accept* prompts his brain to remember that learning to accept himself is why he's here. *Okay, okay, I'll do it. I can do this.* He ignores his insecurity and drops his pants and underwear to the floor.

He returns his gaze to the floor, knowing he's increased the chances of Tasha looking disappointed. She steps close enough to be face to face with him, then lifts his head so that they lock eyes. He sees her examine his pupils, as if studying the space beyond. Her eyes become glossy. A single tear escapes and rolls down her face.

"On behalf of the humans who have entered your life, I want to apologize." She wipes her tear. "You don't hate whores. You hate that you've rarely been touched."

Tasha caresses Reid's back, sending shocks of feel-good throughout his body. She rests her head on his chest and draws him in for a loving embrace. He melts into her affection, realizing that his past girlfriends were not physically affectionate. He's tempted to further analyze her observation; deep down he knows she's exactly right.

She glides her sharp fingernails up and down his back. "Wish is correct about you."

"Correct about what?"

"I see what he sees. It's true. You are the ..." She abruptly pulls away from the hug. "I cannot share any more." She draws a fingernail down his chest. "I'm here to serve as a guide for your body."

Tasha instructs Reid to lie, stomach down, on the massage table and rest his face in the table's breath hole. Reid obliges, yet he can't help but wonder, *What was she about to say? I am the ... what?*

Before he can explore the thought further, he feels a firm slap on his butt cheek from Tasha's hand. He clenches his jaw, sucking in air through the space between his teeth. He lifts his head from the hole and glances back at Tasha with a furrowed brow.

"That was to awaken the sensory response system in your brain," she says. "I'm not attempting to control or dominate you."

Tasha turns Reid's head to fit in the table's breath hole. His sight is blocked, but he can breathe comfortably. He hears her grab a few items from beneath the massage table, then feels the bristles of a soft brush being stroked across his bottom. He then realizes the bristles are coated with some kind of cooling powder which now coats his bum. The brush lifts from his body. His mind races with anticipation for her next move — a slap, a kiss, a pinch? Neither. She dances her fingers across his bottom, then she applies a deep pressure near his lower back.

Reid smiles. "My God, that feels amaz—"

Her fingers suddenly move off his body. His cheek is met with the hard *thwap* of something rope-like. He gasps as the sting sizzles into his cheek and spreads throughout his body.

"Silence, Professor," she says. "Focus on receiving."

He lifts his head and looks back to see her holding a black leather tassel. She whacks his bottom once more, sending a cloud of white dust into the air. He releases a silent scream and returns his mouth to the hole. His brain bounces between absorbing the sizzle of the sting while feeling heavenly from the floating, cooling powder settling onto his bum.

Her hands carefully massage the powder into his skin for several minutes, leaving him to melt into the table. Tasha then steps away towards the bathroom and returns to carefully apply a warm, damp towel to his back, gliding the heated cotton all over his skin. He then feels a tingle of cool and warm across his skin; the towel must have had some kind of herbal ointment on it.

She carefully removes the towel. He hears the clinking of ice cubes in a bucket from under the table. His hamstrings suddenly tighten as handfuls of ice are placed on the area behind his knees. Each knee is quickly wrapped with a large towel, securing the cubes in place. His skin prickles with goosebumps as icy shocks of chill spread throughout his body.

Tasha lifts his head from the breath hole, and turns his neck to the side, allowing him to now see her. She glides away from the massage table, then returns holding a lit candle over Reid's back. He stiffens at the thought of what will come next.

"Contrasting sensations help the brain recognize sensory responses more effectively," says Tasha. "Right now you feel cold. Pay attention to the contrast." Reid's chilled spine is met with gooey hot wax.

"Yeeeeowww." He raises his upper back like a cobra. Within seconds, his eyes water from the piercing sting of the wax. The sensation then transitions into unexpected pleasure as the heat creates relief from the ice. He gradually lowers himself back down onto the table, absorbing the warmth into his back muscles. For the first time in as long as he can remember, he's experiencing his mind being turned off, allowing him to actually *feel*.

Her soft breasts rest on his upper back and her lips are near his ear. "The wax turns into massage oil," she says. He then feels her breasts glide across his back, spreading the oil, while she coos: "Your skin makes me feel amazing. Thank you for being you."

Everything you do makes me feel beyond amazing.

A few minutes pass, then she removes the ice from his legs, and pours hot wax on his thighs and calves. His legs shake from a few seconds of pain, but then relax as she uses her palms to spread the warm oil all over his lower body. He can't get over the plethora of sensations he's felt in such a short amount of time.

He senses a specific pattern to her technique, but can't quite figure it out. There's something about the combination of hard touch, light touch, deep touch, then barely touching that ignites his brain and body in a way he's never felt before.

"Turn over," she says.

He hesitates, knowing his erection will be fully exposed. He starts to turn, using his free hand to cover his excited member.

"I'm sorry about that," he says.

"You are a healthy, sexy man. Don't ever apologize for being a man." She rubs her palms in circles on his stomach.

He slowly relaxes his hand to his side. The cool air hits his member, exciting it further. He tilts his head to the side, again fearful of seeing an expression of distain on her gorgeous face — or worse, hearing some form of verbal insult. But she's silent. He peeks at her out of the corner of his eye and sees white teeth through her smile. Her words suddenly come back into his mind: *don't apologize for being a man*. He realizes she's right, he *is* a man. And he has no reason to feel shame about what his body desires. He twists his head to face Tasha, basking in the joy he feels from seeing her smile back at him.

Tasha continues massaging with a variety of pressures. She pauses and smiles. "There's something about the feel of your skin that gives me so much pleasure."

Reid nods. She didn't need to say those words; strangely, he seems to sense her appreciation through her touch. He makes a mental note to learn how to have others recognize his appreciation through touching them; he hopes this is something Wish will teach.

Her hands move in small circles, nudging close to his shaft. He recognizes the ritual; it's similar to Amber's. Reid's mind ventures into flashbacks of the robbery. He narrows his eyes and looks up at Tasha.

"You're safe, Professor Bradley," Tasha smiles. "Wish told me you had a negative experience with this technique before." She kneads her palms around his pelvic bone, then up to his belly button.

"The Shadow Palm Technique?" says Reid.

She nods and moves her palms in a manner that feels like she's painting a triangle from his hip flexors to his pelvic bone, applying deep pressure to each spot. He rolls his head back and closes his eyes, absorbing the sensually spiked blood rush into his core.

Tasha continues the pattern, inching closer and closer to his shaft. She repeats the triangular pattern faster, casually bumping into his engorged member within the flow. He lifts his hips slightly. He won't be able to hold back much longer. Tasha notices, and slides her hands up to his chest, massaging with a soft touch as if to spread the erotically enhanced tingles throughout his upper body.

Soon, her oil-soaked hands slide down his stomach to his pelvis. She grips his shaft as if she were holding a flower, stroking gently from the head downward. She presses the thumb of her free hand just below his scrotum. He tenses his stomach; he's never felt that area be touched before. His hips begin to shake, causing him to lift his pelvis. Her stroking hand then twists up towards the tip of the shaft, popping open the fire hydrant of his release. His hips twist through the orgasmic celebration. Then he exhales a breathless gasp as he lowers down into the table. His mind is blank, lost in the land of bliss.

"I'm honored to serve you." She rubs the damp towel across his stomach, removing his fluid.

He gazes at the ceiling, absorbing the retroactive sparkles that ooze through his body. "That was — the greatest ... of my life."

"Humans have disconnected from their ability to touch each other with authentic appreciation. I'm honored to reconnect you with the sensation being a human animal. Tomorrow you'll see and feel differently. Take notice of how the world opens to you, and make that reason enough to learn to perform this for others."

"I can't wait to learn what you know."

"Wish will teach you. Trust him. But be aware: his lessons won't be easy. He knows your fears and will push you to explore the scariest places within."

A sudden tightness forms in Reid's throat; he's nervous about what lies ahead. But if it leads to him being able to provide an experience like Tasha just did, he's all in.

Tasha dances her finger across his belly. "The oil comes off easiest with a shower. I'll be gone by the time you are out." She kisses Reid on the forehead, leads him to the shower, then exits, shutting the bathroom door behind her.

He rests his forehead on the wall of the shower, allowing the hot water to pulse on his back. His lips form into a dark smile. Something about the naughtiness of the experience not only excites him but makes him feel connected to something that *is* him.

He continues to let the warm water rinse his body for several minutes. Then he jolts his head upward in swift realization. He never paid her, and he forgot to protect something important: *the envelope.*

He turns off the shower, wraps a towel around his waist, and hurries into the bedroom. Tasha and all of her things are gone. He grabs his pants and digs through the pockets, praying he hasn't screwed things up already. Pocket number one, empty. Pocket two, empty. Pocket three, empty. All pockets, empty. He looks under the bed, then rips off the covers.

He belts out a grunt. The money is gone.

But Wish knows her — he set up this meeting. He grabs his phone and calls Wish.

"She took all the money. I'm so sorry," says Reid. "I took a shower and came out to the bedroom. The money was gone, she was gone."

Silence.

"Hello, are you there?" Reid trembles with fear, then hears a laugh.

"We're gonna have to get you away from thinking with the head between your legs," says Wish. "Relax, she's bringing the money to me."

Reid falls onto the bed. "Oh, thank God. I swear I'll be more on top of things next time."

"How was the experience?" asks Wish.

Reid suddenly feels Tasha's potent touch all over his body. "I think I'm in love."

"You aren't in love. You've been awakened to possibilities you didn't know existed," says Wish. "I usually explain to clients what to expect beforehand, but with you I had to first see that you had the courage to experience the thing you judged. Tasha did her job, and now you have a deeper sense of what the body is capable of feeling. Soon you'll see how this leads to a deeper understanding of yourself and reconnects you to the value of tactile human-to-human interaction."

"It was amazing."

"She was honored to serve. You were her last client. She recently finished her doctoral program at UNLV and is now going to focus on her formal career."

"I want to take her to dinner. Is she single? I swear, I think I'm falling for her."

Wish chuckles. "I figured this would happen. That's why you now need to go pay for another experience with a different prostitute, someone who isn't trained by me. And you need to do it right now."

"Buying sex to prevent love?" asks Reid. "I don't know if any woman will make me feel the way she did. I swear I'll be good to her."

"You're buying sex to understand who you are," says Wish. "And quit saying you're in love with her. You enjoyed how she made you feel; she filled you with the approval that you don't know how to give yourself. Many people fall into the same trap when becoming involved in a relationship. They don't authentically love their partner, they love the distraction the partner provides — distracting them from their self-hatred. Unfortunately, being in that situation leads to abuse and limited self-growth. Frankly, people shouldn't be allowed to get into long-term relationships until they know and accept who the fuck they are."

Reid grins and shakes his head. He's perplexed by how Wish can sound academic and street at the same time.

Wish continues: "Tasha woke you up to what you've been missing in your life. There's a great deal more for you to learn, but at least you've experienced another dimension of the human body. Your brain's sensory response system has expanded; therefore the way you interpret the universe has expanded."

"I swear her hands are still touching me. My body feels like its humming. I'm all in on this method of learning about myself. I'm ready for the next experience — what's the assignment?"

"Walk across Sahara Boulevard and enter the strip mall. Behind the burger joint is a place called Sunny Massage. Ask for a sixty-minute massage, and when the masseuse is almost finished, you must ask her for a hand job."

"Are you serious?" Reid catches his denial. "I mean, yes, sir."

"Tasha left two hundred in the dresser for you to pay the masseuse. Call me when you're done." Wish pauses. "Don't be a pussy when it comes time to ask for the hand job. A man should have no shame when admitting the desires of his penis."

Reid struggles to swallow his gulp. "Okay."

Chapter 8

There's something strange about going into Sunny Massage an hour before midnight. When Reid enters the dimly lit store he finds the front is sectioned off to be a waiting area, with a small couch, a shoebox-sized sliding-glass window, and a closed door he assumes leads to a hallway off which are the massage rooms. He smiles as a thirty-something Asian woman with blond hair appears behind the small window. The glass slides open. He puckers his face as it's hit with cigarette smoke.

"How long massage?" she says without a sense of welcome.

"One hour, please." He hands her cash. She disappears from the window, then opens the door. "Okay, follow me."

She guides Reid down a long hallway off which are empty massage rooms labeled one, two, three, and four. The carpet along the hallway is pocked with cigarette burns and looks like it's never been vacuumed. His skin crawls from the filth. He instantly appreciates how Tasha had the environment set up perfectly — scented candles, soothing music, and everything was clean.

Each door is cracked open and the rooms appear empty. The silence of the place leads him to believe that she's the only person working there. She signals him to enter room number four. There's a massage table covered with a long white sheet that reaches the floor.

"Take clothes off, lie on stomach, cover with this." She hands Reid a white hand-towel and exits.

He examines the towel, then shakes his head. It'll barely cover his butt. He wonders if Wish truly knows what's going on here, but figures the man must know what he's doing because Tasha provided something he'll never forget. He undresses, crawls onto the table, and rests his face in the table's breath hole. Through the weight of his chest pressing on the thinly padded table, he can feel his heart thump.

Something about being here feels off.

She re-enters the room. He lifts his head upward and sees her standing with a bottle of massage oil in her hand. The sight creates a tickle in his member and sparks arousal. He's curious to compare her to Tasha. The optimist in him hopes that her massage skills are so excellent she doesn't need to focus on the disturbing ambiance, and that clients are still happy. She squirts a copious amount of oil into her hands and slaps it onto his back, rubbing her hands across his skin in a circular motion with minimal pressure and zero care. He instantly recognizes the difference between her and Tasha. He hopes this is how she starts, but then she gets herself in the "massage therapist" zone, eager to work out his tense muscles.

Forty minutes pass and she still hasn't improved; she's still oiling and rubbing her hands in random motions all over his back and legs. She's creating more knots than she relieves. He huffs with frustration, tempted to tell her to stop.

She leaves the room abruptly, then returns with a steaming towel in her hand. She dumps it on his back. He howls from the hot sting. The towel feels like it was pulled from a pot of boiling water.

"Oh, so sorry," she says in a tone that almost sounds sarcastic. She rubs the thin, sandpaper-like towel across his skin. He wonders why this place is still in business; nobody in their right mind would pay for such torture.

"Okay, turn over," she says, lifting both the hot towel and covering towel away from Reid.

He flips over and sees her toss the towels on the floor. He moves his hands to cover his flaccid penis, then looks up to see her lift her eyebrows up and down while smiling. *Ugh, I'm supposed to give the hand job signal. I'd rather get the hell out of here.* But he stays true to his assignment: he forms his hand into a fist and motions from side to side.

"You give me good tip?" she says.

He nods while internally rolling his eyes. She squirts oil into her hands, plops them on his package, and begins tugging and pulling like she's kneading dough. His stomach begins to hurt, as if someone's kicked his jewels. He's learned that a man has permission to express his sexual desires. *Can a man also ask a woman to stop pursuing those desires if she's awful?*

The excessive tugging has dried the oil on his shaft, but she continues her stroke. He now feels the burning sensation of chafed skin on his member. He considers telling her to stop, but the polite side of him fears he might upset her. Instead, he lifts his hips, gasping as if feeling orgasmic. Then he moves her hand away, covers his member, and turns on his side. He grunts loudly through a fake orgasm.

She steps back, grinning. "You likey?"

Reid reaches for a nearby tissue and pretends to wipe his fluids from his hands. "Yes, me likey." *I'd likey to get the fuck out of here.*

She takes his used tissue and tosses it in the trash bin next to the massage table. Reid glances in the bin and sees that it contains several used tissues. Nausea spreads across his stomach. She gathers all of the towels and exits. He recalls Tasha saying Wish would be testing his limits, and this massage was certainly that kind of test. He quickly slides his jeans on and pulls out his phone. His nausea shifts to a sense of alarm: Wish sent him an urgent text thirty minutes ago.

Get out of there!!! Det. Jones said Youngblood is out to bust massage parlors tonight. And he's in your area.

Reid shoves the phone in his pocket and throws on his remaining clothes. He cracks open the door to leave, then hears a deep southern voice coming from a man in the lobby.

"I need to look in the back," says the man. "I'm here to inspect the premises and patrons."

Reid slips back into his room. He darts his gaze to the ceiling, then to each wall. No escape route. He hears the woman opening the doors to the other private rooms.

"Nobody here," she says.

Three doors have opened and closed. His room will be next. *I'm screwed.* Then he sees additional sheets folded on a shelf.

"Show me room number four," the voice commands from the hallway.

"No need to look. All rooms empty," she says.

"You're hiding someone, aren't you?"

Reid grabs a sheet, crawls under the table, and covers himself.

Luckily, the sheet that already covers the table hangs to the floor, so he should be difficult to spot. He rests on his knees, curling into a tight ball as the door slowly opens.

"I love cops," says the woman as they enter.

"Oh," the man replies. "Is that so?"

Reid peeks through the sheet and sees the shadow of the man walking around the room. The shadow stops in front of the trash bin.

"There are a lot of tissues in your trash. You won't mind if I take this down to the station and have the tissues examined for semen?" Reid's ears focus on the twangy sound of the voice. The man sounds like Youngblood.

A bead of sweat rolls down Reid's forehead. He considers his options. *Maybe I should just stand up and tell the truth? Youngblood was nice to me before. He was trying to save me from Wish.* Yet he can't ignore the distrust Wish has for Youngblood. Heat builds behind his eyes; he imagines the headline of his school's next newspaper: "Professor Gets Caught with His Pants Down at Massage Parlor."

"I love cops. You very handsome man," says the masseuse.

Reid lifts his sheet slightly, exposing his eyes for a clearer view. He notices her bare feet step closer to the man's shoes. She rises to stand on her toes. *Is she flirting with him?*

"Well," says the man, "I do have some time — for a massage. But only ten minutes. Do five on my back and a special five minutes on my front."

"Lie down. I get oil."

Reid sees the man's clothes fall to the floor and clenches his teeth. *Blackmail.* He cocks his head upward and sees the man's salt-and-pepper goatee as his face settles into the breath hole. It's Youngblood. *But he claimed to be all about ridding Vegas of its sex problems? This could tie into Wish's belief that Youngblood is part of the Collective Shadow, with deep repression issues.* Either way, Reid knows he's got to get out of there, and he figures it's best to leave now while Youngblood is distracted.

Reid slides the sheet off his back, then begins to crawl out from under the table. Youngblood starts to speak and Reid slips back under.

"You've been busy today. That's good. Perhaps we can make an arrangement."

Reid shakes his head. *The man is a hypocrite.*

"I love cops," says the woman. "Time for you to relax. You work very hard."

"Mmmm, good. You understand how to treat us. I arrested a girl in the parking garage across the street who wasn't as open-minded. She had six grand in cash on her. I had patrol take her in. Now I can relax."

Reid covers his mouth with his hand. *Tasha?* He looks up and sees the man's face return to the breath hole. Youngblood exhales for a few seconds, appearing to settle into his massage. Reid crawls out, reaches for the door knob and twists it slowly to keep quiet, then pulls the door open. A sensation of relief overtakes him as he slips into the hallway. In his peripheral vision, he catches a smile from the masseuse and turns his head toward her, then he notices his phone on the floor, partially covered by the table sheet. *Shit.*

Reid's heart damn near jumps out of his chest. He glares at the phone, then at the masseuse, then at Youngblood. The man appears to be relaxed into his massage. From the doorway, Reid reaches towards the phone. Youngblood lifts his head from the hole. Reid freezes in full sight.

Youngblood's eyes are closed.

"Don't mess with my hair, though. I gotta look pretty for all the hookers tonight." Youngblood's head returns to the hole.

Reid quickly snags the phone, then crawls backwards into the hallway. He rises with cat-like silence and steps heel-to-toe towards the front door. The door chimes as he pushes it open, shocking Reid into a full sprint across the street. Afraid to look back, he runs straight to his car, and drives out of the garage while catching his breath.

As he turns onto Sahara Avenue, he glances across at the massage parlor. He sees no sign of Youngblood and figures he must still be inside. Driving down the road, Reid reflects on how the detective is such a hypocrite. *He solicits girls, then busts them if they don't cooperate. Tasha probably didn't give in to his shtick.* Reid continues down Sahara Boulevard and calls Wish through the Bluetooth speaker system in his car.

As Wish answers, Reid starts talking. "Freaking Youngblood came to the parlor." Reid further explains how he managed to escape and how Youngblood seemed to take a "happy ending" bribe.

"You handled yourself well, Professor." Wish goes silent for a few seconds, then speaks. "The man's repression is stronger than we thought. This might work in our favor."

"How so?" Reid squeezes the steering wheel.

"The lives of repressed individuals typically follow predictable patterns. I'll explain more later. Which way did you exit the Sahara Hotel parking lot?"

"I turned right."

"Make a U-turn. There's another stop for you in the opposite direction."

Reid quickly turns the car around. "Youngblood said he arrested a woman in the Sahara parking garage. Was that Tasha?"

"Yes, she just called from the precinct. Luckily, Youngblood didn't have adequate evidence; he's new to Nevada law. Tasha is a chiropractic doctor. She can validate why she was carrying six grand and a massage table. Detective Jones says she'll be free within the hour. Are you certain Youngblood didn't see you there?"

"Uh oh." Reid's eyes lock onto the rear-view mirror; police lights are flashing behind him. He steers the car to the side of the road.

"You okay?" asks Wish.

Reid sees the cops speed past. He watches them for a bit longer before replying. "Two cop cars just flew by me, then pulled into a strip mall off in the distance. Hold on."

He presses the pedal mildly, driving forward for a few seconds, then drifts to a stop at a red light. The stop light is in front of the strip mall that contains the massage parlor. He turns his head and sees the cop cars parked, lights flashing. Instantly, Reid understands what he sees.

"Youngblood just busted that masseuse. He's got her out front in cuffs with the other cops helping out."

"Youngblood is trickier than I thought," says Wish. "But I'm glad you witnessed how he operates. This may come in handy for us to protect ourselves from him. Are you certain he didn't see you there?"

The idea of coming into contact with Youngblood again stirs

Reid's stomach. He glances in the mirror while driving further down Sahara Avenue. "I'm fairly certain. He would have busted me as well. By the way, that second massage was shit. Did you know it was going to be awful?"

"I would have been surprised if it wasn't awful," says Wish. "A good lesson for you: the human brain is a duality mechanism, meaning it recognizes best by comparing opposites — contrasts. For the brain to recognize night-time, it must also have observed the opposite, daytime. The brain cannot recognize beauty unless it has also seen ugliness. For the brain to recognize amazing, it must also experience what you describe as shitty.

"Most people experience the sex act similarly to how you felt with the last masseuse: uncaring, selfish, and surface level. Soon you will learn to be like Tasha, providing the greatest sensory experiences on the planet — connecting people through their erotic passion, instead of their mundane lives of disconnected shame."

"I can't wait to learn more. Does this mean I passed your tests?"

"You have one more test, but first I'll need you pick up something at the Adult Megastore on Decatur and Sahara. When you arrive, ask for Goddess Mindy."

"Who is Goddess Mindy?" says Reid. He shakes his head, knowing Wish has ended the call.

Chapter 9

Could tonight possibly get any stranger? I damn near got arrested, and now I have to go into a porn shop. While pulling into the parking lot, Reid gawks at the massive neon sign: *THE ADULT MEGASTORE, the largest adult selection in the world.* A tingle rushes up his neck and across his face.

He sits in his parked car, nervous to exit as a painful memory enters his mind. He drifts back to the one and only time he visited an adult store. It was in the '90s, before internet pornography existed. He was eighteen, and years of driving past this store had pushed his curiosity to breaking point. He took his mom's car, without her permission, and made the short drive to the adult shop. It was in a rundown part of town, isolated on a piece of land so that any car parked in the lot was clearly for the adult store. Flushed, Reid entered the store and bought the first pornographic DVD he could find that seemed unintimidating. He then hurries out with a purple bag in hand, elated from his rebellious purchase. The high he felt quickly dissipated when he stood in front of his mom's car and noticed the keys were locked inside. He had no choice but to call his mom and explain. Soon, a taxi dropped Reid's mom off at the adult store, and they waited, awkwardly, until help arrived. It took years for him to shake off the shame he felt that day. He remembers clearly what his mom said: "I'm raising you to respect women, not watch movies of them being exploited."

And now those uncomfortable feelings ooze throughout his body. He turns off the ignition, then taps his fingers on the steering wheel as he ventures into thoughts of quitting. A sudden needle-like pain penetrates his heart; the scene of Jasmine moaning with her newfound lover creeped into his head. A reminder: *The work I'm doing now will ensure that I'll never be in that position again. I'm not blindly following a dumb pimp. Everything he's said seems to be on point. And the experience with Tasha is proof that there is more to learn from Wish.*

He huffs a quick keep-on-keepin'-on breath, then steps out of the car and enters the building. He peeks at the grand displays of dildos, leather whips, porn DVDs, blow-up dolls, bachelorette party favors, and lubricants. Though he feels uncomfortable, he wonders if there's a way to be at ease in these surroundings. He ambles further, then halts at the sight of a naked woman posing doggy style on a bed. Reid shifts his gaze to the floor, as if to say, *Sorry for looking at you.*

"May I help you?" asks a female voice.

He looks at the girl on the bed, certain it's a manikin, but does a double-take. Then he turns and sees a woman smile from behind a tall desk.

"That fake woman looks damn near real," says Reid.

"I know, crazy, right?" replies the clerk. "She's a Stacey. The world's first fully robotic sex doll. You can program her into any position you desire and she'll please you. Her breasts are silicone, meaning they're real-fake-tits."

"Men would buy that?" Reid moves for a closer look, realizing there's an entire world of hidden sexual expression that he's only beginning to understand.

"We're backordered for at least a year," she says. "I guess men will do anything to avoid having to deal with the complexities of a woman."

Reid tilts his head back. He's heard of sex-robots being developed, but never actually seen one in person. He turns towards the clerk. "I'm here to see Goddess Mindy."

"Go to row nine. Her office is at the end, on the right, just beyond the butt plugs."

Butt plugs? He tightens his bum cheeks, wondering how people can be into such strange sexual practices. He catches his judgmental thoughts and recalls how Wish said everyone has their own style of finding happiness in their life.

Reid can't resist the icky sensation he feels as he moves past displays of glass dildos, edible clothing, and nipple clamps. He stops to calm himself. *It's just sex. I've got to figure out how to quit being so damn uptight.* He turns down aisle nine, slowing his walk to observe the plethora of butt plugs and anal beads, noticing the many different shapes, sizes, and styles. He widens his eyes at the sight of a giant orange plug in the middle of the aisle, again tightening his bum cheeks together. *Oh, it's just a construction cone, or maybe not?*

"Wish said you'd look like the most uncomfortable person ever to step into this store," a female voice calls out. "My vision is not the greatest, but the energy of your presence certainly suggests he was correct."

Reid turns his head and sees a petite young woman nearing him. She's wearing thick-lensed bifocals that resemble the glass of old-fashioned Coca-Cola bottles. Her arms are covered with tattoos, which extend from denim overalls hanging over a white tank top. Her black hair is whipped up in a bun held tight by a pencil. Although he's not attracted to her, his heart flutters at the sight of the thick lenses, which display her retinas as double-sized. He instantly feels an odd connection to her, as if she's a little sister who needs his protection.

"I'm beyond excited to meet you, Reid," she says.

Reid shakes her hand, noticing her quivering palm. He grins and tilts his head to the side, as if to say, *Don't be nervous.*

She smiles. "I ... I'm Mindy. Follow me." She turns to walk down the hallway, but trips over the construction cone.

Reid rushes to help her up. "I should have warned you about the cone." He lifts her to her feet.

"No, no, no. It's my fault. I should have remembered they put that there yesterday."

Mindy centers her glasses on her face. Reid once again feels a strange connection to her as he locks his gaze on her magnified retinas. Her curled lips form a smile.

"Me tripping and falling was an omen. Look at how present we are now. Thanks for helping me up." She goes to kiss his cheek; her lips hit the side of his nose. They both giggle. "My vision is not that bad, but when I'm nervous it's the first thing to go. Wish has never sent me a male trainee before. You must be a big deal."

"Wish has never trained a man?"

"No. He's always feared that men would abuse the knowledge, use it for evil. But now that society has changed for the worse, he understands that his knowledge must get out to men before it's too late."

"Before it's too late for what?" says Reid.

"It's best for Wish to explain that to you."

Reid's puffs his cheeks with air, then exhales. His patience is wearing thinner every time he hears that Wish will tell him — he's always having to wait. *Why is Wish so damn guarded?*

They enter a small, cluttered office. At one end is a work bench covered with loose wires, tools, and several half-opened vibrators that appear to be getting fixed. Next to the bench is a shelf with a microscope and vials filled with various liquids. In the corner is a desk with a laptop and a small purple box sized to contain index cards. Reid processes the scene and senses Goddess Mindy is some kind of sex toy designer. He continues to explore the room, noticing a uniquely designed candle at the edge of the work bench. It appears to be unused, and is contained in some kind of plastic jar. He grabs it and notices that the bottom portion seems to be detachable. He then lowers his nose to sniff the scent.

"Guess what that is?" she says.

"A candle." He sniffs it again. "Orange and lavender scent."

Goddess Mindy grins. "Exactly what I was hoping you'd say. Yes, it's a candle, but hidden in the bottom part of the frame is a video camera. The camera enables you to record and live-stream whatever you might be filming. Once the candle is lit for twenty seconds, the camera activates; blow the candle out and it shuts off. You could film yourself having sex without the partner knowing."

"Amazing," says Reid. "But why would someone use this?"

"It would go in the category of visual stimulation. A man could secretly film himself with his wife, then send her a naughty clip while she's at work the next day. Obviously, it could be used for evil as well, but we hope that isn't the case. Has Wish taught you about the importance of stimulating all five senses when providing an erotic service to someone?"

"Not yet. But he has mentioned contrasts and the brain."

Goddess Mindy reaches under her desk and retrieves an oddly designed glove. "This glove has the fingertips removed and contrasting materials sewn throughout." She lifts each finger of the glove. "The thumb is velvet; the index is scratchy, like sandpaper; the middle is thin, cold metal; and the ring and pinky fingers are fur. And as you can see, the bottom of the palm has small metal studs for pulsing techniques such as the Shadow Palm. Used properly, this glove will provide never-ending contrasts for the brain, resulting in heightened sensory responses."

Reid examines the glove. "Wish has mentioned the Shadow Palm Technique. What's your interpretation of it?"

Goddess Mindy quickly snatches the glove from Reid's hand. "Don't tell him I showed you this. I didn't realize he hadn't taught you about that yet." She puts the glove back under her desk.

He raises an eyebrow, but knows he won't be able to prize Wish's secrets out of her. He shifts to another topic. "How did you come to know Wish?"

"We met in the UNLV library a few years ago. I was struggling to study for an exam as a pre-med anesthesiology student. Wish was at the desk next to mine, reading the newspaper. He saw my frustration and offered to help. The man was incredibly patient and articulate. He ended up meeting me twice a week and helped me pass those classes. He never asked for anything in return; he claimed that us becoming friends was part of his calling. Now we work together."

Reid scratches his head, then glances around at several disembodied dildos and the chemistry equipment.

Goddess Mindy continues: "Eventually, I choose to get off the path for anesthesiology and go into tech-engineering. As it turns out, the knowledge from studying the human sensory response system has proven helpful for my career, because I now make erotic sensory-enhancement products."

Reid rubs his chin. "How does Wish know that stuff? Was he an anesthesiologist?"

"I don't think so. He never directly answers questions about his past. However, I must admit the man knows the human body better than all of my professors combined."

"I've noticed that to be true of him as well," says Reid. "He keeps referring to the mission. What is it exactly?"

"You never stop with the questions." Goddess Mindy laughs. "It's best he explains it to you, so you'll have clarity with what your role will be in the mission. Most of his knowledge is written on index cards contained in that small purple box. He lets me hold onto it here, because it contains erotic concepts, gathered from his years of research, which I use to create erotic sensory-enhancement products."

Reid exhales a playful yet frustrated breath. "I'm sure I'll have to wait for Wish to tell me what's in the purple box." Goddess Mindy chuckles and nods. "Have you designed anything that seemed like a great idea but actually didn't work well?"

Mindy rolls her magnified eyeballs. "The Ghost Piranha insert." She reaches under her desk and grabs a cone-shaped item that is the size of an expanded condom. It appears to be made of soft white rubber, smooth on the outside, but rippled with small teeth pointing inward on the inside. "The woman inserts this into her vagina. For the man, his penis feels amazing during entry, but upon removal the teeth shred his shaft."

Reid grimaces, moving both hands in front of his privates.

"We thought the pain would be a great contrast to enhance the sensory reception in the penis, figuring it would just scratch the shaft, but it shredded Wish's penis when he and his wife tried it. He ended up with multiple surface abrasions that kept him from sex for a while."

"Ouch. That sounds awful."

"I figure if a woman is really pissed off at her husband, it could come in handy. She could even apply jalapeño lube to increase the burn once the penis is cut. But we aren't convinced it's worth selling to the masses yet."

Reid feels his phone vibrate and digs it out. He sees a text from Wish. It contains an address followed by instructions:

Get the item from Goddess Mindy, then come to my place.

Reid glances at Goddess Mindy. "Wish says you have an item for me? Then I need to go to his place."

"Have you ever been to his place?" she asks. Reid shakes his head. "The cage can be a lot to take in for the unexperienced."

"Cage?" says Reid, then he recalls Wish mentioning something about Amber and a cage after she robbed him.

"You'll see." She grins. "Remember, all that he does is based on service to others, even if it doesn't look like the type of service that mainstream society would approve of."

"I'll keep that in mind. It was nice meeting you, Goddess Mindy."

She reaches under her desk and hands Reid a black leather paddle. "This is for you."

He pauses to examine the item, which resembles a pingpong paddle, but with a longer handle. "Will I be using this tonight?"

"Yes, and don't hold back," she says.

Reid further examines the paddle, then looks at the floor. *I could never hit a woman.* He then feels Mindy's cold fingers lift his chin until their eyes connect.

"Wish knows your fears and he'll force you to face them. He'll push you beyond anything you can imagine. He senses something special about you, as do I. Hopefully, you'll soon see it as well."

Goddess Mindy opens her arms and they embrace in a friendly goodbye hug. Reid exits, walking with a lifted chest, excited to hear about the potential that Wish sees in him. But as he nears his car, he slows his pace, considering what might take place at Wish's home.

He gets into his car and exhales a long sigh while staring at the paddle. *I'm supposed to hit a woman with this?* He recalls how Wish accused him of abusing Jasmine when they first met, then tosses leather-bound item onto the passenger seat. *But wouldn't THAT be abusing a woman?* He programs Wish's address into his phone's GPS and drives off the lot.

Chapter 10

The security guard looks at the paddle in Reid's hand, then smirks as he reaches into the elevator and pushes the button labeled "PH," for penthouse. Reid stares at his shoes, nervous about what might be in store for him. The elevator carries him, alone, to the top floor.

His eyes expand as the elevator doors open, revealing an immaculately designed, dimly lit penthouse.

"Hello?" Reid enters, his body stiffening with each step. "Wish, are you here?"

Reid carefully steps, heel-to-toe, around the sunken living room. He gawks at the rich white-leather furniture, polished silver fixtures, dark-wood floors and large white-fur rug in the center. He examines the rug, noticing its fluffiness, except for one spot that appears mushed from something sitting there often. He wonders if Wish has a dog, and if perhaps the cage has something to do with that dog. He looks around, not seeing anything that looks like a cage. He wants to believe Mindy was messing with him, but nothing involving Wish thus far has been a joking matter.

His gaze moves past the rug to the floor-to-ceiling windows that give a panoramic view of the Strip. Wish's tower is located just across the freeway from the center of the Strip, allowing for this breath-taking view. He then shifts his eyes to the walls, which display various erotic works of art. A certain painting captures his attention — the illustration of a human shadow swinging a long whip.

"Hello?" says Reid. He moves quietly along a hallway that has three closed doors, wondering if maybe he's in the wrong home. A feverish chill rolls down his spine and he grips the paddle tighter. Then he hears a loud *kerwack* from behind the first door. *What the hell was that?* He stops, glances back at the elevator, then returns to face the door.

A sudden vibration buzzes into his toes: rhythmic tribal music has begun pulsing from inside the room. Reid knocks lightly. He leans closer, resting his ear on the heavy wood. He hears talking, but can't make out the words. The music and talking abruptly stop. A few seconds pass — then he hears an eruption of several whacks.

He steps back, cringing at the thought of what that powerful-sounding whip must be doing. He glances at the elevator again, feeling an urge to leave, but something about the heaviness of his feet keeps him in place. He hears the music click back on, followed by three more whacks. He questions if such violence is what Wish has in store for him, but then he hears faint sounds of feminine elation. *Pleasure?* He leans towards the door again.

The door swings open. Reid stumbles backwards and drops the paddle on the floor. He gathers himself, retrieves the paddle, and notices Wish standing in the doorway looking stern. Reid catches a quick glimpse of a dark and strange scene behind Wish before he slams the door and steps closer to Reid. Reid's chest tightens; he's struggling to believe what his eyes claim to have seen. *Was that a woman, blindfolded and tied to metal rods?*

Reid returns his focus to Wish, who is shirtless. His body is sculpted to perfection, with muscles comparable to that of a gymnast. Wish maintains his stern expression, and nods for Reid to return to the living room. Reid turns and walks, hearing Wish slip back into the whipping room. *I swear that was a naked woman tied to metal rods, and she didn't look happy.*

Reid walks quickly through the living room and stands near the elevator. He stares at the call button, contemplating if he should stay. He reaches for the call button, then hears Wish's footsteps, so he stops his hand short of pressing the button. Reid turns, straightens his stance, and smiles like a polite house guest. *Mindy says to trust him.* Wish glides across the living room with a sense of certainty, walking barefoot, shirtless but in black silk pants.

Reid gawks at Wish's superhero-like physique, feeling the doughiness of his untrained muscles. Wish sits in the mushed spot on the fur rug, legs crossed, like a yogi meditating. Reid follows and sits across from him. Wish closes his eyes and takes several deep breaths.

Reid studies Wish's posture, then looks away out of the window at the Las Vegas Strip.

"I've meditated on this rug every day for the past ten years," says Wish. Reid's gaze darts back to his mentor. "Some days, nothing interesting happens. Other days, I experience a vision, a vision that then reoccurs until I experience it in reality. My life experience has taught me that reoccurring visions often prove to be a form of guidance, leading me into the next phase of my journey. So I never take them lightly.

"A few years ago, I had a reoccurring vision that suggested I'd meet a key contributor to our mission at the UNLV library. I didn't know who, or why. But the dream kept occurring, so I kept visiting the library."

"That's where you met Mindy," says Reid.

"Goddess Mindy," says Wish.

"Sorry, I meant Goddess Mindy. Why do you call her Goddess?"

"Every woman is a goddess, possessing important feminine powers that must be utilized to ensure the human race will thrive. She tends to operate with self-doubt, therefore the nickname is a polite reminder for her to not shy away from her feminine strength."

"She says you helped her with anesthesiology?"

"We've learned from each other. She helped me understand what I needed to know about the younger generation of men and women."

"How do you know about anesthesiology?" says Reid.

Wish closes his eyes, ignoring the question. "For the past two months I've had a reoccurring vision of a crisis, which I believe to be an omen. The word *crisis* to the layman means danger. But in Cantonese writing, the symbol for *crisis* translates into two words — danger and opportunity."

"Danger and opportunity contrast," Reid says.

"Exactly, Professor. You're starting to catch on. As I mentioned before, contrasts are vital for the brain's ability to understand anything. We cannot recognize the value of good times unless we experience bad times. Those who have seen the very worst in people possess a uniquely expanded awareness, allowing them to recognize the very best in people.

"The vision portrayed danger and opportunity colliding in the same place, a bar that resembles the Diamond Bar at the Largo Hotel. I've come to believe the danger involves Youngblood — whom we'll discuss later. The opportunity part of the vision involves a young man with gifts that will save the world. I had visited the Diamond Bar twenty-nine days in a row prior to the night we met."

"I don't know that I have gifts. I'm a nerd whose girlfriends cheat on him."

"The vision implied that this young man isn't aware of his gifts, and that my final assignment during this phase of my life will be to serve as his guide. The young man is the one chosen to complete the final phase of our mission, but he must first come to understand himself and the depths of his powers."

A cautious grin forms onto Reid's face.

"The only thing that's held me back ..." Wish releases a heavy sigh. "The vision portrayed this young man as having some kind of physical wound on his head. You clearly have psychological wounds, but the vision showed a physical wound."

Reid drops his chin as flashes of horrific childhood memories pulse through his mind. He was teased and bullied throughout his youth because as a child Reid's head was abnormally large for his body and misshapen. Many of the girls called him ugly and stupid because of how he looked. His well-intentioned mom, fearing the teasing, was afraid to let him cut his hair short, leaving him to look like a boy with a lion's mane.

Reid tilts his head to the side, then uses his hands to spread apart his thick, droopy hair, displaying a lengthy scar, from ear to ear, the result of skull surgery as an infant.

"I had to have surgery on my skull when I was a baby," says Reid.

Wish hastily crawls near to Reid, kneels, and places his hands on Reid's head to examine the scar. "A single cut across your skull, along the ear line." Wish feels the shape of Reid's head. "Your skull was malformed when you were born. You had Craniosynostosis. If you didn't have the surgery, your skull would have grown inward and it would have dramatically impacted your brain function."

Reid pulls away from Wish. "How did you know?"

Wish hops up, eager like a child on Christmas morning. "It's time for your final test. Grab your paddle."

Wish hurries down the hallway and waves for Reid to follow. Reid runs his hand through his hair, flustered by Wish's evasiveness, but also in awe of how Wish knew more about the surgery than he did. Reid grabs the paddle, then looks at the elevator, and is surprised to find he now has no desire to leave. He moves towards Wish and stops to stand with him in front of the door to the mysterious room.

"Our newest member, Molly, is in this room. In my twenty years of research, she's one of the most gifted women I've come across. She's as delicate as a flower. She's also more connected to sexual energy than anyone I have met, including my wife, Dalia. Molly is being tested tonight, just as you are. Your presence will help me assess if she's developed the skills that we've been working on."

Reid figures Molly must be the woman he saw in the room. "Okay, and what is my test exactly?"

"Your test is to be honest — be honest with yourself, then be honest with me and Molly. Any hesitancy or dishonest response will be considered failure."

"That's it?" Reid glances down, sighing with relief. "Goddess Mindy said it was going to be all kinds of scary. She must have been messing with me."

Reid lifts his gaze. Wish is staring at him, unmoved by his comment. "So, what is it that Molly has been trained to do?"

"Molly has been trained to sense your energy. She needs to prove her skill without being able to see you. Her eyes are covered with a blindfold."

"My energy?" replies Reid.

"The energy of your shadow-self."

Reid swallows a gulp. "Is she going to use that to control me?"

Wish smirks. "It's good that you bring up how women can abuse men through their sexual expression, just as you're a pussy who has abused women through giving flowers and ass kissing. Both are forms of manipulation. However, Molly experiences a different form of abuse. She has used her potent sexual energy to abuse herself."

Reid cowers as he sorts through the defensive responses in his mind; but he knows Wish is right in calling him a pussy. He lifts his shoulders, feeling his inner psychologist kick into gear. "How has Molly abused herself?"

"She was born with the same gene as you and me. This gene has programmed us with an extreme form of sexual energy that was designed to ensure the safe evolution of mankind. I'll explain more about that if you pass this test. For now, just know that if this energy is misunderstood, it will be used for evil — either towards oneself, like with Molly, or towards others, like with you."

Reid stands in silence, pondering all that's being shared.

Wish continues: "Molly often gave her sexual energy away to men because she was seeking approval. The gene in her body kept signaling that sex would be her path to the acceptance of self, but because she misunderstood the energy, she kept getting herself into increasingly negative situations. Her actions often resulted in men having complete control over her. Once a man feels he can control a woman, he will often turn to violence when she attempts to break free. You'll see a scar below Molly's stomach. She was stabbed by her ex-boyfriend before she ran away to Las Vegas."

"Is that why women are taught to wait for a few dates before having sex?"

"Women who choose to engage in that behavior can also be considered abusive." A look of disgust forms on Wish's face. "Dishonesty about desire is repression. If sexual desire isn't present, and the woman honestly doesn't crave the man, then delaying sex is fine — society contains plenty of women who don't desire sex until they feel genuinely connected to a man. But if the woman has fiery desire and chooses to hold back, she's repressing the energy. She's behaving in agreement with the Collective Shadow, using her repressed sexuality to manipulate the man from day one. If that ever happens to you, remind yourself that she's part of the Collective Shadow, seeking to fill a void through manipulating others, and make a respectable exit."

"That makes sense. So, what am I supposed to do in the room? What's Molly supposed to do? And how does this relate to what you want me to do tonight?"

"You'll be expected to be honest about your sexual desires. I'm sharing Molly's story because she's an example of what many women and men who have our DNA struggle with. They want to know how they can honestly express their sexual energy in a world that shames such honesty."

"How will I learn to do this?"

"Learning best occurs through taking action. Right now, your assignment will be to explore your repressed truths, then honestly express yourself to me and Molly."

Wish pulls the door open. Reid thinks he hears music, but realizes the sound is his heartbeat thumping through his chest up to his ear. He sees a gate, formed of crisscrossing metal rods, blocking the doorway. He peeks through the rods, curious to find the woman he saw earlier and see if that woman is Molly. Wish lifts a lever to open the gate and steps into the dark room. Reid follows and notices a padlock dangling near the clamp, shuddering as he wonders if Wish locks people in here. Reid steps just past the gate and halts, still unable to see the woman from earlier. He feels hardwood floor beneath his shoes, sticky like a basketball court. The light from the hallway gives him a few seconds to examine his environment, and he sees some kind of metal design surrounding him, but he isn't able to make complete sense of it. Again, he looks for the woman, but is unable to see her as the hallway door shuts, leaving them in complete darkness. He takes a deep breath, hoping to relax, but the sound of the padlock closing on the lever intensifies his nervousness.

A dim spotlight switches on — just enough light for Reid to piece together what he sees. He gasps, looking upward, realizing they're in a large metal cage. *Is this some kind of giant torture chamber? Was Molly the woman I saw earlier? Is she still here?* His eyes slowly adjust, and he observes several metal rods woven together from the floor to a few feet overhead, resembling something like a dome. He's reminded of the playground climbing domes he enjoyed as a child. However, those domes were circular, and this is more of a clunky oval. Reid notices the outline of windows along the far side that would provide a view of the Las Vegas Strip but are blacked out by thick curtains.

His neck hairs raise as he hears the sound of rhythmic, tribal-like drumming pulsing through speakers, activated by an illuminated remote control in Wish's hand. Wish moves his hand like a magician swinging a wand, and a centrally located spotlight switches on above, showcasing a black-leather massage table. At first glance it looks like Tasha's table, except this has various straps and clamps hanging from chains attached to the sides of the table.

Reid struggles to swallow as he looks just beyond the table and sees a blindfolded woman sitting quietly in a chair; he recognizes her as the woman from before. The presence of this woman causes Reid's fear to dissipate momentarily, and his body tingles with an oddly timed sensation of sexual attraction.

Reid walks nearer to her, feeling as though a magnetic force is pulling him. He stops, faces her, and observes the black lace lingerie on her breathtaking figure. *A goddess.* Reid notices something strange about her hands. He glances at Wish with an expression of concern, then back at Molly's wrists: they're resting in her lap, handcuffed. Reid looks at Wish, hoping to receive a comforting signal, but instead the serious expression on Wish's face has intensified. Wish stands tall, legs wide, like a ghostly spirit.

The overhead light clicks off, and a light near the far end of the cage turns on. Reid walks towards the illuminated area and identifies various erotic items hanging from small hooks. Centered amongst the items is a wooden sign with the engraved words:

PROVIDE CONTRASTS TO FULFILL LIVES.
ACCEPT CONTRASTS FOR A LIFE FULFILLED.

Reid squints, processing the instructions. The light clicks off, leaving them in darkness. He hears the sounds of chains clinking from where Molly is sitting. Surging with fight-or-flight adrenaline, Reid holds his paddle in the air with a quivering hand, praying he'll magically develop the skill to ward off an attack. He reaches out with his free hand, only to grasp the cold darkness. The music lowers and Reid listens carefully, anticipating any sound of danger. Instead, he hears Molly's soft, feminine voice.

"I'm honored to serve this man."

Something about her delicate sound calms Reid. He lowers his hands to his sides. Then he hears footsteps, followed by more sounds of chains clinking together.

Several red lights switch on, creating an exotic glow in the cage. Reid rubs his eyes as they adjust to the light, then he sees that Wish has moved Molly from the chair. Now she's standing, her arms extended overhead, clamped to a chain which dangles from the woven metal above. Molly's backside faces Reid. His eyes move along the curves of her irresistible figure.

A sense of befuddlement overcomes Reid. He's noticing a sensation, a foreign sensation he believes he shouldn't be having. A sense of power; dominance. His hands tingle with the urge to explore Molly's silky skin. *I want her. I want to fuck her.* His chest lifts high and sinks low with each breath; he's lost in a world of naughty thoughts.

"What were you just thinking?" asks Wish.

Reid moves his gaze to the floor, flushed. "Nothing. I'm just a little nervous, sir."

"Well, aren't you the polite young man," says Wish. Reid lifts his head, cracking an innocent smile. Wish steps closer, exuding an aura of seriousness. "Politeness is dishonest. It's what gets you cheated on. Politeness is what a boy does to win the approval of his mother. Your boyish behavior ends right now. The boy inside of you must die to initiate the birth of the man you're destined to become."

Reid breaks eye contact with Wish, observes Molly's helpless state, then stares at the floor. He anticipates the sympathetic touch of Wish's hands on his shoulders. Instead, his face is met with an open-handed strike that launches his head sideways. The force causes Reid to drop the paddle and, clanking, it hits the hardwood. Gasping from the sting, he bends forward and grips his knees.

"Stand the fuck up." Wish's voice echoes in the cage. Reid's eyes start to water as he returns to standing on wobbly knees.

"Where's that man inside of you?" yells Wish. Tears race down Reid's cheeks. Wish's open hand explodes across Reid's face once more. Reid drops his hands to his thighs, coughing as he tries to halt his sobbing.

"Stand." Wish's voice pierces Reid's heart like an icepick. "Stand the fuck up."

Reid slowly rises. His body feels boneless, as if every ounce of his masculinity has evaporated. With his forearm, he wipes his eyes, then he looks in desperation at his mentor. *What am I supposed to say?*

"Tell me what you were thinking when you saw her," says Wish.

A thick, chalky sensation clogs Reid's throat. He opens his mouth, but is incapable of speaking. He knows what he was thinking when he saw her. *I want to rip her lingerie off and fuck her brains out.* But those words would never come out of his clean, respectable mouth.

Wish's glare continues to cut into Reid, roughly, like a strong man using a dull knife. Reid drops his jaw, intending to talk, but remains speechless. Again, Wish's open palm explodes across Reid's face. Reid crumbles to the floor, gasping in silent desperation. He reaches towards the exit, intending to crawl to escape, but then halts, remembering the cage has been locked. He curls into a ball, surrendering to helplessness, and looks up at Wish: a towering representation of the man he wishes he could be but knows he never will.

Wish mutes the music and steps closer to Reid. "Real men don't fail other men, and they certainly don't fail themselves. You're failing yourself, son."

The word "son" is something Reid has never heard from another man. His father is long gone. The sound of that word does something. An unfamiliar feeling of strength suddenly enters his body. He's never been led by an alpha male, and this alpha is leading him to a place he's never given himself permission to explore. He rises, straightens himself, and quickly wipes away all remaining tears. He looks Wish directly in the eyes, confident his eyes will not move until he's further instructed.

"What was it that you were thinking when you looked at her?" says Wish.

Reid maintains eye contact. He feels resistance to share his true thoughts, but ignores it. "I want to fuck her." His voice suddenly deepens. "I want to ravish her." A sense of power surges his body, lifting his chest.

Molly opens her legs slightly and slowly sways her hips. Wish steps close to Molly and carefully examines her lower back. He gestures to Reid to move closer for a look. Goosebumps have spread across her back.

"The men of your generation have been taught to hide their masculinity." Wish grabs the paddle from the floor, hands it to Reid, then signals to Reid to follow him away from Molly, near to the entrance. Wish lowers his voice. "You didn't even touch her, but she can sense the masculine energy your soul is emitting. Raw honesty about your masculine desires, from a healthy psychological mind, is what sparks the sexual interest of the female, on an animalistic level. You serve as the spark, igniting her towards feeling feminine. Now, with the item in your hand, honestly express your masculinity to her."

Reid's brow furrows. He's unsure if he's supposed to hit her, and if so, how hard? They go closer to Molly. Wish pantomimes how Reid should swing the paddle towards her cheek. Reid's palms become slick with sweat, challenging his grip of the paddle. He studies Molly's plump, firm behind. He wonders if this is a trick, a test. A week ago, Wish accused him of being an abuser of women. *Wouldn't this be abusing a woman?*

Molly shifts her stance, bringing her knees together, closing the gap between her legs. Her sensual swaying comes to a halt.

"She senses your repression. You're disappointing the female animal in her and she's losing sexual interest. Your lack of certainty is dropping your masculinity." Wish clicks the music back on. His voice booms as the volume of the tribal music increases. "It is time for you to release the erotic ghost that lurks in your soul."

Reid stares at the paddle. *I've been taught to be polite and respectful to women. I'd never hurt one, even though they all seem to end up hurting me.*

A hundred images of his past run through his head. He's been teased, lied to, cheated on, and abused by women. His rage-inspired thoughts make him lift his arm back and prepare to take a ferocious swing with the paddle. Reid clenches his jaw and launches the paddle towards Molly, like a baseball player swinging for a home run.

The explosion of a loud whack echoes throughout the cage, but the paddle didn't strike Molly. The paddle falls to the floor and clanks against the hardwood. Reid feels his wrist burn with a sharp sting; it's locked tightly in Wish's grip. The grip releases and Reid's arm plops to his side. A perplexed look forms on Reid's face.

"This isn't about revenge," says Wish. "Abusing someone else to mask the emotional pain created by your own unacceptance of reality will never give you the contentment you seek. A truth you must accept is that pain must exist in our lives — without it, the brain wouldn't be able to recognize pleasure."

Wish strides towards the entrance and unlocks the gate. "You can leave now — if you want."

Reid stares at the ground. He takes a few steps towards the door, then stops, pausing to gain clarity on a decision. He turns his head and reads the sign once more. *Provide the contrast to fulfill lives.*

Reid moves, but not to exit, instead towards the area of hanging sex toys and sensory enhancers. He grips a white-fur mitten and plucks it off a hook. Above the hook is a business-card-size placard that reads, *With this item, how will you serve?* The word "serve" triggers the original mantra from Wish, and his commitment to being a man of service. Reid slides the soft glove onto his left hand and returns to Molly, moving with an aura of certainty.

Reid channels his contrasting experiences from Tasha and the awful masseuse, recalling the potent sensations he felt when touched by the hand of someone who genuinely cared. He extends his free hand to touch Molly's back, using his fingers to study her body like a sculptor admiring the finished product. The tips of his fingers tingle with delight as they glide along the smoothness of her skin. He pauses when he notices a two-inch long, one-word tattoo on the middle of her back, *Acceptance,* and wonders if she got the tattoo because of Wish's teachings.

His hand brushes across her stomach, feeling the ripples of a scar above her right hip. He figures this must be her stab wound. Molly sways her hip to the side, seeming to want to move his hand off her scar. Reid glances at Wish, as if to say, *Did I do something wrong?* Wish remains stoic and nods at the sign; a reminder for Reid to practice acceptance and provide contrasts.

Reid focuses on the thought, *I accept all that you are.* He channels the thought into his fingers as they touch the edges of her scar. Molly slowly returns her hips to the center, fully allowing his hands to explore her wound. Wish's mouth forms an approving smile, like a coach who witnessed the desired outcome from his teachings.

Reid's hand pulsates with a pleasing vibration, absorbing how it feels to connect with every inch of her skin. He then pets her skin with the fur glove, making circles along her back and stomach. Molly coos. Reid grins, then alternates his movements between touching with his bare hand and the fur glove, noticing her body prickle with goosebumps.

Wish picks the paddle up from the floor, then waves for Reid to follow him to the other side of the cage. Wish hands the paddle back to Reid.

"Her deep femininity must be boosted by your deep masculinity. You expressed masculine energy through your caring, soft touch, but she'll eventually become numb to your touch unless you provide a sensory contrast. Help the brain recognize sensations; provide a sharp contrast of pain so that she can experience deep sensations of pleasure. Express your caring masculine strength through the paddle, knowing you are serving her."

Reid exhales a cautious breath. He and Wish return to Molly. Reid studies the paddle like a young knight holding his first sword. *I'm a man of service.* He extends his arm back, feeling the hand that holds the paddle tremble. He glances at Wish for approval. The pimp nods. Reid then focuses on his target: her voluptuous butt cheek. In a swift motion, he swings the paddle to her bum, creating a loud *thwap*. Molly gasps and lowers her head.

"Come from the place of service," says Wish. "Serve her with all of the care in your heart. She needs this from you. Don't deny her your gifts. Your service will remind her that she's a living human being who feels. Rescue her from the world that thrives on her feeling numb." Wish moves two steps away from Reid. "By providing these sensory contrasts within her, you reunite her brain, body awareness, and inner goddess."

Reid studies the hand that holds the paddle. The tremble is gone. He's perplexed by the seemingly positive sensation and glances back at his mentor for guidance.

"This is who you are, Reid. The more you express your

masculinity, the more she'll feel her femininity. Human existence is rooted in the charge created by masculinity and femininity. Modern society has taken us away from that charge. It's time for you to embrace the feeling of being connected to the animal that you are."

A surge of strength, confident strength, flows through Reid. He swings the paddle again, connecting to her cheek with maximum force. She groans, sucking in air through her clenched teeth. His bicep and forearm pump full of blood as he repeats the whack twice more. *This shouldn't feel good, but it does.*

Wish grins and takes the paddle from Reid. "Now provide the contrast. Remember, you're not inducing pain for revenge, or dominance, or to mask your insecurities. You are a man of service acting as a guide who's activating her brain — the sting of the paddle increases the depth of the bliss that she'll feel from your soft touch that follows."

Reid moves his fur-gloved hand across her lower back, then along her bum. He eyes a slight discoloration on the skin of her bum. *Damn, I hit her hard.* He then glides the fur-covered hand over the mark, hoping his touch will ease the sting, or give her deep bliss as Wish described. She drops her head, sways her hips slowly, and releases light, euphoric moans. *Bingo.*

"Well done. Keep in mind that not every woman will derive pleasure from the force you just used," says Wish. "Her sensory response system requires a stronger stimulant; some women are more sensitive and will do fine with simple massage techniques to provide contrasts. I'll soon teach you how to calibrate your approach based on the physiology of the woman you are servicing."

Molly coos again. Reid looks with amazement at the sight of her shoulders rising and falling from deep breaths. He then turns his head to face Wish and narrows his eyes. *Guys like me don't get women who look like her.* He glances back at Molly. *And we sure as hell don't get women like her ... to feel like that.*

Wish brings his palms to a prayer position. "She appreciates the pain you provided for her. Soon, you'll also learn to have an appreciation for all the pain you face in your life. You'll funnel all experiences through your understanding of the necessity of contrasts.

You'll accept that painful experiences *must* exist — in order to feel the bliss from the touch that follows."

Reid nods slowly, but then sees something strange when Wish moves the paddle from one hand to the other. The top part of the paddle has peeled apart; a sharp point of wood is splintering outward. He looks down at Molly's bum and sees that the outer edge of her right cheek is cut and bleeding. Reid examines the glove. It's splattered with blood. *The discoloration on her cheek was smeared blood. The edge of the paddle must have caused an abrasion.* He holds the blood-spotted glove up to his face and cringes. *What the hell did I just do?*

"I'm so sorry." Reid drops his hands, then looks at Wish. "I made her bleed. I swear, I don't hurt women. This isn't right."

"You did well, young man. I'll take care of her. Your work is done for the night."

Reid leans towards Molly's ear. "I'm so sorry, Molly. I swear I'd never hurt a woman. I'm beyond sorry."

Molly is motionless and silent.

This went too far. Reid yanks off the glove, drops it to the floor. He walks towards the gate of the cage, seeing that Wish left it unlocked. Reid pushes it open and hurries out of the room. He takes the elevator down to the parking garage and drives off.

A swell of thoughts clogs his mind while he waits at a stoplight. *How does beating a bound woman contribute to serving the world? Get your head straight, man. Is this some kind of sick game Wish is playing? Am I really the one Wish has been looking for? I made that poor girl bleed. She's already experienced enough violent men. I'm not THAT guy.*

As Reid finishes turning his car onto Las Vegas Boulevard, his phone rings: a call from Wish.

"Don't worry about Molly — she's fine. It was just a little cut. Sometimes erotica can lead to a Band-Aid or two," says Wish. "By the way, it's too risky for you to stay at the Sahara Hotel. Youngblood may have found a record of our room there. Go to the Lexi Hotel instead. It's a modest place behind the Hard Rock Casino. Tell the front desk you're a guest of mine. They'll set you up with a room."

"Okay," says Reid. "Was I able to help you assess Molly?"

"I assessed both of you. You both passed your tests. You stepped into your fear of connecting with your masculinity. Her assignment was to connect with your repressed self without speaking or touching you, only focusing on what remained of her feminine expression."

"How so?"

"The world is made up of the charges created between masculine and feminine dynamics. The key is to understand that opposite charges working together enhance each other. Her raw feminine expression allowed you to feel comfortable exploring your raw masculine expression. Once you became comfortable with the dynamic, your inner guard was set free, and the repressed wounds of your psyche were allowed to rise to the surface. It's not a coincidence that your hand went to her scar. Your desire to touch her scar and understand it was a projection from your shadow-self. Your shadow knows that its path to freedom begins with you first understanding and accepting your own scar. She's never let anyone touch her there, not even me."

Reid grins and shakes his head, wondering how Wish knows this stuff so well. A psychologist often has to work with someone for months to get them to recognize and admit the source of their issues. He completes the turn onto Harmon Road, and heads in the direction of the Lexi Hotel.

"While touching her, I noticed my focus shift to accepting all that she is, especially her scar. It felt like I was touching her with appreciation."

"Yes, because your subconscious was simultaneously accepting your own scar. You know you've reached a new place of self-acceptance when, suddenly, you accept the apparent flaws of others. However, this awareness is only the beginning. You'll be working on these issues for a long time." Wish pauses. "You both experienced significant growth tonight; a great sign for the potential I see within each of you. I'll see you in the morning."

"What's our plan for tomorrow?"

"We are going to a special place, a place that will help me explain what the mission is, and your role from this point on."

"What should I wear? Where will we be going?"

"Wear gym clothes. We're going to a nearby suburban town called

Henderson. There is something very important I'll be sharing with you
— the thing I've spent my entire life researching."

"I'm dying to know. Can you share it now?"

"No," says Wish. "I have to be certain you aren't going to fuck with
its powers."

Chapter 11

Wish moves his hands along the steering wheel of his topless, midnight-blue, 1981 Mercedes coupe. He turns the car off Las Vegas Boulevard onto the 215 Freeway en route to Henderson. The wind swoops across the car seats. Reid dips his head forward, unable to avoid the heightened tingles caused by the breeze.

"My body is extremely sensitive today," says Reid. "I feel ticklish all over, and I'm never ticklish."

"You're feeling the retroactive effects of your experiences last night," says Wish. "Tasha awakened your body from its sensory slumber. Our senses dictate our reality. With repressed senses, we then have a repressed interpretation of reality. Most psychological issues are routed in a person's ability to accurately understand reality."

"So to improve someone's psychological issues, we must first address how that person interprets reality."

"Correct, Professor. Also, our repressed self creates a limitation on our bodies sensory capabilities. Last night, your brain's pleasure receptors improved due to your courage in exploring your repressed self with the guidance of Molly."

"What do you mean, my pleasure receptors improved?"

"As I've said before, the human brain is a duality mechanism. It understands things by comparing opposites. If the brain only experiences minimal challenges throughout life, then it's only capable of feeling minimal joy. You faced a huge challenge and walked through a fear. The bigger the challenge you face in life, the more the brain's pleasure receptors will grow. It's a neuroscientific way of understanding why happiness comes from action towards overcoming challenges, and depression is created by non-action."

"I'm surprised at how quickly I can feel different."

"Your recent life experience with your ex has primed your brain to be ready to change. That's why you must see the experience of Jasmine's infidelity as a blessing."

Reid stares at the tips of his shoes, delving into thoughts of Jasmine. He stops himself and glances at Wish. "But I still have negative emotions. I'm still angry."

"The emotional part of your brain is the last to heal. It's normal to have angry thoughts. The key is learning how to talk yourself through those thoughts, pointing out the blessings that may occur as a result of that challenging experience."

"A blessing I see right now is that last night was wild." Reid smiles. "Amazing and scary at the same time. So, my willingness to step outside of my comfort zone is why I feel so different today? It was just one night, but I feel like I've grown a lot."

"Self-growth always occurs from being outside your comfort zone. Unfortunately, most people aren't willing to explore beyond their safe, comfortable lives, and our society supports that. We live in a world that fears mankind developing the inherent self-power that comes when a person is fully self-aware, mature. When someone is disconnected from their self-power they're often insecure and confused, which makes them easier to control by those in charge.

"As you continue to train with me and my staff, you'll shift to experiencing the world as a human animal, not a brainwashed peon, because you'll know who the fuck you are. The wind will tickle, food will taste better, music will cause you to dance without a thought, and colors will pop with brighter hues." Wish stops at a red light, then extends his hand for a shake. "What you're feeling right now, the sensory overload, is the feeling of being a real human. Welcome to earth, my friend."

Reid grins and shakes his head. He then glances around, studying the suburbia that surrounds them: the hotels and casinos from the Strip have given way to grocery stores, schools, and parks.

"Looks like you can have a normal family life out here," says Reid.

"Normal family life doesn't exist anymore," says Wish. He steers the coupe into the parking lot of a large, scenic park. They hop out and walk through a crowded picnic area. Reid absorbs the scent of freshly cut grass combined with charcoal smoke from active grills.

"I see normal family life all around us. People grilling, socializing, having a good time," says Reid.

"Take a closer look. Who is socializing?"

They continue down a gravel path, passing a variety of families. Reid observes adults kicking soccer balls around and hears music played throughout the park.

"It looks like everyone is socializing," says Reid.

"Everyone of a certain age," says Wish.

Reid shifts his focus, then notices a commonality amongst the children and teenagers present but not in the adults. "Most of the kids are sitting alone, staring at their devices."

"That's our mission," says Wish. "Technology is separating us. We must educate the world on the importance of human-to-human connectedness, physical connectedness, tactile interactions. Otherwise the planet will be in grave danger. Empathy and respecting and valuing one another develops in the human brain through tactile experiences."

"Tactile? Meaning human-to-human touch?" Reid asks.

"Yes, tactile deprivation is the single most common experience of violent criminals. Prisons are filled with violent humans who haven't been touched enough and haven't touched others enough. It's safe to assume that empathy was underdeveloped in their brains. And now we exist in a society where man's most important relationship is human to computer, not human to human."

Reid observes the many families spread throughout the park, and sees very few people touching, except for older couples holding hands. He and Wish continue their walk for several minutes, cruising towards a quiet section of the park.

Wish continues: "With human-to-human sensory deprivation, people will disconnect from valuing the sacredness of each individual life. Man's psyche is already shifting to see everything in the world as one-dimensional. And that's why we're seeing an increase in acts of horrific violence." Wish stops walking. "People will soon view each other like disposable characters on the movie screen, not fully caring when a someone suffers or dies."

"When do you predict things could get out of control?" says Reid.

"They're already out of control," says Wish. "And one major gateway to these problems, approval seeking, is sourced from misunderstood sexual energy. We now have reported cases of ten-year-old boys being addicted to porn, and soon most men will be having sex exclusively with sex-robots, because those things, like porn, never say 'no.' Men will never have to face rejection. These males will grow up to be entitled, selfish, and confused by their sexual energy. And when rejected by a real human female, it's likely they will respond with boyish, negative, self-centered behavior, such as abuse, violence, rape, and even murder.

"This failing system taps into man's instinct to reproduce. If the woman doesn't see the man as valuable for reproduction, then he feels further isolated and shamed, and develops more hatred. Men who engage in criminal acts of violence are rarely skilled lovers who can go out and attract a high-quality woman."

Reid shakes his head, then recalls what he observed at the Adult Megastore. "I just saw the Stacey sex-robot for the first time. I'm guessing Goddess Mindy is committed to the mission; is she okay with working at a place that sells a Stacey?"

"The robots can be used therapeutically, like marijuana, but many individuals go beyond use and into abuse. Abusing those artificial sex pleasers will dramatically affect how men utilize their sexual energy. Japan, which currently produces and sells the most sex-robots, is reported to be suffering a population crisis. There's a shortage of new babies being born, because men are leaving their wives for robots, or ignoring their wives due to porn addiction."

"But it's impossible to slow down the growth of technology," says Reid.

"Ain't nothing slowing it down, but there's one activity that, if done correctly, will almost always guarantee both participants will be off their cell phone."

Reid's mind flashes exotic images of his sexual experiences the night before. In those moments, he wasn't thinking about emails or social media posts. "You think sex will keep people off technology?"

"To some extent, but there's something stronger — beyond basic fornication. Sex is either for reproduction or childish escapism. There's something more potent; this is the thing I've spent my entire adult life researching." Wish places his hand on Reid's shoulder and squeezes. "Promise me, you ain't gonna fuck with its powers."

"I promise."

Wish nods, walks away, and waves for Reid to follow. Reid walks a few steps behind, sorting the thoughts inside his head. He used to scoff at the idea that sex can lead to self-growth. But the new sense of confidence he feels, combined with the pleasure sparks shooting through his body since he woke, seem to be proof that Wish is onto something. Now he's starting to see the bigger picture of Wish's mission — it's more than promoting self-growth for happiness; it's the thing that will help save the world.

The men enter a secluded area covered by overhanging trees that form a cave-like environment. Beams of sunlight shine through, but the trees block most of the heat, creating a cooler environment. They take a seat at a picnic table centrally located in the covered area. Wish removes his fedora, sets it on the dusty table, and takes a deep breath.

"The thing I've been researching is called the Erotic Sensory Experience. A practitioner using erotica-based techniques provides the client or partner with the deepest sensations of pleasure the human body is capable of feeling. The ESE goes beyond what people experience with basic sex, because it's tied into freeing a person from the denial of their shadow-self, which is almost always sourced from sexual repression. Proper execution can initiate the recipient down the path of liberating the unknown self, thus resulting in self-actualization and an authentic connection to earth and mankind."

Reid's mind flashes to his experience with Tasha. His body tingles with pleasure, as if Tasha is touching him. Chills spread throughout his body. He quickly rubs his arms, hoping to bring back warmth and not appear giddy.

Wish grins, seeming to notice. "You've only been exposed to a few basic concepts thus far."

Reid nods and returns his arm to his side. "So, is technology the enemy?"

"Technology by itself is neutral; it requires a human to program it and a human to choose to use it. Self-actualized people know how to use technology for life enhancement and support. Unfortunately, they're becoming a minority. The real enemy is the Collective Shadow. As I told you before, the CS is an invisible force created by large groups of people who don't accept themselves, which means their brains haven't developed the ability to be fully accepting of others.

"Our world is becoming occupied with people who are numb to fully knowing themselves, resulting in the largest Collective Shadow mankind has ever seen. The CS will soon dominate technology, drastically multiplying the CS's strength. Non-actualized beings will give their personal power away, without knowing, and become slaves to a higher ruler, who will preach unacceptance and destroy anything that tries to steal its powers."

"So, the Erotic Sensory Experience is the cure?"

"It's one cure. Many of the highest powers in the world — religions and government leaders — do very well for their followers. But there are also people in power who promote unacceptance. These powers gain their strength by first manipulating the sexual expression of the individual. Repressed sexual energy is repressed self-power. Therefore, the sexually repressed individual can easily give their self-power away. We've seen countless examples of repressed individuals giving their power to a higher source, then being instructed to kill non-followers, and receiving sex with a virgin as the reward." Wish shakes his head. "Doesn't make sense to me, because sex with a virgin is fucking awful."

Reid chuckles.

Wish continues: "Bottom line, the men and women who have experienced the ESE have a deeper sense of connectedness to the world and themselves. Their brain develops more empathy. They discover the untapped source of power stored within and use that energy to serve."

Reid watches Wish amble to a nearby tree and glide his fingers along the bark, as if he were touching a beautiful woman with deep admiration. Wish speaks over his shoulder. "We need to spread knowledge of the dangers of sexual repression, teach others how to provide Erotic Sensory Experiences, and promote the uniting powers that occur as a result of these experiences. It may be the last bit of hope we have to stay connected to each other in the future."

Reid nods. "You see me as the one to bring the knowledge to others?"

Wish walks towards Reid. He ignores the question and opens his arms wide.

"Stand," Wish says. "Humans increase their empathy when being touched by another. Hug me for sixty seconds." The men embrace. "Pay attention to what your heart feels."

Reid cringes while holding Wish. He wonders if anyone will see them, but then recalls they're far from the busy section of the park. Wish moves his hands up Reid's spine, then squeezes him in closer. Reid jolts his head back and looks at Wish with a furrowed brow.

"Forty-five seconds more, kid. Just relax. It's a simple hug. Squeeze close to feel my heartbeat."

Wish yanks him in tighter. Reid gasps for air, then relaxes his breathing and surrenders to the remaining time. He begins to feel the heartbeat of his mentor, and it ignites in his brain a positive sensation of being protected. The hug continues until they hear a rustle from the bushes. A menacing voice calls out to them.

"Look at these fucking fags."

Reid and Wish pull apart. Reid sees three Caucasian men, covered in tattoos, with shaved bald heads. The man who spoke stands in the center with a large hunting knife in his hand. The other men pop their fists into their hands, appearing ready for a scuffle.

"I was hoping to find some faggots today," says the knife-wielding man. "God wants us to fuck you up."

"Yeah, we're gonna fuck you up," says the goon on the left.

Reid takes a step backwards, trembling. He looks at his mentor. *Should we run?*

As if he were going through a typical day at the office, Wish strolls towards the picnic table. He grabs his fedora, spins it between his fingers, and slides it onto his head. He glances at Reid, smiles, then flashes a playful wink. "Our first visit from the Collective Shadow."

Reid wants to yell, *Now is not the time for philosophy!* But he keeps quiet, resisting the urge to run.

Wish tips his hat to each of the men. "We're honored to serve you today, gentlemen. What is it that you desire?"

"Fuck you, nigger. God hates you."

The knife-wielding man looks to his comrades for confirmation. Reid notices a tattoo on the man's neck that reads, *Ain't white, ain't right*. A chill shakes his bones. He looks around, hoping someone may pass to witness the situation, but fears they're too secluded from the crowds.

Wish remains calm. "I'm honored to represent what your God hates. How else can I serve you today? Would you like to learn how to get laid?" Wish winks at Reid, then looks back at the assailant. "Clearly, getting laid is your biggest challenge right now."

The comrades chuckle at Wish's strange comment.

Reid takes a step back. *Don't rattle this guy any further — jeez.*

The knife-wielder shoots a *shut it* look at his friends. He then puffs his chest towards Wish. "I get laid plenty, old man."

"Doubtful," says Wish. "You might have sex with a female from time to time. However, judging by the lack of self-love you are portraying right now, I can safely assume that she must also hate herself. What you call sex is merely a two-minute escape from your self-hatred. That doesn't count."

"Two minutes?" scoffs the knife-wielder. "I satisfy plenty of bitches, old man."

"Bitches?" Wish looks at the other men. "You are probably referring to one of these guy's sisters. That doesn't count either. You don't conquer your fear of rejection by settling for bitches."

Reid sees each of the goon's nostrils flare.

Wish continues: "Your anger stems from your inability to attract a woman you really desire."

"You don't know shit about me, old man."

"Perhaps you are correct. But I do know that men who've developed the skills to connect sexually with the women they desire don't stroll around parks with a knife." Wish dips his chin and chuckles. "Because they're too busy fucking the women they desire."

Reid's body stiffens. *Now is not the time for your lecture. Please don't get them angrier.*

The knife-wielder scoffs. "Faggot nigger is talking shit. You're about to die, mother fucker."

Reid presses his toes into the ground, ready to burst into a full sprint. Except he won't abandon his new friend, his insanely relaxed new friend.

"I'm honored to be the visual representation of what you dislike about yourself," says Wish. "And if I knew you'd grow as a man by killing me, I'd sacrifice my life." Wish takes a step closer to the goon and kneels. "The problem is, killing me won't free you from the burden of what's going on inside of you. You'll feel good for an hour, then return to hating yourself. And just so we are clear, I don't hate you. I look forward to how much your brain is about to grow. I'm excited for you."

The goon drops his arm while holding the knife tight. His eyebrows have raised at the sight of Wish kneeling. Reid cringes at what he observes on the inner forearm of the assailant: a swastika tattoo. Wish places his hands in the prayer position and continues the sermon from his knees.

"You're free to stab me as much as you like. However, your friends should know that each stab will be a representation of how much you hate yourself. It takes a courageous man to admit the depths of his self-hatred in front of his friends. Prove to all of us how much you dislike who you are today."

"This faggot is crazy," says the assailant. "Just give me your fucking money."

Reid digs in his pocket for his wallet. "Come on, Wish. Let's just give them what they want."

Wish shoots Reid a stern look, signaling to him to remain silent. Wish then turns to face the goons. "I'll give them my money. But first, I want an answer to my question."

Reid narrows his eyes, then takes his hand out of his pocket, leaving his wallet.

Wish points at the man with the knife. "When are you going to admit to your friends that you're a homosexual?"

Reid feels a sudden sense of security as he realizes Wish knows exactly what he's doing — calling out this man's projections. And he remembers that Wish has already proven he can handle a man with a knife by taking down Amber's boyfriend.

"I'm no faggot. He's fucking lying," says the assailant.

The two comrades look at their friend with expressions of disbelief. The assailant grunts, then lunges towards Wish with the knife pointing forward. In a swift move, Wish dodges the attack then grabs the man's arm and flips him to the ground. The knife flies out of the goon's hand and falls near Reid's feet. Reid quickly scoops up the knife. Wish then pins the man down into an arm-bar hold; placing his legs across the man's chest, with one of the man's arms between his thighs and the elbow joint against his hip.

The men step forward, intending to assist their friend. Reid holds the knife in a ready-to-fight position. He feels a sudden surge of energy — masculine energy, similar to what he felt the night before with Molly.

"Stand the fuck back," yells Reid.

The men freeze. *Wow.* Reid sees Wish shift his body to increase the pressure of his grip on the goon, then hears the man groan in pain. Reid then glares at the comrades, who are looking at each other, befuddled.

"Take a step closer and you two will face the wrath of my lover," says Wish. He blows a kiss to Reid.

My mentor is crazy.

Again, Wish shifts his weight to apply more pressure to the goon. The man belts out a gut-wrenching scream. Wish remains calm as he speaks.

"In a few seconds, you will see this man's life change for the better. His brain is about to increase its ability to feel a depth of pleasure that he never knew existed. Pay attention, gentlemen. He is a human who feels — as am I, as are you."

The grappled man pleads for mercy. The friends remain cemented in their stance.

Reid continues to point the knife, but with a shaky hand. He looks at the trapped assailant, feeling a hint of sympathy. *He's about to feel great pleasure? But that can only come from ... uh oh.* Reid cowers as he hears the horrific sound of the man's scream. Then he peeks to see the swastika tattoo start to bulge on the man's forearm. *Oh no.*

Wish's voice booms through the man's desperate cries. "Young man, your lack of acceptance of others is merely a reflection in your brain — a signal that you do not accept yourself."

Wish twists slightly. Reid sees blood squirt out of the swastika; he squints and turns away, then returns to a protective stance, seeing Wish through his peripheral vision.

"To *accept* all that exists in your life will free you from suffering." Wish shifts his body up, then jerks downward in one swift motion. The man howls. Wish speaks through the cry. "Let this be the start of the new you."

Reid tries to fix his focus on the other assailants, but he can't ignore the sound of a bone cracking. He sneaks a look. Bursts of blood dance around a white bone piercing through the swastika-stamped skin. The sound of the man's never-ending horror echoes in the surrounding trees.

Wish carefully releases the man and rises to stand. Reid remains ready to fight; his chest rises and sinks from rapid breathing. Wish takes the knife from Reid, then tosses it towards the men. Reid gawks at his mentor, shocked to see him return the knife.

"Thank you for existing, fellas," says Wish. "Without bad guys in this world, our brains wouldn't be able to recognize the good guys." Wish reaches into his pocket and pulls out a wad of cash. He peels off five hundred-dollar bills, and drops them near the bloody mess. "I told you I'd give you money. This will help with the medical fees. It's been an honor to participate in the game of life with you today."

Reid stares at Wish, dumbfounded. *This man is insane. Who lectures at a time like this?*

Wish walks away. Reid follows, but glances back every few seconds, eventually seeing the comrades gather their busted friend and stumble off in the opposite direction.

Though his heart is beating rapidly, Reid continues walking in step with the unshaken Wish. Soon they near a pond. Reid's stomach churns with discomfort. He's unable to get the image of the bone piercing through skin out of his mind. The contents of his stomach erupt through his throat. He bends forward and vomits.

A few minutes pass, then Reid glances up to see Wish in the

distance, washing his blood-soaked hands in the pond. Reid turns to heave again until he finishes. Using the back of his hand, Reid wipes his mouth, then rises and turns around to see Wish holding a piece of gum out for him. Reid smiles, takes the gum, and chews it.

"Those men were part of the Collective Shadow," says Wish. "For that to happen so soon is a significant omen."

"An omen of what?" asks Reid.

"The Collective Shadow knows we are uniting."

Chapter 12

"As much as I prefer you to discover yourself through your own experiences, there's something you need to know right now," says Wish. They're sitting across from each other on a picnic bench.

"First, you must understand that not everyone is wired like you and me. Some people who are sexually conservative are not sexually repressed; it's how they're wired genetically. We're different. We're a specific type of breed within the human race born with a higher level of sexual energy than most. There was a time, long ago, when our breed was called upon to ensure the survival of the human race."

"How so?" says Reid.

"The easiest way to understand our wiring is to think back to the early days of mankind, when there were only a few villages of humans. Let's say that in one village there were forty fertile adults. If all forty of those people only reproduced with each other, massive inbreeding would occur; we'd have too many unhealthy babies. Eventually, the human race would fail in its evolutionary course and cease to exist.

"Of those forty people, roughly two or three men and women evolved with a gene that gave them the desire to look for sex outside of the village — which was considered highly dangerous and against tradition. Their potent sexual wiring guided them past those fears; they understood that they were serving a greater purpose. Our ancestors engaged in sexual experiences outside their village, which prevented mass inbreeding and ensured healthy evolution for mankind. And today, society still has people wired with the highly juiced sexual gene, but unfortunately, they're misunderstood and shunned by those who don't have it."

"So, you're saying you have that gene?"

"As do you," says Wish. "The average man wouldn't have the stamina to bring their woman flowers every single day for several years."

Reid smirks. "I was foolish to do that."

"I'll ask you this: when you were a young teen did you cry yourself to sleep because you couldn't relate to women?"

Reid drops his head. "I did, many nights I did. Too many nights I did."

"Most boys cry over a toy or a game. You had this sense inside that others couldn't understand; the tears came because you knew you were different. But nothing exists in our society that explains why you felt the way you did. So you repressed the desire you felt within, fearing disconnection from others. Luckily, you courageously allowed that part of yourself to come out last night."

Reid glances down. *And I wouldn't have acted that way with the knife today had I not tapped into that strong aura last night.*

"Our ancestors understood that their calling was to prevent extinction, to save the human race from inbreeding. They risked shame, abandonment, and even death at the hands of their fellow villagers by venturing into the unknown. But they stayed committed to the calling, leading by example, and teaching others who had also evolved with sexual curiosity in a land that supported repression."

"Sounds like the naysayers to our ancestors were an early version of the Collective Shadow," says Reid.

"Precisely. And now our breed is being called upon again. Except the human race doesn't need rescuing from inbreeding; it needs rescuing from isolation."

Reid furrows his eyebrows and remains silent.

"My calling for the past twenty years has been to research and master the Erotic Sensory Experience. I didn't always understand why I'd been driven to do so, but along the way I learned how events can occur in our lives to guide us towards our purpose. Many events have occurred in recent years which validated my research and created insight as to the purpose it will serve. However, I never felt like I was going to be the one to share this with the world. I always knew that I'd pass my knowledge to a young man who was equipped to share my findings. This young man would be another one of my kind." Wish pauses. "It's you."

Reid struggles to swallow his gulp. "What's my role in all this?"

"Your responsibility will be to get the information out to the world, through books, lectures, social media, or whatever the hell you kids use on your phones. Get the information out there by any means possible. You need to reach those who are wired like us, because they'll be your secondary messengers. Our kind needs your help the most. They're drowning in the sea of the Collective Shadow, feeling lost and confused, and probably tolerating mundane sexual experiences."

"I can see people not liking what our message is about."

"We don't have to worry about the people who are wired in the opposite way to us, those who are naturally sexually conservative, because many of them have understanding hearts and practice acceptance. Our enemies are those who suffer from repression, who are confused by what they've been taught about their sexual energy. They're often enslaved to a higher leader or doctrine which continually keeps them from their truth. They'll post negative comments about your books, protest against your lectures, and organize hate groups. They'll do whatever it takes to thwart your overall mission, because we represent what they're afraid to admit about themselves."

"This seems like a giant task. I don't know ... I was happy just being a professor."

"You're happy helping others have better lives, but soon the four hundred or so students you get to help each semester won't be enough — you won't want to keep this knowledge from saving the rest of the world. You'll need lots of help. You'll need to connect with our army, the Erotic Army."

"The Erotic Army? But sex and dating have always been so hard for me. How can I be the leader of an erotic army when I can't even talk to a woman?"

"Give me your all," says Wish. "I'll make sure you become the man that you need to be."

"Why me? You know this stuff so well. Shouldn't you be the messenger?"

"I can't connect with the younger, technology-obsessed generation. You're part of them. You teach them every day. Plus, I've broken many laws to conduct this research. My employees have serviced many high-profile individuals. If I became famous from sharing the knowledge, these high-profile individuals could get worried and have me eliminated within seconds. My work is almost done. Soon it will be time for me to retire from my business."

"What's your business exactly?"

"There are five women I have trained to be masters of the ESE, my wife and four others. These women are sexual mystics — in short, Sexmysts. They all have the gene, like us. All of their work is part of my research, but it has also allowed us to be financially secure while serving others. They understand that our business will end when I retire, though."

"Sexmyst — that's what Tasha said she was. So, what exactly is a sexual mystic?"

"A mystic is someone who shows you parts of existence from an unknown dimension. We provide enlightenment through erotic experiences. But the Sexmysts aren't allowed to turn tricks with any ol' boy. The client must meet with me and prove that he or she is involved for the exploration of the self."

A warm sensation moves through Reid's core. He recalls Tasha's magical techniques, and remembers his first experience with Amber's unique touch pattern. "Was Amber, the girl who robbed me, a Sexmyst?"

"Amber was in training to be the fifth Sexmyst, but she violated our agreement. She's been replaced by Molly, the blindfolded woman you shared the experience with last night."

"How long has Tasha been working for you?"

"Tasha was with us during her eight years of college. As I mentioned before, she's now a doctor and officially retired," says Wish. "All of the Sexmysts are highly intellectual. With the exception of Amber, they're all college-educated, working professionals. I took a chance by rescuing Amber from the streets."

"I'm willing to help any way I can," says Reid.

"This is my offer to you, Professor." Wish reaches into his pocket, retrieves a folded sheet of paper, and hands it to Reid for perusal.

The Agreement

I will teach you all that I know. You agree to master this knowledge, build on its foundation, and teach your findings to the world. You will be fully committed to promoting personal growth and human-to-human connectedness.

Following my teachings will make you a master of providing the Erotic Sensory Experience, a male Sexmyst. You will seek to enlighten the lives of the women you come across, repairing the damage that many men or society has caused them.

Rules within the Agreement

a. *You agree to follow all instructions (even if they break societal laws).*

b. *You are not permitted to fall in love with anyone. But you are expected to fall in love with yourself.*

c. *You are not permitted to ask about my past or my future.*

d. *You continually work on your mind, body, and spirit, knowing it's all connected to the purpose of serving others.*

Violation of any of the above sections will result in the termination of the Agreement.

Reid looks up from the paper. "Wait ... I can't fall in love?"

"It sounds clichéd, but you can't love anything until you love yourself. Plus, you cannot develop the necessary skills for this by spending time with only one woman. Variety is essential to your growth."

Reid nods. Wish signs his one-word name at the bottom of the contract and hands the pen to Reid. Reid takes a breath, hesitant to move his hand.

"Your life will never be the same, Professor. Are you sure this is what you want?"

Reid takes another breath. "Everything inside of me says to follow this path. My schooling never felt right. My girlfriends never felt right. My career feels hypocritical. But this, being here right now, feels exactly right." He signs his name.

"I've never trained a male to be a Sexmyst," says Wish, "because the powers can easily be used to seduce and manipulate for selfish desires. If you fuck with the powers, our agreement will end and I will no longer protect you. Most likely, you'll end up with a life of suffering, like Amber, and all the other members of the CS."

"I give you my word. I'll only use the knowledge to serve others."

"You'll be tapping into an energy within yourself that the Collective Shadow fears. Remember, people who aren't willing to work on themselves greatly fear people who are. That's the essence of the Collective Shadow. As you get closer to your true self, the forces within the Collective Shadow will attack with increasingly difficult obstacles to prevent your success. Many of these obstacles will be masterfully disguised."

"Detective Youngblood?"

"Youngblood is my obstacle, not yours. He's the final dragon that I must slay before I can enter the next phase of my life. I embrace his presence. He's provided us with the urgency to get you equipped with becoming a Sexmyst before Detective Jones retires."

"It's amazing how you can find a way to accept everything that comes into your life."

"We either accept or we suffer," says Wish. "Youngblood exists to provide a contrast within my brain, ensuring I'll enjoy retirement and never look back. It's not a coincidence that he's in my life at the same time as you. Another blessing from Youngblood is that you'll learn how to navigate a Collective Shadow challenge by observing me deal with him."

Reid nods and remains silent.

"We don't have much time. I'll need you to be here this summer to train with me. To earn money, you'll exchange the casino chips that the Sexmysts have earned from service. They usually get paid with cash, but every now and then a client pays with casino chips. I have many months of chips that need to be cashed out, and it's too risky for me to do it, because the casinos know my face. Your cut will be ten percent."

"I can be here every weekend starting now," says Reid.

Wish shakes his head. "After this weekend, you'll need at least forty days of seclusion. It's important for you to take time to heal your emotional wounds from your ex, develop your physique, and define the characteristics of the man you aim to become. You'll be creating the foundation for your future self."

"Why do you feel we don't have time?"

"Detective Jones is retiring this summer, which means I'm retiring this summer. Jones has been my safety net for many years. With Youngblood taking over, all of us could be screwed. It's time for my business to close. I've been investing small installments of money over the years for retirement, which is tricky when running a cash-only business that's illegal, but I haven't invested enough to retire comfortably. I've worked out a plan with an international investor for a one-time, five-hundred-thousand-dollar cash payment that he can make work in my favor. It must be transferred before the end of the summer, and I'm three hundred thousand dollars short. The Sexmysts and I do a fifty/fifty split, which means the Sexmysts will do a big push to the finish line."

Reid pauses to appreciate Wish's willingness to disclose the operation. He thinks the details through and this opens his mind to question further. "How much do the Sexmysts charge per session?"

"It varies. Anywhere from five thousand to twenty-five thousand. Some men are allowed to experience two Sexmysts at once, which doubles our profit during that session."

"I'm looking forward to learning from you and helping as much as I can this summer. What about a place to stay?"

"I've made arrangements for you to stay at the Lexi Hotel. When you aren't working, you'll be going out and meeting women who are in need of what you will learn to offer."

"Meaning I'm going to be a gigolo?"

"No," says Wish. "It's best you spend time with women who aren't paying for services. You'll provide them with the experience they deserve while learning about the uniqueness of the sensory response system.

"You'll be exchanging a great deal of cash, and in some cases it will need to be stored in your room. Because of this, you're not permitted to take a woman back to your room. Andrew, who does night-time security at the Largo Hotel, will be able to open a room for you there when you need to provide an ESE."

"Okay, I can't wait. Will I be meeting Andrew?"

"Yes, I'll be dropping you off to meet him right now." Wish stands, speaking over his shoulder as he walks in the direction of the parking lot. "Andrew is the gateway to your forty days of seclusion. A symbol for the start of your quest, and a physical representation of your potential. He's going to teach you how to work out, to master your physique."

Reid hurries to catch up. "Is he a personal trainer or something?"

Wish chuckles without slowing his pace. "Andrew is everything you probably wish you could be."

Chapter 13

"Has a man named Andrew checked in?" Reid asks the girl at the check-in desk of the Las Vegas Fitness Center.

She releases a love-laced sigh and smiles. "He's here. Thank God he's here. My day is always better when that gorgeous specimen of a man enters those doors. He's upstairs, probably looking amazing on the bench press — wearing orange shorts and a navy-blue shirt. You must be the friend he was expecting. Go on up."

Gorgeous specimen of a man? Reid hunches forward as he walks up the stairs. His leg muscles wobble with each step up, a reminder of his out-of-shape body. He arrives, short of breath, and enters a long and wide room filled with gym equipment. The gym has a few patrons, but isn't crowded. Reid spies a man in the distance who appears as described, and moves towards him.

"Andrew?" says Reid, standing before an ice sculpture of a man lying on the flat bench. His mouth falls agape at the sight of the man's gigantic hands spread across a bench-press bar loaded with at least three hundred pounds.

"Spot me, bro," he grunts.

Reid took a few weight-training classes in college, but it's been years since he's lifted something heavier than a textbook. He stands behind the bench, observing multiple veins pop throughout Andrew's shoulders as he presses the weighted bar up and down with ease. Reid stands, knees slightly bent, with his hands near the bar, ready to assist. However, Andrew is able to guide the bar to rest on his own. Reid looks up at the ceiling, as if to thank God that his help wasn't required for this set.

Andrew stands and sips from his water bottle. Reid tilts his gaze upward, seemingly forever, to see Andrew's face. He's six inches taller than Reid, thin in the midsection and wide-shouldered, like a body builder.

"Sup," says Andrew. He reaches out with his bear-sized hand and they shake. "Wanna see a video of a chick I banged last night?"

Before Reid has time to process the question, Andrew taps a button on his phone and shoves the screen in front of his face. The video portrays a large, muscular man thrusting away on a petite brunette. Reid nods approvingly to be polite, but inside he's irked.

"Chick wanted to do some extra cardio after the spin class, bro," says Andrew. "Wish gave me the candle video camera for my birthday a few weeks ago. Best gift ever — been filming all of my bangs."

Reid is immediately reminded of all the meathead jocks who teased him in high school. He holds a fake smile, while trying to repress his rage from being forced to meet this douche bag. *I fucking hate guys like this.*

"Did you know her before the class?" says Reid.

"Nope, after class I just asked her if she wanted to do some extra cardio with me."

"I'd never have the balls to say something like that."

"Aren't you the one from Wish's vision, bro?" Andrew slaps Reid on the back, nearly launching him across the bench. "You're the legend who doesn't know he's a legend."

Reid shakes his head, keeping the same fake smile, unable to tell if the jock is making fun. He's reminded of the insecure feelings he experienced as a pimple-faced teen. He can't help but steer the conversation to the one thing that gives him credibility. "Where did you go to college?"

"Never went to school, but I've banged a girl from every major college west of the Mississippi River."

Reid drops his head and places his hands in his pockets. "How do you know Wish?"

"We met at an Aikido academy. He's a bomb martial artist. Don't want to mess with the old man — he'll jack you up."

Reid lifts his head. "I've witnessed that."

"Yeah, we also both love banging chicks. Except he's more spiritual about it."

"Did he teach you to be good with women?"

"No, I've been banging chicks my whole life. He calls me a natural, whatever that means. But he did teach me to accept myself."

Reid knows exactly what being a natural means: Andrew was born with the ability to be comfortable with women, something Reid would have paid his life savings to learn. Reid wonders if Andrew has the sex gene that Wish talked about.

Andrew studies Reid up and down. "Wish predicts you are some kind of special talent," he says, then leans in closer. "Your skin looks like shit."

This asshole just has no filter. The comment triggers Reid to scan Andrew's complexion. He sees that it's damn near perfect: olive-toned, free from zits and wrinkles. *The man looks like a god-damned Greek god.*

"What's your secret?" says Reid.

"Food. The skin you have is created by the food you eat, bro. Your body looks like it has been made by burgers and fries. And your muscles look like they are built to lift pens and pencils."

"I'd like to look like you," says Reid.

"I know." Andrew flexes in the mirror. Reid slumps his shoulders. Andrew catches himself intimidating Reid. "My bad, bro. Wish says you recently broke up with your girlfriend. A break-up is always good motivation to get your ass in the gym."

"I felt so weak around her. I don't ever want to feel weak around any woman, ever again."

Andrew nods, then leans forward to clear the weight plates off the bench-press bar. "Today I'll show you the workouts you'll be doing for the next six weeks to become summer-ready. Gonna get you ripped so you can bang a bunch of chicks."

Reid grabs a plate off the bar to assist putting them away. He's curious as to why Andrew doesn't seem to respect the sacredness of sex with women that Wish talks about.

Andrew walks Reid around the gym, shares some resistance-training basics, then guides him through an intense workout. In spite of his arms feeling sore from lifting, Reid warms up to Andrew.

"Wanna know something cool that I learned from Wish?" asks Andrew. Reid nods. "Do you like tits?"

"Of course," says Reid.

"Do you like a round booty?"

"Definitely."

"The curves of a woman, from her tits to waist to booty, signal to the male animalistic brain that she's fertile. A twelve-year-old girl is shaped like a stick; then as she gets older, she goes through puberty and begins to develop curves. The curves indicate to the male animal that she's now able to have babies."

Reid lifts an eyebrow.

"Not that we'd actually be with a woman that young. But it was a signal to the caveman and it's just as strong today. Wish makes sure his women display these curves, as it's essential to attract the male. He says there's a specific shape for men that is attractive too."

"Six-pack abs?"

"Abs that pop can help, but they're not essential. The V-shaped figure is what draws the female eye, broad shoulders to a narrow waist. Wish even has some mathematical equation for the perfect V-shape. I can't do that math shit. I'm a visual dude." Andrew studies Reid from top to bottom. "We gotta develop the muscles on your back and chest, and the deltoids, while trimming the body fat from your gut."

They continue their workout. Reid soon views Andrew as a fun-loving guy, and his insecurities ease. Andrew further explains his security job at the Largo, which mostly includes monitoring the hallways outside the rooms throughout the night, although he boasts that from time to time he gets to *kick some ass.*

They walk out to Andrew's car, and he opens the trunk and reaches for a printed spreadsheet of the workouts Reid will be doing back home. The backside of the calendar displays guidelines for supplementation and eating.

"Add a teaspoon of MCT oil and collagen powder to your protein shake. The oil will help you burn fat faster and keep you full. Collagen will make everything bad ass, including your skin. Eat all the veggies and animal muscle that you want. Everything else must be low carb or no carb."

Reid examines the spreadsheet. "I hope I can meet hotties like your video girl in these spin classes."

"For sure, bro." Andrew peels his shirt off, exposing his washboard stomach. "Wish might ask you to go to the club with me tonight. If so, you should definitely come."

"If he says so, I'll be there," says Reid. "Just promise me you'll keep your shirt on."

"It's going to be like a hip-hop music video, bro. You, me, and thirty women with their hands all over us. The shirt will probably come off, but not by me."

"Thirty women and just us? Awesome." Reid gulps, figuring they'll all want Andrew and he'll be left cowering in the corner, just like his life in high school.

Andrew grips his cell phone, types for a few seconds, then glances at Reid. "Wish wants me to drop you off at the mall. He's waiting for you there."

Andrew and Reid make small talk in the car. As much as Reid's insecurities tell him to hate the guy, he senses this is a man who is completely comfortable with himself, and that's highly likable. *Why doesn't Wish see this guy as the chosen one? He's damn near perfect.*

Reid enters the mall and follows directions texted by Wish, which guide him towards a British fashion shop. Reid sees Wish standing in front of the store.

"Andrew was pretty cool." Reid huffs a quick breath. "I have to be honest, he seems like he's much better at this stuff than me."

"He is, for now," says Wish. "He's maxed out what he's been born with. You haven't, and that's why you feel intimidated."

"I'm projecting." Reid shakes his head and smirks.

"I hear men and women complain all the time about how they can't attract a partner because of height, weight, beauty, or handsomeness. Until you max out what you've been born with, you have no right to complain. We can't change our face or height. But just about everything else is within our control. Fitness, charm, finances, and fashion, among many other things, are things we can choose to master.

"Andrew seems like a god to you because he's your age and represents your potential. Truth is, he's a puppy who will only grow to be a teenager. You'll soon see that as well. But still, he's a good man to have on our staff."

Reid nods with a sense of understanding. Wish enters the store and Reid follows.

"Alright, Professor, it's time for Fashion 101," says Wish. "Rule number one: ignore American styles and focus on European trends. British, Italian, and French fashion consistently highlight the male physique in a manner that is attractive to the female eye."

"This stuff looks like it will barely fit me," says Reid. He grasps the sleeve of a slim-fitting suit. "Andrew talked a bit about what draws the female eye. What are you referring to when you say 'attractive' to females?"

"The female human-animal is predisposed to seek a man who signals that he will give them safety, reliability in terms of providing resources, and healthy genetics for reproduction. Your strengths in these categories must be portrayed in every interaction you have with a female, but without being too showy. Your girlfriend cheated on you because you kissed her ass and neglected to improve yourself. That left her with no choice but to take on the role of treating you like a son who needed to be raised, instead of treating you as her man. She eventually lost her physical attraction to you, because no woman wants to fuck her son."

"Don't hold back your opinions," jokes Reid.

Wish ignores him and continues: "Often, a woman cheats when she's ovulating. She'll seek out men like Andrew, who fulfill that instinctual sense of what they are missing. As much as it seems you'd be a good father for being thoughtful with flowers and gifts, her motherly instincts suggest you'd give her babies who'd grow up to be pussies like you — meaning they wouldn't survive in the wild."

Reid's chin falls to his chest. "Why was this never explained to me in all my years in college?"

"The psychology you learned was developed during the feminist movement. I fully support women's rights, but unfortunately, the man's penis got cut off during the process. Your mommy-approving behavior stems from this. Listen to me: you have permission to be a man. And once you've developed, I expect you to share those same words with other men."

Reid lifts his chin. The words "permission to be a man" connect to that voice which seems to rest in his gut. He examines a suit, noticing it's tailored for broad shoulders and a slim waist. "Andrew mentioned something about a math equation for our body shape?"

"The golden ratio," says Wish. "The female human-animal is genetically wired to seek out men who most accurately showcase broad shoulders and a narrow waist, a symbol of strength. It's a non-conscious signal to the feminine psyche that the man is strong enough to keep her safe from danger. Women are prewired to always seek safety, protecting the babies. That V-shape should closely equal the golden ratio, meaning your shoulder width should be one-point-six-one times the width of your waist. Through fitness training, your body must become a close representation of the golden ratio V-shaped frame. And all clothing, especially your suits, must show the V-shape."

Wish slips away momentarily and returns with his arms full. He hands Reid a navy-blue slim-fitting suit, white dress shirt, and brown wingtip shoes.

Reid examines the items while noticing photos of famous soccer players spread throughout the store. "These clothes are what all these soccer players wear?"

"And women all over the world would gladly deliver their vagina to any of those soccer players. They possess the natural body types that most women find attractive, not the blown-up baboons you see in many American sports. Andrew is actually too big, so he only caters to a small percentage of women. But that's fine; he has to be himself." Wish points to a poster of a soccer player who might as well be a model. "You'll be styling your hair like this man."

The corners of Reid's eyes tremble with fear. The man in the poster looks amazing with the hairstyle, but the sides of his hair are cut short. *People will think something is wrong with me if I expose my scar.* He lowers his gaze to the floor and runs a hand through his hair.

Wish places a hand on Reid's shoulder. "Accept all that you are, and the world will follow by accepting you as well."

Reid straightens himself, cracks a half-smile, and takes the suit into the dressing room. He slips on the suit and steps out to face his mentor, gasping for air. "It feels like it's trying to suck away my internal organs."

"During your forty days of seclusion, you will sculpt your body to fit this suit. Failure to do so will mean the end of our agreement," says Wish. "Andrew gave you the workout plan and food guidelines?"

"Yeah, and he also showed me a video of some girl he had sex with last night."

Wish raises his palm to his forehead. "That fucking child. Always seeking approval."

"Why did you give him the candle camera?"

"Field research," says Wish. "I can't stand sex with women under thirty; their brains are so disconnected from their bodies, and they mimic the shit they see in porn. The frustration is such that I can't think clearly for research. Andrew fornicates with many women in their early twenties. I can keep a clear mind while studying his game tape. I need to see how the sex has evolved with the young adults who grew up in the internet porn generation."

"What have you noticed?" Reid asked.

Wish huffs with disappointment, shakes his head, then stomps off to the other end of the store. Reid adjusts the lapels of his suit in the mirror, not surprised by Wish's response. Gone are the days when children were raised without internet or cell phones; many learn social skills through technology, and sex is no different.

He returns to the fitting room and changes back into his workout clothes. He brings the new outfit to the register and hands it to the clerk. As Reid pulls out his wallet, Wish's hand reaches over Reid's shoulder and drops a few large bills onto the counter.

"Happy belated birthday, kid," says Wish. Reid bows with appreciation, wondering if the joy he feels resembles how it would have felt to receive such a gift from his father.

The men exit and enter a nearby barbershop. Wish guides the barber to cut the style he feels is best for his protégé. Reid holds back his nerves while sitting in the chair, facing away from the mirror. He knows he can't violate his agreement with Wish.

"I'm jealous of your scar," says the barber. Reid smiles, but is hesitant to believe the man.

"Your scar gives you an aura of mystery," says Wish. "Aside from all the shit I mentioned about a woman's attraction instincts, the single most important factor in attracting a female is what they don't know about you — your mysteriousness. In movies, the attractive men are never computer engineers who work a nine to five and play Scrabble on the weekends. They are men with an edge. Women can't quite figure them out, but know enough to feel safe and taken care of. Your scar will raise a thousand questions in a woman's mind."

Reid squints as the barber spins the chair to face the mirror and he sees the final result. Slowly, a smile forms on his face. He tilts his head to see the long scar on display from ear to ear. *This actually makes me look a bit ... like a bad boy.* He holds his next breath in his chest, studying his new, edgy look in the mirror. *This feels good. Really good.*

The men drive back to the Lexi Hotel as the Las Vegas sun sets and the Strip lights start to glow. Wish instructs Reid to wear his new suit, even though it's a tight fit, when joining Andrew at the nightclub later that night.

"Andrew will tell you when and where to meet. He's highly skilled at attracting women in a nightclub environment. Observe his methods, and copy them if you must. Soon you will create your own style for interacting with women, but for now mimicking Andrew will serve as a solid starting point."

Chapter 14

"Reid, my man, you're looking fly. A fresh haircut and a dope suit," says Andrew.

"Thank you. This new hairstyle is out of my comfort zone, but I'm glad you dig it," says Reid. "So, what are we doing tonight?"

Reid pumps Andrew's hand. It's a quarter to eleven and they are at a casino bar inside the Aria Hotel.

"In order for Las Vegas nightclubs to survive, they need to look like they are full of beautiful women. My friend owns a promotion company that recruits groups of attractive women and brings them into nightclubs. He needed tonight off, so we're covering for him. We'll be walking in thirty girls and they'll be split between two bottle service tables. You'll be at one table and I'll be at the other. Fifteen girls each. Think you can handle that, big boy?"

Reid's face goes pale. "I'll need a few drinks. What do I have to do with the girls?"

"You'll have access to unlimited free booze. Our role is to keep the girls entertained so they won't leave and go to another club. It's the best deal ever, bro. Just be yourself and you'll probably take a girl back tonight." Andrew slaps Reid on the back.

Just be myself? Ugh, that's the same awful advice I've heard my entire life. Being myself means getting cheated on, laughed at, teased, and humiliated.

They stroll towards the entrance of the hotel's nightclub. A group of thirty or so college-aged women stand near the entrance. A few of the women recognize Andrew and run over to him, glowing with excitement. He gives each one a bear hug and introduces Reid. Reid smiles and shakes their hands, releasing a breath of relief. *So far, so good.*

A bouncer organizes the group into a single line, then guides them towards the entrance. Reid, with his fifteen women following behind, stands tall as they stroll past the hundreds of people waiting in line. Andrew walks in front of his fifteen and looks over his shoulder, shooting a smile at Reid as if to say, *Freaking amazing, right?* Reid gives him a thumbs-up. He can't believe he gets to be one of "those" club guys.

The group enters the main ballroom of the packed nightclub. Reid absorbs the thumping sounds of hip-hop music, bobbing his head slightly as they stroll past the crowd. They arrive at two maroon semi-circle booths centrally located in the club. Each booth wraps around a low-profile table, on which rests a large bottle of vodka, ice, juice mixers, and glasses.

A nervous chill combined with feverish joy pulses through Reid. Everyone in the club appears to be noticing their entrance. The women file around the booth. A few women take a seat, and the others stand around the booth and talk with each other. Reid studies the layout, noticing a second-floor balcony where patrons can hang with their drinks and see below. He assumes Wish might be looking on from there and commits to making him proud.

Reid turns his head to study the action at the neighboring table. Andrew is in the middle of his women, igniting what looks to be the world's greatest dance party. The women have their hands all over him, like groupies reaching for a rock star. A girl starts unbuttoning Andrew's shirt. Reid shifts his gaze downward. *We've only been here a few minutes and the shirt is coming off. Ugh, just like god-damn high school — the jocks get the girl and I'm a loser.*

Andrew leans towards Reid's table. "Get in there and make them drinks, brotha."

Make them drinks? Okay. Yeah. I suppose I can do that. With quivering hands, he grabs three empty glasses, then adds ice and vodka to each. He turns to three girls sitting at the edge of his booth and politely taps one on the shoulder. All three turn around, notice the glasses in his hand, and wait for him to say something. Reid's knees become wobbly. His mind races with what he should be saying in this moment. The women glare at Reid, as if to say, *Are you gonna offer us drinks or not?*

Think of something quick. Uh. Um. Shit. Just say anything, dammit.

Words squeak out of him like he's a pubescent teenager. "H-hi, ladies. May I offer you a drink? What would you like with your vodka?"

They each mouth the word "cranberry," then give him a semi-friendly grin. He adds the cranberry to each glass of vodka, hands the ladies their beverages, then repeats the same process with each woman at the table. The tremble in his hands shifts to steady-calmness as his confidence improves with each interaction. *This is the easiest way to talk to women. No woman will reject free booze.*

He finishes serving all fifteen women, then leans towards the girl next to him. "Where are you from?"

"I'm local," she says, then quickly turns away. *Rejected.* His shoulders cave forward. He then hears elated screams coming from Andrew's table. He quickly glances their way. The muscle-man's shirt is off and he's performing like a one-man Chippendales show. *I'm supposed to mimic that? There's no way.* Reid scans the club; it seems that every woman is screaming for Andrew. *He's perfect and I'm an ugly loser. Does Wish expect me to be Andrew?*

Reid feels a tap on his shoulder. He turns and sees the first three girls hold empty glasses up to his face. He nods and acts as their bartender once more, quickly refilling their drinks.

"How come you're not drinking?" says one of the women.

"Oh, yeah. I forgot." He reaches for a glass and fills it three-quarters full with vodka and a splash of orange juice. The drink reminds him of the night he met Wish. *A screwdriver for the guy who always get screwed over.* He pours the drink down his throat, then adds more vodka and orange juice.

He glances at Andrew's table. Security is asking him to put his shirt on. He buttons it up, then high-fives the guards. Andrew then stands in the center of his booth, towering above the women while dancing subtly with a welcoming smile.

Reid can't believe what his eyes see next. *Andrew's women are pouring him drinks.* Reid clenches his teeth, then examines the women at his table. They look like a group of zombies with glowing faces: each girl is staring at her phone. Reid swallows his drink. *Fuck, man. I'm in Vegas. I can do this.* Reid remembers Wish's instructions to mimic

Andrew.

Reid stands in the exact same spot in his booth as Andrew next door, then starts dancing like Andrew, bouncing slightly from side to side while smiling. The women at Reid's table soon stand up and follow.

Reid feels a vibration in his pocket. He slides out his phone and reads a text from Wish.

Notice how your dancing got them to change. It's human nature to want to conform. The feminine energy is prewired to respond to masculine energy. Be the leader of your group and you'll be the most desired.

Wish is here? Reid canvasses the balcony, but doesn't see a fedora anywhere. The phone vibrates with another text.

You don't need the approval of these women, or any woman you'll ever meet. Own your penis and balls. Stand proud in your masculinity — let that energy pulse through you.

Reid slides the phone back into his pocket, then rolls his shoulders back. The urge to yell out a lion's roar is strong, but he refrains and shifts the energy to further study Andrew. He notices that Andrew isn't talking much, just moving his body in a way that women seem to enjoy.

Reid gulps down another stiff drink. His buzz increases; he feels drunk and free from inhibitions. He continues his coy dance, then locks eyes with a cutie a few feet away. He smiles, and she smiles back. But then she turns her back to him. He sulks, feeling he missed an opportunity, but then wonders if her back-turn was a way to invite him to come closer.

He takes a step towards her, places his hands on her hips, then grinds his core along with her backside. The woman launches forward, freeing herself from Reid's grip. She turns around and shoves Reid, causing him to fall back into the booth.

"Gross," she says. "Don't touch me. You're fucking creepy."

The entire table of women freeze in their dancing to take notice. Reid quickly rises, but feels his remaining self-esteem ooze out of his toes. Each woman backs away with a look of disgust, as if he's a convicted sex-offender. *I swear I'm not creepy. I'm a caring professor who passionately wants to help others.*

The girl who shoved him hurries away. Minutes pass, and she returns with a bouncer following her.

"Come with me, sir," says the bouncer.

Reid sets his drink on the table and follows the bouncer out of the VIP area. Although the music is blasting, he feels as if the club has gone silent and everyone is glaring laser beams of judgment. He follows the bouncer to the back of the club, where the bouncer rips open an exit door. Without notice, Reid is shoved outside with great force. He stumbles onto the pavement, scrapes his knees, then rolls onto his back. As he lies there in shock, the smell of rotting food begins to irk his nose. He crawls to the curb and sits, realizing he was thrown out like trash near the hotel dumpsters. He wraps his hands around his bloody knees, curls into a ball, and sobs.

Why is it so easy for Andrew? The guy uses women for sex and they happily wait in line for it. Why does life seem so easy for everyone else but me? He runs his hands through his hair, noticing his new hairdo, then pauses to feel the exposed scar on each side of his head.

"I hate this fucking scar!"

A familiar voice calls out from behind, "What else would you like to blame?"

Reid turns to see Wish standing tall, wearing all black. Wish slides a cigar off the brim of his fedora and puts it in his mouth. He then digs a lighter out of his pocket, adds a flame to the cigar, and puffs.

Reid's knee throbs with a needle-like sting as he hobbles up to stand and face his mentor. "I'm not the sex god or whatever you think I am." He looks at the ground. "Maybe I'm some kind of runt who'll confirm that Andrew is the one you are looking for."

The tip of the cigar glows reddish-orange as Wish inhales. Wish's gaze pierces through the exhaled ball of smoke and into Reid. A black Cadillac Escalade pulls up in front of both men. Wish mashes the cigar against the bottom of his shoe and walks nearer to the car. He opens the rear passenger door, then glances back at Reid.

"You're correct. You're not a sex god." Wish steps into the SUV. "You're more than that." Wish slams the door and the car drives off.

What does he see in me? I'm not worthy of any of this.

Reid limps back to his hotel, each step releasing a hit of pain as his torn pants graze his scraped kneecaps. When he arrives, he falls onto the bed, head spinning with drunkenness, and passes out.

Chapter 15

Reid rubs his eyes as the sun beams onto his face through the hotel room window. His head throbs with the essence of a hangover. His heart aches as he replays the shameful images from the night before. He grabs his phone to type a message to Wish. He considers typing something like, *Thanks, but no thanks; I'm not the one,* but chooses to wait a few minutes to make sure it's the right decision.

Reid squints as he notices an envelope has been slid under the door. He steps out of bed, feeling the sting on his knees as he stumbles over to grab the letter. It's from Wish.

Professor Reid Bradley,

Forty days of seclusion begin today. The goal is to cleanse yourself of negative emotions, to study true masculinity, and to rebuild your body, mind, and spirit with a solid foundation. During this time, you must pay attention to the judgments you make of others in your day-to-day life. These judgments serve as the projected signs of weakness from the inner self, pointing out what needs work in order for you to feel whole.

— If you judge the person with money, silently thank them and commit to making more money.

— If you judge the person who is fit, silently thank them and commit to becoming fit.

— If you judge the person who is sexual, silently thank them and commit to being sexual.

Love your judgments, because they are your guides towards self-mastery.

Remember, you are a man of service. Your natural gifts will soon inspire millions around the world. There is a young man somewhere right now who is in desperate need of what you are destined to teach.

We don't have time to waste; you must remain focused.

At work, commit to serving your students.

At home, commit to exploring, then listening to, the inner self.

At the gym, commit to creating your physical being (completing the plan set forth by Andrew).

During this time, you must be alone as much as possible. Journal when you wake and before sleep. No women, no masturbation, no television. Only read the books that I suggest. Dive into the depths of yourself and listen to the messages released from your shadow-self.

Be aware that the Collective Shadow will continue to attempt to throw you off by tapping into your fears and insecurities. You must also be aware that the CS will attempt to ruin your progress with seemingly positive temptations. Remember, the CS wears different masks; it won't be as obvious as thugs in a park.

I am committed to our agreement, to serving as a guide for you to become the man you have always wanted to be. You must commit to focusing on the self. I'll be expecting you to fit into the suit.

Our next meeting will be on Saturday, June 1st, 9am. Desert Memorial Park, Palm Springs. Unless it's an emergency, we will not communicate until that day.

Remember, those who are wired like us are praying for you to succeed. They're ready to meet their leader.
— Wish

Reid rubs his head. The pulsing hangover makes it difficult to consider all that Wish has written. He starts to pack his clothes, then stops to examine the damage done to his suit pants and jacket. He realizes they can't be fixed, but stuffs them in his bag anyway. He then takes a shower, hoping to alleviate the headache. As the water sprays on the back of his neck, his mind wanders into a daydream.

Reid is an invisible spirit who enters the dorm room of an eighteen-year-old male college student. The boy doesn't speak, but Reid can read his mind. He instantly recognizes what this young boy is experiencing, because he went through the same thing. The boy is lying on his bed silently crying to himself, hoping the kids in the hallway won't hear. It's a Friday night and everyone is out partying, but he's stayed home, frightened and full of shame because he doesn't fit in. People think he's nice, but really they only use him for help with homework.

The boy rises to stand in front of his mirror. His brain fills with hopeful thoughts — *maybe tonight is the night I make friends, or maybe I'll finally feel what it's like to kiss a girl.* He musters all the creativity he has to put on a seemingly cool outfit, though the pants are a bit tight. He sucks in his gut to secure them. The young man bends over to tie his shoelaces, then feels the rear seam split apart down the center of the pants. His momentary courage dissolves into shame. He stands in front of the mirror, shoulders slumped forward, studying what could have been.

"Why is life so easy for everyone but me?" says the boy to the mirror. "Everyone else knows what to say, how to look, and what to do. Why is it so hard to fit in, to be cool?"

He bursts into tears as he falls to his knees in front of the mirror. "I'd give anything to know. Please, I'm begging you. Help me ... teach me."

The urgency brings Reid back to reality. He jumps out of the shower, determined to never quit. He hears several young men crying because they don't fit in, just as he used to. Heat builds behind his eyes as he finishes packing. *I was forced to take chemistry, geology, and history in school, but why the hell is nobody teaching people how to relate to one another?*

As he zips up his luggage, he realizes that Wish is the mentor he has been begging for his entire life. *The guy might be harsh, mysterious, and a bit scary, but I'm committed, even if it means jail time or death. I promise I'll master this and find that young man someday. And if that young man scraps up his suit in the process, I'll give my last dime to buy him a new suit.*

Reid grabs his bag, then attempts to pull open the hotel room door, but something has jammed it. He pulls harder. The door yanks open and knocks him back a few steps. Reid gathers himself, then notices something dangling on the doorknob. It's a new suit, with a small note from Wish attached.

It was once said that the suit makes the man.
What if the man first makes himself, then puts on the perfect suit ...?
What does he become?

Reid hurries back to southern California, eager to begin the forty days of seclusion, determined to be a new man who wears a suit that fits perfectly. During the first two days, he moves his remaining items out of the home he shared with Jasmine, without her being present, and into his mom's house. Jasmine and Reid agree to no longer have contact, which allows Reid to quickly fall into the rhythm of his routine.

He wakes up at a half past six, gulps a protein shake, and writes in his journal. He works from eight to four, then does forty minutes of lifting, followed by an hour of spin cycling. Yoga on Fridays, Saturdays, and Sundays. His commitment to consistent training and proper eating serves to change his physique, mood, and thinking process for the better.

Each night, he studies erotic massage books and video clips online, soaking in the knowledge like a sponge. He combines his "hands-on" experiences from times spent with Wish, Molly, and Tasha with the materials covering erotic tactile experiences.

While studying one evening during his second week, he notices a strong point of emphasis that stands out from a massage book: how each individual's sensory response system is different. He recalls Wish mentioning that not every woman would enjoy the aggressive paddling he did on Molly; some women are plenty satisfied with simple massage techniques for stimulation.

Reid looks up from the massage book. "But how will I be able to tell if she's the type to enjoy being bound and paddled, versus being satisfied with simple massage? I'm supposed to provide something she doesn't know her body is capable of feeling."

The question makes his creative wheels move. He connects this knowledge to Goddess Mindy's "glove of contrasts." Each finger on the glove had a different sensory trigger attached; soft, scratchy, hard, cool, and furry. Then there were nubs on the palm of the glove, for the Shadow Palm Technique. He shakes his head while grinning, excited to someday learn the mysterious technique. He returns his focus to the contrasts that the fingers of the glove would provide, and realizes that such an item might be useful in seeing how the woman's body responds during the early stages of an Erotic Sensory Experience — a means to understand how she is wired. *But I don't have the glove.*

He reads the massage book further, learning how a massage practitioner tests their client's sensory response system, gauging the client's response through applying light touch, then medium, then hard, and calibrating the session from there. Reid scratches his chin. He thinks of a way he could test a woman on a future date, then begins to visualize and write out the details of the date.

This exploration into sensory stimulation with women has him aroused, very aroused, and often. He struggles to remain committed to not masturbating during his seclusion phase, but stays true. As a form of relief and mental practice, he finds value in writing short erotic fantasies with scenes of himself acting as the man he visualizes himself becoming.

In tonight's story, he approaches a woman in a bar and knows the perfect thing to say. He sits next to her, enjoying her awestruck expression due to his irresistible charm. She's wearing a short white skirt, and her legs are crossed towards him. While conversing with basic getting-to-know-you questions, he places his hand on her thigh, feeling the silkiness of her freshly shaved skin. He leads the conversation to the topic of massage, asking her what style she prefers. Then, based on her answer, he applies pressure, a tad stronger than she anticipates, to gauge her sensory response system.

He drops the pen on the notepad. A tingle rolls down his spine. He realizes he's creating his own style. He's creating the "Reid" he's always wanted to be.

He's excited to finish his final week of isolation. His body itches with the desire to showcase his new self to Wish and the women who visit Las Vegas. Aside from feeling improved within, he starts to notice that his external environment is responding to him differently as well — women seem to be acknowledging his presence. He's getting flirtatious looks at the grocery store, mall, and even his college. He realizes that when a person consistently works on themselves, people seem to be drawn to that energy. This is especially evident when a gorgeous woman of Pacific Island descent approaches him during a workout at his gym.

"What's your story?" she asks. "Every guy here hits on me during my workout, except you."

Reid is filled with prideful joy — more proof that all the hard work seems to be paying off. He's tempted to be the lothario he's been writing about, but he knows he must stay focused on isolation.

"Forgive me. I'm not allowed to talk to anyone."

"You married or something?" she says.

"No."

"Girlfriend?"

Reid laughs. "Definitely, no."

"You don't like my big tits?" She lifts her hands to grab each breast and squeeze.

He darts his gaze to her cleavage, then quickly returns his focus to her eyes. "I need to do this set." He grins internally while lifting a set of dumbbells overhead for a series of shoulder-press movements. *One more week.*

"Go ahead. I'll wait," she says while gawking at him in the mirror. "There's something about you I can't figure out. I've been watching since you started here last month. That scar on your head is sexy. What's the story with that?"

This must be the mysteriousness factor Wish mentioned. While completing the presses, Reid can't help but notice the woman's impeccably sculpted body, and he feels temptation rise.

"My name is Drea. What's your phone number?" she asks. "You're a challenge. I'm gonna get you somehow."

Reid's controlled breathing becomes short. *Zero sex and masturbation is making it difficult to say "no" to this woman.* He returns the dumbbells to the rack, then stares at the weights. He reminds himself to stay disciplined. But he can't avoid seeing what's reflected in the mirror, inches above the weights. Drea is bent over from the waist, bum facing the mirror, with her hands on the floor, giving the illusion that she's stretching her hamstrings, but Reid knows damn well what she's doing.

He turns towards her. "I'll give you my number, but I can't do anything with you until after next week."

"Why? Your divorce become final then?" Drea hands Reid her phone.

"I made a commitment." Reid types his number into her phone.

"Next week, okay?"

"We'll see about that." She kisses Reid on the cheek and struts off.

Reid finishes the rest of his routine feeling boosted with unusual strength. He recalls his past rejections from women, then shakes his head in awe, knowing the interaction with Drea went smoother than any he's ever had before. He leaves the gym, glowing from his response to Drea and how it lacked approval-seeking. But while driving home, he suddenly feels a knot form in his neck. He broke his agreement with Wish; he wasn't supposed to interact with a woman of interest. Yet he can't deny how good it felt to be desired, to see himself on Andrew's level. As he nears home, he settles on figuring it was just a minor glitch and Wish won't find out. *Hell, she approached me.*

At home, Reid eats a healthy dinner consisting of baked chicken, broccoli, and a sugar-free mint-chocolate protein shake to minimize his cravings for sweets. His mom offers to cook, but she understands Reid's commitment to work on himself. Reid hasn't told her about Wish, figuring it's best to hide the fact that his new mentor is a pimp. Instead he's explained that the transition away from Jasmine has inspired him to improve his overall health.

While journaling after dinner, he can't stop fantasizing about Drea. Luckily, he didn't get her phone number; only she has his. Having gone thirty-four days without touching himself, any image of an attractive woman sparks his member to stand tall. But experiencing Drea in person, sensing her hunger for him, triggers his loins to near-explosion. He chooses to channel the energy into writing the fantasy as a short story. Halfway through the first paragraph, his phone buzzes with a text. He looks at the message, sent from an unsaved number.

Join me in the shower?

Reid narrows his eyes. A picture text follows; Drea is topless in front of her bathroom mirror. He leans back and chuckles. *Sometimes technology can be considered a good thing.* Another picture comes through, showcasing her naked rear end, followed by a text.

I need your strong hands all over me right now.

Reid sets the phone down and exhales deeply, hoping to calm the stiffness in his pants. He returns his pen to the paper with the hope that writing the fantasy will deflect the lure of reality. Nothing comes to mind. He slams the pen onto the pad and grips his hair with both hands.

Drea continues to send erotic photos, each one steamier than the last. Reid has been taught how sex can be used to serve others and inspire them towards personal growth. His mind locks on how he can serve Drea with the new concepts he's eager to try. Should he be the one to deny her such pleasure and self-growth? He's a man of service, isn't he?

His phone hums as it receives more erotic pictures, and another text.

I am all alone in this big house. Free me from my boredom ...

He drops his forehead onto the pad of paper, fighting his desperation to provide the experience this woman is yearning for. *For the first time in my life, I finally feel like I know what to do with a woman, and I'm not allowed to do it.* His brain conjures images of Molly bound to the metal cage, cooing as he causes contrasting sensations throughout her body. The muscles of his forearms cramp with tension as he grips his phone, typing a response, then deleting it. *Don't respond, damn it. Don't respond.* His fingers dance across the keypad; he's eager to share the new version of himself. He types and presses "send."

If I came over, the last thing you would experience is being free.

Drea responds: **OMG, you know exactly what I want. Come over now.**

"Ahhh." Reid throws his phone across the room into a pile of clothes. *Come on, Reid, don't fuck with the mission.* He drops his head into his hands and considers possible options. *Maybe Wish would be proud of me for servicing this woman? He would be honored to know I contributed positively to her life, giving her an enlightening sensory experience. Ugh, but my commitment is to be in isolation for forty days. Or I could serve her, keep it secret, knowing I got in a round of practice for providing ESEs. Wish did say that it was urgent that I master this as soon as possible.*

He sits quietly, hoping to channel a response from the voice of his shadow, but it's dormant. *Goddammit!*

Reid hears the phone vibrate amongst the pile of clothes. He grabs it and sees Drea's address listed, along with the following text.

You have 30 mins to get here. Tonight will be your only opportunity to have me.

His chest tightens. He considers calling Wish to explain or even ask permission, but Wish wrote in his letter that they wouldn't talk until the end of Reid's seclusion. He explores each option a bit more, unable to deny how much he's dying to express his newly understood sexual energy and try the new techniques.

His mind arrives at its final decision. *There's no way Wish will find out.* He puts on a newly acquired fitted black t-shirt and slim-fitting jeans, proudly displaying his V-shaped torso. He opens his sock drawer, and grabs two condoms and the paddle that was gifted to him by Goddess Mindy. He then looks around the room, hoping to find something he could use to bind Drea's hands together. He reaches to the top shelf of the closet, grabs an old shoe, and yanks the black shoelace free, then stuffs all of the items in a small bag.

Reid strides towards the front door, but halts to examine himself in a mirror that has been there since his childhood. The reflection portrays a different person than usual: a man with an aura of darkness, an edge that makes him feel strangely secure. He leaves, gets in his car, and drives to Drea's place, an ocean-side mansion.

Reid parks alongside the curb next to her gated driveway. He steps out of his car and scans the gate for a call box of some sort. Seeing nothing of the kind, he fishes for his phone to call her, but then the gate suddenly opens. Reid shrugs mildly, then walks up the driveway, seeing Drea standing by the door holding a drink.

"Drink this." Drea hands Reid a shot of dark liquor, then nods for him to enter. Reid swallows, forcing himself to keep a neutral expression as his throat burns from the whiskey. They walk towards a tall liquor cabinet, then she pours Reid another whiskey shot. "Drink again. I don't want you to cum too soon."

Reid swallows the warm, ethanolic-tasting liquid. He grimaces, then quickly neutralizes his expression. He scans Drea's hourglass figure, stuffed into a skin-tight black tank-top and a long, grey, flowing skirt. The sight releases an onslaught of sexual excitement into his core.

Drea takes Reid's hand, then leads him on a brief tour of the dimly lit home. While he scans the cold, minimally designed space, Reid's body stiffens — something about being here isn't right. The place looks like a palace he's seen in movies, a place owned by drug lords. It doesn't seem home-like; there's a staleness, an uninviting aura. But he can't put his finger on why this seems so off. They enter the living room and sit on a stiff white-leather couch.

"I know men quite well," Drea says, then pours another shot. Reid downs it with a straight face, though he's questioning why she's adamant he needs to drink.

As he hesitantly places the small bag on the floor, he can't ignore the excitement between his legs. The room begins to spin as the buzz of alcohol kicks in. He focuses on her cleavage, her magnificently showcased cleavage. Reid realizes in this moment he's not that teenager who gets called names and laughed at. He's not the nerd who hides while the meatheads get the girl. She desires a stud, and that is who he's now become.

"You like my tits, don't you?" Reid nods, grinning like a child eager to play with a new toy. She slides her bra off, then pulls down her tank-top. The breasts stay in the same position, lifted and perky. "They're all yours. I just got them done."

She caresses the back of Reid's head and pulls him to her cleavage. He ravishes her breasts — fondling, squeezing, and sucking the gelatinous mounds. His hands glide around her body, then down her stomach towards her navel. Just before he touches her pelvic area, Drea slaps his hand away.

"Not yet, young man," she teases. "You need more shots. Don't want you to cum too soon."

Reid grins slyly, not wanting to show the full extent of how much he agrees with her. He gulps down another shot, then kisses her soft lips. His hand inches down her side, then towards the navel, only to be slapped away again.

"One more shot," she says. "Then you get my goodies. I promise they're the best you've ever had."

"You are quite the tease." He swallows the dark liquid.

She rises and takes his hand. "You bring a condom?"

Reid nods and grabs the small bag, then Drea leads him upstairs to a bedroom. He feels a sudden tremble in his stomach, a signal of some sort of problem. He hasn't seen any pictures of a husband or kids. She isn't wearing a wedding ring. Everything appears safe. Yet he can't help but sense a voice from his gut calling out, trying to give some kind of guidance. But his buzzed mind ignores the warning.

They enter the dimly lit bedroom, fondling and kissing. She drops Reid's pants and tease-kisses around his erection, then she glides her breasts up his body and they kiss once more. Reid slips his hands under the waistband of her skirt and starts to pull it down. Before it can move, she slaps his hands away.

"I need to see you put the condom on first, sexy boy."

Reid reaches into his bag for a condom, feeling the shoestring and paddle before grabbing a condom. A reminder that he's there to provide a sensory experience. *But how do I handle a woman who is controlling everything?*

"Condom comes on, and the skirt will come down. You boys can be slick with pretending like you have a condom on."

Reid smirks and decides to skip the idea of using the items in his bag. He tears open the condom and slides it into place. She turns her back towards him and drops her skirt and underwear, then bends over with her hands on the bed. She spanks her bare bottom while gazing seductively at him.

"Put it deep in my ass, you big, strong man."

In your ass? His tranced-out mind suddenly becomes present. The anal option has never been on the menu for Reid.

He steps towards her, feeling uncertain about how to proceed. He touches her bare bum, then moves his hands up her back, then across to her front and down her stomach, nearing her private area — only to be slapped away again. Reid steps back, looking befuddled.

"You're such a tease," says Drea. "Just stick it in me, deep, so I feel it in my stomach."

Reid shrugs, then steps closer to her rear end. He grips his stiffness, presses it to her opening, then feels a strange resistance meet the tip. He figures he must have misguided his aim and reaches between her legs, searching for her dewy opening, but instead he discovers a firm sack. He quickly rips his arm away and jumps back.

"What the fuck is that?"

"Come here, baby. You know you want this." She stands tall, then turns to face him. Reid catches a glimpse of Drea's erect penis, then darts his gaze to the floor.

He locates his clothes and quickly gets dressed.

"Don't leave. You and I could be something special," says Drea. "I promise you'll get used to my penis — other boys have."

I can't believe I risked everything for this. Reid feels his heart race but he remains silent as he runs out of the room, down the stairs, and out to his car, feeling adrenaline drown out the alcohol buzz. He drives away, controlled, but looking back just in case she follows. The shock of what occurred manifests in a tremble of disgust in his stomach.

Minutes pass. He pulls over, opens the car door, and vomits onto the pavement. He cleans his mouth with bottled water, then sits silently, wondering what would happen if Wish found out. He feels certain that Wish may not learn of this escapade directly but will see the shame in Reid's eyes. He's tempted to call Wish and own up to his mistake, hoping to receive understanding by turning himself in.

Reid glances at his phone and notices a text from Wish that was sent an hour ago.

You came into my mediation tonight. The energy was confusing, neither masculine nor feminine. Does this make sense to you?

Shit. I gotta tell him. He calls Wish that second.

"I'm sorry, sir," says Reid. "I made a mistake tonight." Reid goes on to explain the story.

"You've failed," says Wish.

"But it doesn't count, right? She was a man or a whatever. I left before anything happened."

"Don't give a fuck what she was," says Wish. "You violated the agreement. You're not worthy of continuing our mission. We are done. Goodbye."

Reid hears the phone signal cut off. His mouth falls open as he drops the phone into his lap. Images of his future slipping away release tremors throughout his body. He musters just enough strength to drive home, and stumble out of the car and into the house. He crawls into bed, thinking about how the knowledge he had been desperate to discover had been at his fingertips. He questions whether the experience with Drea was another version of the same story of humiliation that has continued to occur in his life: the girls teasing him as a teenager, his girlfriends cheating on him, women rejecting him when he finally had the courage to approach. He felt like he was becoming everything he dreamed of being, and that humiliation was something he'd never experience again, but he got duped.

He runs his hands through his hair, thinking of how sly Drea was in duping him. He suddenly sits up with an epiphany. Drea was sent by the Collective Shadow. He recalls how Wish said to watch out for a CS member, likely wearing a disguise. Reid chuckles, thinking about how he didn't expect *that* kind of disguise. He continues to explore his thoughts, realizing that if he quits now, the Collective Shadow will have won. *Wish might be out of the picture for now, but maybe if I continue working on myself, I can win back his trust.*

Chapter 16

It's the final week of the spring semester. Reid's strong motivation to earn Wish's trust has dissipated. Wish won't answer Reid's calls, leaving him to wander in a land of hopelessness. His depression takes him away from the gym, his journal, and even eating. He slouches into classes, poorly dressed, unshaven, and lacking his usual desire to serve the students. Reid finds it easy to not care, believing most other professors don't care all that much about their students either.

Each night, he returns home and locks himself in his bedroom. He can only muster the strength to watch James Bond movies on repeat. He hopes for some inspiration; instead, the movies are a constant reminder of the man he'll never become. Friday night, the day before he was supposed to meet Wish, is the same. Until he hears a knock on the bedroom door.

"Son, we need to talk," says Reid's mom.

Never being one to ignore his mom's request, he moves from the bed and opens the door. Reid stands in front of a concerned woman whose eyes fill with tears as she speaks.

"I'm sorry … I have failed you, son."

"What are you saying, Mom? You've been nothing but amazing to me."

She walks to the couch, sits, and takes a few breaths. Reid follows and sits next to her.

"When your father left me while I was pregnant with you, I was emotionally destroyed. I swore to raise you in a way that would guarantee you'd never feel such pain. This mama bear felt she had to protect her only child."

Reid places his hand on her nearest shoulder. "Mama Bear did great. I never got in trouble, I made good friends, and I graduated from college."

She smiles briefly, then lowers her chin. "When you were a teenager, I'd hear you cry yourself to sleep every night. My intuition knew why, but I was afraid to share. Now I hear you crying at night again, as an adult. I've realized that I can no longer keep you from the truth."

A warm sensation rolls through his body. *What truth?*

"Son, I've realized that my methods for your upbringing were not to protect you, they were to prevent you from discovering the other half of yourself." She takes a deep breath as she fights back the tears. "I was afraid you'd develop traits genetically passed on by your father."

"What traits? I don't want anything to do with that asshole."

"He had a way with women. Nobody ever made me feel the way he could. I got pregnant with you and wanted marriage, but he knew he wasn't able to be monogamous. He was also seeing another woman. He pleaded with me to have an open relationship. I refused, so he left. He continued to see that other woman, and they died in a car accident before your birth."

She cries. Reid moves his hand to rub her back lightly. His face burns from seeing her sob. He's always been obsessed with making sure the women in his life are happy; perhaps he sensed his mother's heartbreak while in the womb. But then Reid further explores what she just described. He wonders if his father had the same gene that Wish claims Reid has.

Reid's mom wipes her eyes, then glances at him. "All these years, I blamed his death on the way he was wired. I hated that those characteristics took my son's father away." She reaches for a tissue. "Truth is, your father was a good, honest man. He did the right thing by being upfront with me. He was excited to help raise you."

Reid's head falls into his hands. His father was a man he hated. And now, his father has become someone he desperately wants to know. All the conversations they could have had ... his dad could have taught him how to deal with the girls in high school, how to never get cheated on, how to be a man. He sees his mom's apologetic eyes, then shifts his gaze to the floor.

"A month ago," says his mom, "you were walking around this house with purpose. You were connected to something, a mission of some sort. But something happened, and now you are hiding with Mama Bear for safety."

"I'm grateful for your safety net," says Reid.

She shakes her head. "My protection is preventing you from experiencing the life that's waiting for you. You've fallen into your old patterns."

"What do you mean?"

"Whatever you were involved in a month ago was the correct path. I saw glimpses of your father, the other part of who you are." She sobs. "You cannot stay here anymore, Reid. You need to leave and continue that journey."

"You're kicking me out?"

"Everything inside of me wants you to stay, where I can keep you safe." She takes her hand off his back and stands. "But I can't teach you how to be a man."

"Who will teach me?" Reid shakes his head, knowing he blew his chance with Wish, the man who understood all that he was desperate to learn.

"I don't know, but you can start by asking your father." She hands Reid a faded index card with an address written on it. "This is where he's buried. Perhaps you'll find inspiration there. I know he would love to help you."

They embrace in a loving hug. Reid experiences a profound sense of relief from learning that his father was a good man. His body fills with a sudden surge of energy. *Maybe this was the inspiration I was seeking?* He takes a shower, shaves, and knocks out a few push-ups before bed. He had been dreading tomorrow, knowing it was supposed to be the day he'd return to Wish. But the idea of visiting his father outweighs all of the pain. He tries on his suit; Wish would have been happy to see that it fits perfectly. He shrugs his shoulders. *At least I'll visit my father in style.*

The excitement prevents a good night's sleep. He continues to imagine all the things his father could have taught him. *Perhaps how to play sports and fix stuff around the house, but it sounds like Dad knew women.* He flips on his nightlight to read the address of the cemetery. His eyes expand with shock.

Henry Bradley is buried at — no freaking way — Desert Memorial Park in Palm Springs. That's where I was supposed to meet Wish.

He looks up at his ceiling. *Synchronicity?*

Chapter 17

Reid wakes up early and embarks on the hour-and-a-half drive from Huntington Beach to Palm Springs. He arrives at Desert Memorial Park a few minutes before nine, in case Wish planned on showing up anyway. He steps onto the modest-size graveyard, roughly half the size of a football field. There aren't any large statues, only ground-level gravestones surrounded by manicured grass. Reid scans the yard, hoping to find his Las Vegas mentor, but he only sees grass and squirrels dancing about.

He finds a grave map near the entrance and locates his father's burial. He adjusts the lapels of his suit and struts towards the grave. Reid quickly arrives and reads the stone that bears his father's name, Henry Bradley.

"Hi, Dad. I'm your son, Reid." Tears roll down his cheeks; he wipes them away. "Mom said she's sorry for taking so long to connect us. Let's not blame her, though. She did a great job with me. Perhaps you were able to witness some of my life from above."

Reid examines the inscription on the grave of the name, date of birth, and date of death. His father passed away one month before his birth.

"She said you were a great guy, and that … you were special with women." Reid reaches to touch the stone then drops to his knees, no longer able to control his tears. "I'd give anything to be able to talk with you about women. It's so hard for me."

Reid continues to sob; his forehead lowers to touch the stone.

"Can you help me? My struggles with women cause me more pain than anything else in my life. Can you guide me, or give some kind of a sign? Please."

A warm desert breeze flows across Reid's neck. The tingle causes him to lift his head. He squints, and in the distance he sees a man enter at the far end of the cemetery. He finds it impossible to take his eyes off the man, who appears ghost-like as he glides into the graveyard, dressed in white from head to toe but for a tan fedora which almost appears to float with him as he moves. The man stops in front of a grave at the far end of the yard. Reid squints again and comes to a conclusion.

The man looks and moves like Wish.

Reid leaps up and jogs towards the man. As he nears, he only sees the man's back, but he notices his skin tone is similar to Wish's. The man is holding a bottle of dark liquor. He pours it into a small glass.

"You're here," announces Reid.

"Yeah, baby," says the man. "Excellent observation." *The man's tone sounds just like Wish's.*

Reid walks in front of his mentor, then steps back as he sees it's actually not Wish, but someone significantly older.

"Forgive me, sir," says Reid. "I thought you were someone else."

The man swallows his drink, then speaks slowly. "Most people ... think other people are different than who they really are." The man winks. "Everyone we meet is a projection of how we see ourselves."

"That sounds like something my friend would say."

"Your friend is worth keeping around."

"I agree." Reid looks away and mumbles to himself, "But he doesn't want me around."

The man pours another drink. Reid sees that it's a bottle of whiskey. His stomach immediately grumbles, a reminder of the night with Drea.

"Drink this, baby. Let's salute a great human being," says the man.

"Respectfully, sir, I can't. Whiskey gave me a bad experience last week."

"Pointing the finger of blame at other things prevents you from pointing it at yourself."

"It's scary how much you sound like my friend," says Reid.

"It's scary how much you sound like a young man I once knew as well." The man carefully pours more into the glass. "If Ol' Blues Eyes, Frank Sinatra, asked you to take this drink, what would you say?"

"The chairman? My goodness, he loved whiskey. Didn't he? I'd drink it in a second."

The man hands Reid the drink, then signals to him to look down at the tombstone.

Reid's pupils expand. "Francis Albert Sin-a-tr— holy shit. He's buried here?"

"The chairman respected people who had the courage to face their fears," says the man. "The pack is only as strong as its weakest member."

Without hesitation, Reid swallows the dark liquid, expecting a burn. Instead he tastes sweetness, and looks confused.

"Don't worry, baby, it's just cola. But a good lesson: stepping into your fears is never as painful as your mind convinces you it will be."

"No wonder you drank it with such ease."

"All of the ol' Vegas performers knew I was allergic to alcohol. But I drank cola in a glass like this to connect with the audience members who were drinking booze."

"You knew him, Ol' Blue Eyes?"

"I warmed the crowds up for all the big Vegas acts over the years. Loved taking a stiff group and getting them riled up for the big show to follow. Retired years ago. Live around the corner now."

"Wow. How often do you visit Frank's grave?"

"Every Saturday morning at nine."

A chill shoots down Reid's spine. He pieces together what he's noticed. *This man used to work in Vegas, visits the graveyard every Saturday at nine, and philosophizes like Wish. Maybe they know each other?* Reid considers asking, but figures it's not polite to assume the man is friends with a pimp. And the man is from old-school Vegas, which means mob-run Vegas. Reid figures he should play it cool.

"Who are you here to visit?" asks the man.

"Well, I was originally supposed to meet the friend I was telling you about. But we had a falling out. As it turns out, my mom told me the truth about my dad last night. He passed before I was born, and he's buried over there."

"Is that so?" A large smile comes across the man's face. "I noticed you fell to your knees over there. You okay, baby?"

"I was asking him for help with being good with women." Reid rolls his eyes. "It's silly, I know."

"Fathers can be helpful, either by their presence or by their lack of presence. Both are a blessing. The key is to seek guidance from men who have the skills which you desire."

Reid can't help but feel a sense of connectedness to this man. He recalls Wish's words about how you should pay attention to the signs life gives you in the exact moment you are ready to grow, knowing that there aren't random coincidences in life.

"You said you could perform for an audience that is cold and have them laughing within seconds?"

"That's correct, baby."

"Do you think those skills would help me talk to women?"

The man chuckles with a sense of humility. "I've learned a few things over the years." He turns to leave. "Join me for breakfast. My wife, Connie, is the best cook."

Reid hesitates, unsure if he should join a stranger.

The man extends his hand to shake Reid's. "My name is Henry, by the way."

Hearing his father's name alerts Reid. It's an omen; he should follow.

"Breakfast sounds wonderful. I'm Reid."

They stroll to Henry's home nearby, on an upscale single-story estate, common in Palm Springs. They enter through the backyard and sit in cozy chairs surrounding a glass dining table next to a sparkling pool. Reid slides off his suit jacket as the desert sun begins to beat down.

"That suit fits you well," says Henry. Reid grins, knowing he at least got the part about fitting into his suit correct during the forty days of seclusion.

The sliding glass door to the house opens. A vibrant woman steps out and walks towards them holding two glasses filled with ice tea. She appears to be twenty years younger than Henry. She moves with a light-footed step, the kind of step that signals hours of fitness training.

"Hi there. I'm Connie." She smiles and extends her hand to grip Reid's. Her smile shifts into a frown as she turns to Henry. "You didn't kiss me goodbye, and you forgot to take the trash on your way out."

She plops the drinks on the table and stomps back to the house.

Henry stands, nodding at Reid with a sly grin. He jogs to catch Connie before she re-enters the house. Reid watches Henry face Connie and gaze deep into her eyes. Henry says something and pulls her in for a hug. Her head cowers momentarily, then Henry lifts her body several feet off the ground. He then lessens his grip, allowing her to slide down his arms into a loving kiss. Connie smiles, Henry playfully spanks her bottom, then she hops back into the house as if nothing was wrong.

Henry returns. "Breakfast is going to be extra-delicious now, baby."

"Why do you say that?"

"Her feminine energy was just boosted."

"What do you mean? She seemed pissed at you."

"This is where your generation fails," says Henry. "She wasn't mad at me. I left without saying goodbye, and my behavior triggered a red flag in the part of her feminine instincts that's programmed to sense safety and security in the male. The instinct exists within a woman to ensure the babies will be protected. We don't have children or plan to, but that instinct never goes away. Some people would label her behavior 'nagging,' but it's natural response by the female human-animal. She's seeking reassurance that her man is loyal, will reliably provide resources, and is able to protect her."

"Wasn't she also upset about the trash not being taken out?"

"When a woman is complaining, the male must address problem as it relates to the feminine instinct first, before fixing the actual surface level issue she's complaining about. I didn't apologize until after I reassured her that she's with a good man. I did this by igniting her with my masculine energy — lifting her over my head and looking deep into her eyes. That action immediately reminded her of my strength as a male and my commitment to protecting her. Then I whispered my apology in her ear while squeezing her hands tight. Her fears subsided, and she simultaneously felt a boost in her femininity. This energy will come through in her cooking, which is why I say it will be extra-delicious."

"Wow, I get it. My friend always talked about masculine and

feminine energy being exchanged in the bedroom as well."

"Your friend is a wise man," Henry adds. "Such men are rare."

Reid and Henry engage in small talk while they wait. Connie returns with two magnificent plates of eggs, bacon, and potatoes. She hugs Reid and gives Henry a tender kiss goodbye, explaining that she'll be gone for the afternoon to play golf.

The men eat and continue to talk about Henry's life in Palm Springs. Henry shares how he enjoys the simplicity, but misses the thrill of entertaining people.

"I'd be scared to death to do what you did," says Reid.

"I did it for forty years," Henry responds. "And I threw up before every show."

"Really? It never got easy for you?"

"My skillset improved, but fear is something that never really goes away. We just get better at managing it. I've learned to appreciate the role fear played in my career, so much so that I'm appreciative to have never moved past fear. Fear was the contrast that made the laughs from the audience feel so special."

"This is getting weird." Reid sits back in his chair. "Forgive me, but you sound exactly like my friend."

"Why?"

"The power of contrasts. Loving the role of fears and challenges in our life. He would say that we must explore those in great depth, in order to be able to experience equal depth with their opposites — comfort and self-growth."

"You've been a good student." Henry finishes his tea. "Wish taught you well."

Reid leans forward. "You know him?"

Henry nods. "Wish told me a month ago that you'd be here. But he called last week to say you failed the training. I didn't expect to see you at the cemetery. Wish mentioned a young man with a scar."

"I was put in a predicament last week. I made the wrong choice and failed." Reid glances at the pool.

"This mission may not be over for you," says Henry. "Wish is a stubborn cat, very protective of his research. He doesn't want to train a youngster who's gonna abuse the knowledge. That man put his life in great danger to make those discoveries."

Reid sits there shocked as he considers he may have another shot with Wish. Could it be possible? He glances at the pool, then back at Henry. "What do you mean? How was his research dangerous?"

"It's better I let him do the explaining. There are certain things he will deem it safer for you not to know."

"Does he know I'm here with you?"

"No, baby. But the synchronicity of your father being buried next to Frank is something we can't ignore. And Wish wouldn't want us to ignore that as well."

"What are the chances of that? It's pretty amazing," says Reid.

"When your brain is seeking information or guidance with great passion, occurrences are certainly not random. Step one is to recognize the signs that appear to be guiding you. Most people handle step one quite well. It's step two where the majority of people fail."

"What's step two?"

"The signs you follow always bring you to a point where you need to face a fear. You either walk through that fear or stay stuck in that spot forever. We only grow when we walk through a fear."

"Wish has guided me to face fears I didn't even know I had."

"His unique gift is to recognize an individual's greatest self before that individual even knows the self exists."

"I'm dying to have him guide me. How often do you talk to Wish? I desperately want to continue our agreement, the mission."

"I can call him anytime. If I tell him you're worthy, he'll probably take you back."

"I promise I'm worthy. Please call him."

"Hold on, baby. I gotta see you in action." Henry takes a bite of food. "Rest assured, Wish believed you had more potential than any man he's come across."

"He did? I'll do anything. How can I prove myself?"

"I'll need to see you step into your fears, baby." Henry stands. "You're gonna put on a show today."

"A show for who?"

"You, me, and the people who are seeking a connection."

Chapter 18

"Palm Springs is known for three things: old folks, golf, and pool parties," says Henry. "Today you're going to go to the pool party at Hotel Zaza and interact with every single person there."

Reid's face tightens. He's never been to a pool party. He's always assumed the pool would be full of beautiful girls falling for musclebound guys, while everyone pointed a finger at losers like himself.

"I don't have a swimsuit," says Reid.

Henry goes into his house and returns with a swimsuit in his hand.

"These were Wish's. He left them with me years ago."

Reid takes the navy-blue swim trunks, eyeing them like a pair of shoes worn by his favorite athlete. "They look to be a perfect fit. Thank you. Maybe they'll bring me luck."

"Wear them, and imagine yourself channeling Wish's strengths. You may not be able to walk in the man's shoes, but today you can swim in his shorts."

"These are awesome," says Reid. "But I really don't function well in a party environment." He goes on to explain how he got thrown out of the club last month. "I don't want to be called creepy ever again," says Reid.

"You got called 'creepy' because you weren't being authentic. Your actions were rooted in approval-seeking," says Henry. "What would Frank Sinatra do if he saw a beautiful woman at a bar?"

"He'd walk right up to her, without hesitation, and say, 'Hi, I'm Frank Sinatra.'"

"Exactly. Why would she be impressed and curious about him?"

"Because he's fucking Frank Sinatra."

"He courageously did the work to fully understand who he is;

therefore, he's comfortable expressing himself to the world, regardless of the outcome. Until you can do that, your life will be that of a victim, constantly seeking the approval of others, because you haven't figured out how to approve of yourself."

"Wish says my approval-seeking behavior stems from when I had surgery as a baby. And because the surgery happened when I was an infant, I started my first few months of life believing there was something wrong with me. Since then, I've relied on validation from other people to prove different. How do I go about resolving that?"

"Acceptance. Accept that which is stored within your shadow-self; accept your uncomfortable truths. Sinatra's life is an excellent example of exploring your dreams as well as exploring your dark side. He was a famous performer, but he yearned for the gangster life. He was connected to the mob in more ways than you can imagine. His willingness to express his light and dark sides gave him supreme self-understanding and unwavering confidence. Humans are drawn to the people who emanate complete self-acceptance. It's a place every human yearns to be, yet few have it figured out."

"My dark side seems to be tied into sex and sexuality with women," says Reid. "I'm deathly afraid to approach a woman. I don't know what to say."

"Love the fear, baby. Fear must exist for you to enjoy the reward that comes after." Henry touches Reid's shoulder. "And when socializing, be genuinely curious while remaining true to your intentions. Authenticity stems from being clear about your intentions. Your mission today is to meet every person at the pool and discover something you admire about them."

"How will I know if I'm being authentic?"

"You'll notice a shift in how the social environment responds to you. Women won't be able to take their eyes off you. Men who are complete strangers will ask you for guidance. Humans want to be around authenticity; it helps us feel safe. That's why we retreat from those who seem shady."

"Makes perfect sense; I do want people to be happy. I hope I can do what you ask."

"Go to Hotel Zaza, and tell the front desk that ol' Henry sent you.

They'll set you up with a room. Be prepared to meet every person at the pool. If things go well, you might end up with a date for tonight."

Reid lowers his shoulders. *I've never been able to secure a date in my life, except with Drea, but that doesn't count.*

"Relax, baby. I ain't asking you to jump out of a plane. Just say hello and ask people what brings them to Palm Springs."

"What do I say if they ask me why I'm at the party all by myself?"

"The truth."

"Really? Won't they think I'm weird?"

"People don't pay attention to the actual words you say, they pay attention to how comfortable you feel while you say those words."

"So I'll say, 'I'm here to work on my social skills.'"

"Exactly. Go to your hotel, get settled, and be at the pool by noon. I'll come check on you at two o'clock. If you pass this test, I might be able to convince Wish to change his mind."

Reid walks back to his car and drives to the nearby Hotel Zaza, energized with his new opportunity. He checks in, freshens himself in the room, and puts on Wish's swimsuit.

He studies the swimsuit on his body while in front of the full-length mirror, hoping to somehow channel Wish's masterful knowledge. The swim trunks fit perfectly around his waist, highlighting his newly sculpted physique. He cracks a smile while playfully flexing in the mirror, admiring his form. Even though he didn't complete the fitness program, the work he did complete made a significant difference. He wonders how women will now respond to him — perhaps by touching him, like they would Andrew.

The clock strikes noon. Reid enters the outdoor complex and sees a rectangular pool with a bar situated at the side. He hears music blasting from a DJ playing opposite the bar. The pool is only a few feet deep, but is packed with people enjoying themselves. He struggles to swallow his gulp. *I'm supposed to talk to everyone here?*

He ambles to the bar, orders a beer, then slips into the pool with the beer in his hand. He's surrounded by women who appear to be having the time of their lives. *Just say hi, dammit.* The warm water does nothing to soothe his insecurities. The music continues to thump away, reminding him of how Andrew danced while smiling. *Andrew would be dancing all over this pool and the girls would be swooning. I've got to try to at least move a little. Maybe when the next song comes on.* Reid finishes his beer and stands in silence.

Two hours pass. He's had four beers and zero interactions. The tension in his neck seems to be increasing by the second. Henry will arrive soon. He scans the pool, hoping to discover an easy opportunity to speak with a woman, but they're all in groups — large, intimidating groups. *Just speak to someone. Grow some balls, man.*

He can't shake the feeling he had when he was kicked out of the club a month ago. The disgusted stares of the women there are clear in his mind. He considers going back to his room to gather his thoughts and then return with more strength. But deep down he knows he'd just be running from fear. He takes a step towards the edge of the pool to exit, sensing that if he leaves, he won't return. He convinces himself to try to start at least one conversation; he'll go down in flames if he must.

Reid notices a group of four girls standing in a circle, talking and laughing. He takes a deep breath and counts *three, two, one,* then leans into the group.

"Wha-what brings you all to Palm Springs?"

They glance at Reid, then look at one another. *I promise I'm not creepy. Please ... a basic conversation is all I'm hoping for. My mom thinks I'm a good person.*

"I gotta go to the bathroom," says one of the women. "Let's all go." They wade away and exit the pool.

Reid drops his head. *Rejected again. This is never going to work. Henry is an old man; why did I believe his stupid advice?* He places a foot on a step to exit the pool. *Try one more time. Maybe those girls were people I wouldn't want to talk with anyway.* He notices a man and woman who are talking a few feet away, and turns to them.

"Hi. What brings you guys to Palm Springs?"

They ignore his question, lock lips, then shove their tongues down each other's throats. *Oooookay, never mind.* He shakes his head with comical disbelief. *At least that didn't sting.*

Maybe I'll just try to get rejected by every person here. Maybe that's what Henry intended? "What brings you to Palm Springs?" *is a stupid question.*

He swims towards the center of the pool to eye his next victim. But before Reid has another thought, he hears a roar of laughter near the bar. A group of women are gathered in a circle, laughing hysterically. A moment of calm passes, then the group goes silly again, except this time a few women cower forward. Their movement allows Reid to see who's causing this burst of joy. It's Henry.

Shit. He's here. Reid's nervous thoughts dissipate as he observes how these women, fifty years younger than Henry, appear to be hanging onto every word he says.

He hops out of the pool and moves nearer to the group, eager to see the master at work.

"Ladies, enough of hanging with this old cat," says Henry. "Y'all go back in the pool and schmooze with some of the classy fellas floating around in there."

The women hiss, then separate and return to the pool.

"Hey, Henry," says Reid, hoping the women recognize he's friends with the king of charm. They hurry away, unimpressed.

Henry's playful expression shifts to a look of concern. "You've been here for two hours, and I've only seen you pound beers and stand like a water statue. You half-heartedly talked to a group of girls, and you tried to interrupt a couple who were kissing. I ain't no professor, but that looks like a failing grade."

"I'm stuck in fear."

"What was your assignment?"

"Talk to everyone here. I tried, but they responded like I was bothering them."

"Young fella, this ain't an assignment to have everyone here like you. You just have to ask each person at this pool, 'What brings you to Palm Springs?' There's no expected outcome. Am I clear?"

"But how did you get all of those women to surround you?"

"I asked them, 'What brings you to Palm Springs?'"

"I just said that to some of those girls and they were creeped out. It's a weird question."

"It's a neutral question. Your intentions behind the words are what people notice. Were you genuinely curious about the people you talked to, or were you hoping for their approval?"

Reid puts his hands on his waist.

Henry continues: "People don't want to be around someone who's trying to get something from them. They want to be around authenticity, which leads to positive emotional experiences. Get your butt back in the pool and find a way to care about each person you speak with."

Reid stares at the pool.

"Hurry your ass up," says Henry. "You've got fifteen seconds to talk to a group of women, or else I leave and I won't help you reconnect with Wish."

It's a stupid question. Nobody will think I'm normal, even with good intentions. Reid grunts with frustration, then re-enters the pool. He moves towards a group of three women. *Seek to make their experience better, nothing more.* He huffs a short breath, then cuts into the group. "Hello, ladies. What brings you to Palm Springs?"

All three smile and one girl points to her friend. "It's Stephy's birthday, woo-hoo!"

"Awesome," says Reid, lifted by their friendliness. "I want to make her birthday experience better."

"She needs a birthday kiss from a cute guy."

Stephy grabs the back of Reid's neck and pulls him in for a smooch. Their lips connect for several seconds and Reid hears cheers from her girlfriends. Stephy releases Reid and shoves him down into the water. The silence of being under the surface centers Reid's mind on the magic of the moment. *Wow.*

Reid returns above water. Stephy and her friends dance their way towards the DJ. Reid looks at Henry, who expresses a wide smile. Henry slowly moves his hands like he's hitting a speed bag, a signal for Reid to keep going with the assignment.

Reid turns around and asks another group of women the magic question.

"We're from San Diego. We just came here to party. Come take a shot with us."

He follows the women out of the pool to the bar. They order shots, including one for him. He swallows the shot, then further engages the group by asking questions sourced from his authentic curiosity.

"Which of you is the craziest of the group and why?" says Reid.

They all point to a short blond who is wearing a bright-pink bikini. She immediately bends over and wiggles her behind. Reid laughs.

"I don't think she's proven herself yet."

The blond jumps into his arms. "Carry me back to the pool." He holds her tight, then tosses her into the air. She screams playfully and falls back into his arms. He then carries her back into the pool, with her friends following behind.

Reid introduces these girls to a group of men. "Fellas, these are my friends from San Diego. Come say hello."

"Thanks, brother," says one of the guys. He pulls Reid aside. "We just saw you talk to all these girls. You're some kind of master at this, aren't you?"

Really? If you only knew the madness that goes through my head. "Thanks, man. I just enjoy learning about people."

The group welcomes his energy and they continue into a long but fun conversation. Soon enough, Reid makes his way around the entire pool. He introduces one group to another group. Then another and another.

"I don't understand why you said you need to work on your social skills," says a woman named Anika. "You seem to know everyone at this pool."

At first, Reid's caught off guard by her comment, but then he canvasses the pool and realizes she's correct. He's befriended everyone. An hour ago, he was a frightened boy hiding in the crowd. Now he stands tall in the center of a group of new friends, bouncing to the music without a care in the world.

Henry nears the edge of the pool and waves for Reid to come close. Reid wades through the crowd, hearing pleas for him not to leave. He high-fives his new friends and lifts himself out of the pool, then walks to meet Henry by the exit. Henry looks like a proud teacher who's about to say, *I'm impressed.*

"You did well, baby," says Henry. "I've never seen that pool fueled with so much energy. You were the matchstick that started that fire."

Reid bows to his sensei. "I don't know how to thank you."

"Thank me by taking that young lady on a date tonight." Henry nods towards the pool. "The one you were just speaking with. She's here by herself and she's been eyeing you the entire time."

"Really?" Reid turns and spies Anika. He smiles her way, and she reciprocates.

"Tell her to meet you in the lobby at eight o'clock and that you'll be taking her for food and drinks across the street at the restaurant lounge called Sota. Do not say you'll be taking her to dinner."

"What's wrong with dinner?"

"A man who takes a woman to dinner is trying to impress her. It gives off the energy of a boy seeking his mom's approval. She'll sense it at her core and you'll be placed in the 'just another guy' category."

"I can't stand being thought of as just another guy."

"I know. And so does Wish. More proof to confirm you are wired like us."

"What do I say to Anika?"

"Tell her your plans, do not ask her." Henry points to the pool. "Set up the date, and plan on meeting me in the restaurant a half-hour before you meet her."

Wouldn't it be rude to just tell her to meet me? Reid ignores the thought and shifts his focus to doing as he's told, since Henry has steered him correctly thus far. Reid hops back into the pool and wades to Anika.

"Hey, cutie. I was just telling my friend back there how cool you are."

A flirtatious grin forms on her face. They engage in small talk. He learns she's visiting from Canada for a work conference that finished that morning.

"Tonight is my last night in Palm Springs," says Anika. "I don't want to head back home without a fun story to share. You seem to be the kind of guy who attracts fun anywhere he goes."

Me? Reid has always wanted to be that guy. He can't believe this is happening. Everything Henry has shared has worked so far. He figures he'd better stick to the plan.

"Let's make tonight worthwhile then," says Reid. "Drinks, food, and witty banter. Meet me in the lobby at eight o'clock."

She grips each of Reid's biceps, then gazes up at him. "Finally, a man who knows how to take control."

Holy shit, that actually worked.

"I'll see you at eight." He kisses her on the cheek, exits the pool, and beams all the way back to his room, feeling as if he's James Bond.

Reid rests until the early evening. He then puts his navy suit on and strolls across the street to the restaurant to meet Henry. He enters the dark-wood restaurant lounge, hearing smooth jazz playing at a volume that's perfect to speak over in a relaxed tone. He sees Henry sitting in a half-circle booth in the back corner and joins him.

"From this booth we can see most of the couples on a date here," says Henry. "Tell me what you observe about the woman in the red and the man she's with."

Reid examines the couple situated ten feet away, sitting across from each other.

"The woman is sitting back in her chair, and the man is leaning forward as he talks."

"Yes," says Henry. "I've been sitting here fifteen minutes and that man has been leaning towards her the entire time."

"Maybe he can't hear her very well." Reid studies the woman, then catches her looking back at him with a gaze that matches her slight smile. He quickly turns to Henry. "Did you see that?"

"I'm not surprised," says Henry. "Body language is everything. That man is begging for her approval. He reeks of desperation. I'm not surprised her eyes found the nearest alpha-male."

"Why me?"

"You have a date in an hour. You aren't desperate right now. Women can sense desperation; it gives them an uncomfortable feeling. In fact, most women here turned their head towards you when you entered. Your posture portrays a man who has worked on himself. The combination of self-assurance and lack of desperation are irresistible to a woman."

"Heads always turn when Wish enters a room." Reid knows he's not close to being on Wish's level, but he feels uplifted by the compliment.

Henry is staring at the man who continues to fail his date. "Men like him hope a fancy meal and a sports car will make up for the work they are afraid to do on themselves. He's trying to buy her approval. That's why I say to never take a woman to dinner. You can get food together if you're hungry, but never take her to dinner hoping to impress her — there's a big difference. It's never your job to impress her. If handled correctly, your masculine energy will have her feeling so satisfied just sitting next to you, the last thing she'll think about is food."

"Wish often talks about boy behavior versus man behavior. So, the act of trying to impress is like a boy seeking his mom's approval."

"Exactly. I'm impressed how you process this stuff quickly."

Reid continues to connect the dots. "If the girlfriend constantly has to deal with her boyfriend's mommy-approval-seeking behavior, the girlfriend starts to feel like a mom raising a son. Then, as Wish says, she feels like a mom fucking her son, instead of being ravished by her man."

Henry smiles. "Most women cheat because of the dissatisfaction you just described. Our society is filled with thirty-, forty-, even fifty-year-old men who have the psychology of thirteen-year-old boys. Many women have given up on seeking sexual pleasure from men, because it's always a let-down. As a result, many women have turned to the next thing that can provide a feeling similar to sexual pleasure — food. They even have a nickname, calling themselves foodies."

"Foodies are sexually repressed?"

"They might as well be calling themselves lack-of-good-sex-ies. It ain't the woman's fault, though. For many of those women, their bodies are craving a sensory experience that men are failing to provide. And now we have amazing chefs who have mastered contrasting sensations on the pallet."

"Can't someone just be passionate about food without the sexual dissatisfaction?"

"Yes, if they love food as art and want to cook as well. But the women I'm talking about don't cook; they hang with a man, then base their opinion of that man on which upscale restaurant he chooses, since he can't satisfy her in any other way. My wife loves food and loves cooking, but those passions are authentically tied into her artistic expression."

"Makes sense," says Reid. "But you told me to bring Anika here tonight. Shouldn't I be taking her for coffee or to a bar without food?"

"Nope, you're bringing her here to prove that you can provide a sensory experience — an experience so good, the last thing she'll think about is food, baby."

"Oh, shit." Reid lifts his hands to his forehead.

"I believe you have the skills to do this, son. And from what I observed earlier, Anika is seeking what you've been taught to offer."

Reid's hands return to his lap. "I don't even know where to start."

"Foreplay begins the moment you see her in the lobby."

"Foreplay? You want me to fondle her in the lobby?"

"Foreplay is the beginning phase of providing the Erotic Sensory Experience, setting the tone for what she'll soon feel. From the moment you see her in the lobby, you must establish that you're the male and she's the female. Don't just give her a hug — wrap your arms around her tightly, lift her off her feet, and stare into her eyes. Make her feel your masculinity. Then grab her hand, unapologetically, and lead her to this restaurant. Then open that front door for her." Henry points to the large wooden doors that allow for restaurant entry.

"I know I'm supposed to open doors for a woman. Mom taught me that."

"I'm sure your mom is a wonderful woman. However, she taught you to open doors out of good manners, as a way to be polite to females. I'm talking about opening a door for a woman because you're a fucking man. There's a difference. You don't do it to be polite, to kiss her ass with the hope that she likes you. You do it to make sure she's safe. When you two arrive, open that door and briefly scan the room to make sure everything is safe, then allow her to enter. As she walks through, she'll experience your masculine energy, which will boost her feminine essence, making her feel even more like a woman. This is, instinctually, how most women yearn to feel around their man."

"So, I need to be a dominant leader?"

"Dominant is a word that has become misunderstood. Most men who consider themselves dominant do so because of their own insecurities. They want to control their partner to make up for their low self-esteem."

"Attempting to control my partner is something I'll never do again. Wish helped me see that I was controlling my ex in just about everything I did."

"Wish and I aren't teaching you to be a low-self-esteem dominant male. You're learning to become the highest form of male sexual expression: a conscious dominant."

"A conscious dominant?"

"You will dominate or lead, while remaining conscious of her unique physiological and psychological needs. This form of dominance comes from a man who has high self-esteem and the desire to serve.

"So much stuff to be aware of while hanging with a woman ..."

"Overwhelming at first, but with experience this will become automatic."

"Are you sure I'm ready? Shouldn't I read some more books about this stuff?"

"Your desire to do more research is your fear talking. Taking action is where the real learning will occur. I believe you're ready to take action. You've learned the power of contrasts with touching and other sensory responses, and you've learned how to authentically express yourself socially. Once you include your attention to the masculine and feminine exchange during an interaction, you'll be on your way to becoming a conscious dominant — a real man."

Maybe I can see an example of a good interaction here? Reid scans the room and sees many men begging for approval from their dates. He shakes his head, then notices a different dynamic between a couple sitting at the bar.

"They seem to be having a good time," says Reid. "They haven't even touched their food."

"Excellent observation. It's safe to assume they have a vibrant sex life — sitting next to each other, physically taking in each other's presence, instead of relying on sensory pleasure from food." Henry glances at his watch. "Your date will be in the lobby soon. Go meet her."

Reid stands and adjusts his suit. "Will you be here during the date?"

"Yes, and so will Wish."

Reid's eyes expand. "He's in town?"

"Yes," says Henry. "As a male human-animal, you don't need approval from a woman, but you do need approval from the elder men in your village. Make us proud. If she chooses to eat, you fail."

Reid turns and walks away. *I wanted one more shot with Wish.* He slows his stride. *This is it.*

Chapter 19

Reid maintains his wide stance as Anika walks towards him in the hotel lobby. She's wearing a flowing black dress. He opens his arms wide as she nears, absorbing her into a bear hug.

"Wow, you look really nice in that suit," she says. "I don't think I'm dressed nicely enough. Perhaps I should go cha—ahhhhhh!"

Reid lifts her off the ground, just as he saw Henry do with his wife. He feels the delicateness of her frame in his arms as he spins in a circle. He centers himself, then fixes his gaze on hers. Her nervous chatter goes silent. Batting her eyelashes, she slides down his body until her toes touch the floor.

"I love the choice of clothing you made for tonight." Reid tilts his head slightly to the side. "Your choice is an honest expression of you. It's perfect. I find you-being-you … fascinating."

She smiles as she lowers her chin. "Thank you. This is my favorite little black dress."

"Are you hungry?" asks Reid.

"I'm starving."

Reid expected that answer, but still he stiffens, searching for a way to distract her from expecting food right away.

"I've got something special planned for us first." He grabs her right hand and leads her out of the hotel. "You're gonna love this place. Lots of good people-watching."

"I can't wait. I love people-watching."

They go to cross the road towards the restaurant. Reid notices a man dressed as if he lives on the streets walking in their direction. A sudden sense of being the protector rises within. He releases Anika's hand, then quickly switches positions with her to ensure the man passes on his side.

"You are quite the gentleman," she says.

"Your safety will always be the most important thing to me."

They approach the entrance. Reid steps ahead, pulls open the door, glances inside, then looks back at her.

"It appears safe for you to enter," he says. She steps into the restaurant and playfully curtsies. Reid grins at her display of femininity, while silently praising Henry's brilliant guidance.

He glances at the booth where Henry sat earlier — it's empty. No sign of Henry or Wish, which causes Reid to wonder if they'll actually show. Yet he knows Wish can be slick with his methods of observation, and remains true to the assignment.

Reid leans towards Anika. "We sit at the bar." Without hesitation, he interlocks his fingers with hers, then leads her towards two chairs.

"I can't get over how attractive it is that you take the lead."

Reid stops, pulls her to face him, then gazes into her eyes. He studies her retinas as they dance left and right. He smiles to take in the moment, then helps her onto her chair.

"Ms. Anika, what is your drink of choice?" Reid slides onto his chair and waves at the bartender, who appears to be helping patrons at the other end. The bartender nods and extends a finger to signal he'll be by soon.

"Vodka soda," says Anika.

"Perfect, me too." Reid looks back at the bartender, whose conversation with a patron doesn't appear to be wrapping up. He waves at the bartender again, hoping to speed things up, but the man doesn't notice. Reid then turns his head to scan the scene behind him once again. Still no sign of Henry or Wish.

"What can I get you two to drink?" says a male voice. The tone is strong and powerful, not exactly friendly. Reid twists his head back towards the bar, widening his eyes as he identifies the man who spoke. It's Wish, and he's dressed like the other bartender, wearing a white button-up shirt and a black skinny tie.

"Hopefully, you two won't order fluffy drinks," says Wish. "This is my first night on the job."

Reid sits up straight, adjusting the lapels on his jacket. He's tempted to voice his excitement, but figures Wish's costume implies that their friendship must be kept secret. Plus, he senses it may take away from the masculine dynamic he's created with Anika.

"Awe," says Anika. "Are we your first customers?"

"Yes, ma'am," says Wish. He bows to Anika, keeping his focus on her and ignoring Reid.

He's still pissed off with me.

Anika leans towards Reid. "It's so cute that today is your first day. This is why I love Palm Springs. You never know who you're gonna meet."

Cute? If you only knew of the powers this man possesses.

"We're quite simple, sir. Vodka soda for both of us," says Reid.

"Vodka soda. Excellent choice; that's a simple assignment for me," says Wish. He shifts his friendly gaze away from Anika and stares harshly at Reid. "It always baffles me when people screw up simple assignments."

Reid stares back at Wish, hoping to somehow discreetly apologize for his past actions, but nothing good comes to mind. He chooses to remain silent, aware of the subtext within Wish's words. *I'll prove myself right now.*

"May I offer to show you our food menu?" says Wish. "We have amazing appetizers. The best food in town."

Reid continues his frozen stare. He senses Wish is going to make the assignment extra-challenging.

Anika sits up. "Ooooh, yes."

Reid cuts her off. "Not yet, kind sir." He smiles at Wish, then tilts his head to lock eyes with Anika. "I want to get to know this beautiful woman's mood for a few minutes and see if I can guess what she'd want to eat. She may even want to order something special that's not on the house menu."

"I understand," says Wish. "A good man always knows what his woman wants."

Anika giggles, oblivious to the sub-interaction. "You are a delight with your kind smile and little tie. I love that we are your first customers."

"Thank you, ma'am. I'll go in the back and get you two some bread." Wish turns to leave.

"Wait!" says Reid. Wish halts. "Umm — I'm allergic to flour. It's dangerous for me to even be near it." Reid turns to Anika. "I'm sorry, m'lady. Bread isn't healthy for us anyway."

Anika nods. "I'm starving, but I certainly don't want you to have an allergic reaction."

"I see," says Wish. "I'll fix your drinks." Wish scoops ice into two glasses, adds vodka and soda water, then sets the drinks in front of them. "I'm going to the kitchen. I'll be back in a sec."

Reid sighs with relief. He dodged a bullet, but figures more are coming. Anika and Reid engage in light conversation, but he struggles to listen wholeheartedly. His mind races to come up with responses to challenges Wish might throw his way. *Perhaps Wish will bring out a dish that's a gift from the chef. Or perhaps —* Reid cuts off his meandering thoughts, knowing he doesn't have much time. He needs to focus only on Anika. He asks her about her weekend and she delves into the details of her conference.

Wish returns from the kitchen and stares at Anika's hand as she lifts her glass for a drink. Wish crosses his arms and smiles mischievously.

"Forgive me for butting in," says Wish. "How long have you two been married?"

"Oh, we aren't married," says Reid. He places his hand on Anika's back. "This is our first date."

"I'm embarrassed, forgive me," says Wish. "I just assumed, since she was wearing a wedding ring. Nothing wrong with having some fun on the side. Your secret is safe with me."

Reid quickly turns his head and sees the bright diamond ring that rests on Anika's left ring finger. He lifts his hand off her back, startled that he hadn't noticed the ring.

Wish appears to be shaking up another drink.

"You're married?" asks Reid.

"Yes, I'm wearing the ring so you don't fall for me. It's best you know the truth so we can have fun."

Before Reid can respond, Wish places two shots of blue liquid on the bar. He hands a shot to Reid and one to Anika. Wish pours himself a shot of mescal. They lift their drinks to toast.

"To the completion of an assignment, no matter how far we're pushed out of our comfort zone." Wish downs his shot while eying Anika's ring.

Anika swallows her shot. Reid hesitates, perplexed by the undertone in Wish's words and still sorting through his shock from learning Anika's marital status. He questions if Wish would be accepting of him being with a married woman. And after everything he's experienced with the infidelity of Jasmine and the other women in his past, he questions if he could violate his morals as well. He swallows the blue shot.

"Wow, that was really good," says Anika. "What's it called?"

"Liquid Viagra," says Wish. "The old men around here should love it, for obvious reasons. It was my assignment to have the drink recipe down by tonight." Wish focuses his gaze on Reid and winks. "I love completing an assignment." He turns and strides off to the kitchen.

Reid shifts uncomfortably in his chair. *Is Wish hinting that I'm not on task?* Henry told him the assignment is to provide an Erotic Sensory Experience that's so potent Anika forgets about food. *Or is this now a test of my morals?*

"Can we order some food now? I'm starving," says Anika.

Reid's head is warm; he knows he has to quickly decide how to handle the assignment. Wish might be hiding somewhere around here, watching. He figures Wish should at least see him demonstrate his skills.

Reid straightens himself, hoping to get past his nervousness and channel the conscious dominant within. He places his hand on Anika's thigh. "Let me see if I can figure out the type of food you would want to order. I have to first learn a bit about your brain." With his fingers, he lightly draws circles on her lower thigh, grazing her knee. He recalls the scene he wrote during his seclusion after reading the massage book — the test he was going to perform on a woman to understand her sensory response system. "If you were to get a massage, would you want it to be soft, medium, or hard?"

"I like it hard."

"Good." Reid stops circling his fingers, then squeezes tightly on a nerve center in her lower thigh. She grimaces slightly, then grins as he speaks. "Do you prefer iced tea or hot tea?"

"Iced tea. My body always seems to be hot."

Reid removes his hand from her thigh, then grips her chair and slides it closer to him. He returns his fingers to her knee and inches them up along her inner thigh then back down again, applying varying massage techniques of soft touch, light scratches, and deep pressure. He sees her moisten her lips.

"Since your body operates hot, I'll assume you don't like spicy foods." Reid continues the massage pattern, noticing her struggle to pay attention to anything beyond his touch.

"Yes. This feels amazing." Anika's eyes roll to the back of her head, then close.

With his free hand, he pinches a small ice cube from his drink, holding it between two fingers as it melts. He then places the cold fingers around the back of her neck. She flips her hair to the side, then coos while she lowers her chin. With his thumb and index finger, he squeezes the back of her neck, aiming to relieve tension under the chilled skin.

He removes his hand from her leg, grips his drink, and slowly sips, allowing his lips to become icy from the cool liquid. He then leans close and kisses her cheek, absorbing the contrast between her warm face and his cold lips. He feels her cheek raise as she forms a smile, then he slowly peels his lips away. Her eyes do something he has always wanted to see in a woman — they squint with a sense of naughtiness and intrigue, as if to say, *Take me right now.*

Wish returns from the kitchen. "Are you two ready to see the menu?"

Reid looks at Wish, then at Anika. Her erotically entranced gaze hasn't altered.

"We're ready for the check, my friend."

"Drinks are on me," says Wish. "Have a lovely evening. Don't do anything I wouldn't approve of." Wish winks at Reid, then exits back into the kitchen.

Reid's heart skips a beat. It seems Wish was happy with what he observed with him and Anika. Would Wish not approve of Reid continuing the ESE? Or would Wish not approve of him walking away from a woman who is in need of an ESE, because things don't seem well in her marriage?

Reid rises, grips Anika's hand, and leads them to exit the restaurant. As he opens the door for her to leave, he feels a strange sensation in his groin. His member rises into a pulsating erection, stiffer than any he's ever felt in his life. Since Wish ended their agreement after Drea, Reid had returned to pleasing himself. He normally isn't aroused in public with such intensity. While they walk, he processes possible reasons, then halts with a realization. *The Liquid Viagra shot — was real Liquid Viagra.*

Before she notices, Reid stuffs his thickness under his belt. They continue their walk back to the hotel, silent with sexual tension. The moment they enter the elevator, she mauls him with kisses. Reid enjoys her sweet scent, but then struggles between the thoughts in his head above his neck and those in the swollen head below his belt. *I shouldn't be with a married woman. Jasmine crushed me; I can't do that to someone else.* Yet his unforgiving erection and desire to test his new techniques, keeps his lips glued onto hers.

"I want to do it in my room," she says. "Four-thirty-six."

The elevator doors open at the fourth floor and they walk the few steps to the room. Standing in the hallway, their lips connect again. He grips her bottom with both hands, lifts her, and presses her against the wall while continuing the kiss. His resistance weakens as their passion increases. He then slowly lowers her down and she fishes in her purse for the room key.

"I can't believe I'm about to cheat on my husband." She grabs the key-card, then pulls Reid in for a deep-throat kiss. Her words have activated his resistance once more. He puts his hands on the front of her shoulders, tempted to push himself away and leave. But she pulls out of the kiss first and gazes at him. "I don't know what it is, but I can't help myself when I'm around you."

Her admiration melts Reid's heart. He made this happen. He finally attracted a woman, a real woman, on his own. His crotch is screaming for the pressure to be released, but at the same time, his mind continues with reason. *Don't forget how you felt when you caught Jasmine cheating.* Reid pictures Anika's husband sitting home alone. *This man trusts his wife to do the right thing. She's vulnerable right now.*

I can't be that guy who takes advantage of her.

She pops the door open, grabs his pants-covered erection, and leads him into the room. The door slams shut. She hops onto him, her fingers interlock behind his neck, and her legs wrap around his hips. They lock lips for a few minutes, then she slides off his body and stands before him. With her hand, she reaches under her dress and slides her black panties down to the floor.

"I can't believe I'm actually doing this. I'm gonna cheat on my husband."

Reid huffs a short breath, conflicted by his morals and the assignment. He knows that if he fails, Wish will be gone forever. He sweeps her up into his arms, then lays her on the bed. He studies her body, her immaculate body. He glances at the door, then returns his gaze to hers, silent as he musters the courage to make a decision.

"I'm honored you find me attractive," says Reid. He bends forward and kisses her head. "I can't go through with this. Perhaps we were meant to hang in another life."

Reid goes to the door, opens it, and steps out to exit.

"Really? You're leaving me? Well, I'm going to fuck someone tonight!" yells Anika.

The door slams shut. *I hope that was the right thing to do.* He takes the elevator down to his floor, then returns to his room. He sits on the bed and calls Wish.

"Did you fuck her?" says Wish.

"No. I don't mess with other people's wives. Even if that was part of the assignment, I have to stick to my morals."

"You made the correct decision. She was looking for escapism, not personal growth."

"Oh, thank God." Reid falls onto the bed. "I thought you wanted me to handle her business."

"I'd never force you to be with a married person who doesn't enter the experience with a growth-oriented mindset. Sexmysts are not wired to provide escapism. Such behavior would be siding with the Collective Shadow."

"I'm relieved to learn that we share the same moral compass," says Reid. "How did you get the job at the bar? You surprised the shit out of me tonight."

"Henry is friends with the owner. Those two old farts got a kick outta watching me fumble while making drinks."

"By the way, did that Liquid Viagra drink have real Viagra in it?"

"Yes, making the drink wasn't part of the plan. But then I saw her wedding ring and heard her response when I asked about her marriage. I had to know that you'd make the right decision in spite of the medical assistance. I'm impressed. You've earned a second chance."

Reid sits up. "Really? Yes, I promise I won't screw up anymore."

"I'm sure you'll screw up a few more times. But you bought a few extra lives by walking away from a married woman who wanted you. I've learned that your heart is in the right place. Get some rest, and plan on meeting me at the Diamond Bar on Friday night next week. Pack enough to live in Vegas for the summer. You're not teaching summer school, correct?"

"Yes, I'm off for the summer and actually looking for a place to live."

"I'll get you set up at the Lexi Hotel. Glad you're back, kid. You impressed me tonight."

"Thank you, sir."

"I'll have a big client in town next weekend. I'm going to need your help. Stay fit and stay sharp. You'll need to bring your A-game. We clear?"

"Yes, sir. See you on Friday."

Chapter 20

Friday arrives. During the week, Reid had returned to his healthy habits of working out and quality eating. Now he's pumped to embark on his new adventure. While driving to Las Vegas, he feels a new sense of security, as if his father's spirit is riding along, ready to serve as a guide through the next series of challenges.

When he arrives at the Lexi Hotel, he unpacks his belongings for the summer, then slips on his navy-blue suit and polished wingtip shoes. He studies himself in the mirror, admiring his new look — not through the lens of cockiness, but with appreciation of the results from the journey thus far. He then takes a cab to the Largo Hotel, where he meets Wish at the Diamond Bar.

They sit in their usual high chairs at the bar, sipping chilled mescal. Wish is wearing a black suit, with a high-collared white dress shirt underneath, an orange ascot around his neck, and a black fedora. He scans Reid from head to toe, then tips the edge of his hat.

"I forgot to tell you in Palm Springs that you did well transforming your body. The suit now fits perfectly. I was disappointed that you failed in our agreement, but you seem dedicated to learning from your mistakes."

"Absolutely. I'm excited to be back."

"A man's commitment to his boundaries," says Wish, "will dictate his success with women, business, and overall life. Tonight, we'll be testing your ability to stand by your boundaries."

"Boundaries? As in, psychological boundaries?"

"Yes, our boundaries are like walls that guard our self-respect — the rules we have for ourselves and how we'll allow ourselves to be treated. If a friend asks you for five dollars, it's no big deal to say 'yes.' But if he asks you for five hundred dollars, an irritable sensation will creep into your body, a signal that someone is attempting to penetrate the wall which guards your self-respect. If you say 'yes,' allowing the wall to be penetrated, you'll instantly feel overwhelmed by that irritable sensation, as if self-respect is being sucked out of your body. Mr. Nice Guys like yourself allow their boundaries to be penetrated too often, resulting in the constant draining of self-respect and, worse, self-esteem."

"I hate that I'm a Mr. Nice Guy, but I can't help myself. How will I know when it's the right time to say 'yes' or 'no'? Obviously, there could be an appropriate time to lend a friend five hundred dollars."

"Certainly, I'd give you five hundred dollars without feeling irritated, because I know you would use it to fund a growth-oriented activity. We're not born knowing how to protect our boundaries. Life experiences will teach you when to say 'yes' or 'no.' Since you've said 'yes' too often in your life, you need to go out and practice saying 'no' — especially to beautiful women."

"But I turned down Anika in Palm Springs."

"You did well denying the married woman in Palm Springs, but she didn't create enough of a challenge, she didn't spark you as much as you sparked her. You'll need to test the strength of your boundaries against stronger, wiser women. In Vegas, there are women who earn their living by penetrating a man's boundaries, doing it hundreds of times a month — strippers."

Reid swallows his drink. He then straightens his suit jacket, hoping to minimize the nervous chill he feels within.

"You must master your control over your boundaries, and numb yourself to the powers of femininity," says Wish. "Tonight you're going to a strip club by yourself, Mick's Cabaret."

Reid stares at the empty glass and crosses his arms tightly over his chest as flashes of his first trip to Mick's come to mind. He was running from the reality of Jasmine's infidelity, while feeling conflicted with allowing himself to explore his sexual nature. He sees himself crying as he drove off the parking lot at Mick's, uncertain which path to take next. Yet deep down, he understands that was all part of the path that led him to Wish.

"It's good that you feel fear," says Wish. "Remember, fears like this that we must conquer must exist; it's how the pleasure receptors within the brain then grow."

Reid nods his head up and down several times, motivating himself into a state of courage. He then shifts his gaze to Wish. "What exactly do you want me to do?"

"At the strip club, you'll be approached by several women. You must say 'no' to the first twenty women."

"Just say 'no'? But won't I be rude?"

"You'll be an asshole."

"You want me to be an asshole?"

"Yup, just until you interact with twenty women. You must work through your discomfort of saying 'no.' After twenty interactions, if you meet one who appears genuinely interested, feel free to engage further."

"What do I say to a stripper I like?"

"Do exactly what you learned from Henry: be authentically curious; boost her femininity while remaining authentic. Then find out if she's a seeker of what you have to offer."

"I still don't know exactly what I have to offer."

"At this point of your training, you know more than most men. Use your masculinity to highlight her feminine energy. Touch her in a way that provides contrasts to deepen the sensory recognition. Soon you'll learn the rest. A strip club will be a good place for you to practice what you've learned thus far. Think of it as reps in the gym."

Wish turns away, looks across the bar, then faces Reid again. "I wanted us to meet here in case Youngblood is watching. I still haven't seen him. Detective Jones says Youngblood's been gathering information nonstop, even during his days off. I swear that man seems to be driven by something more than a promotion."

Reid twists his head to study the surroundings, wondering what type of trouble he could be in for associating with Wish. But in his gut he knows the risk is worth it. He feels Wish tug his arm, and shifts his attention back to the conversation.

"Tonight, you're going to help me with a large transaction. My top client is in town. Youngblood works alone, and he can't be in two places at once. You'll help us keep him confused. Here's two thousand in chips from Treasure Island." Wish palms Reid the chips via a handshake. "Play blackjack, fifty-dollar hands, for fifteen minutes, then cash out. I'll be expecting fifteen hundred in return; you keep the difference."

Reid secures the chips with his thumb, then slides them into his pocket.

"Have fun playing blackjack, kid. I'll be meeting you at Mick's Cabaret later."

Wish and Reid exit in opposite directions. Treasure Island is a twenty-minute stroll from the Largo. Reid's commitment to his fitness routine ensures he maintains a comfortable pep in his stride. His once jelly-muscled legs now flex firmly with each step, a physical reminder of how far he has come.

He arrives at Treasure Island with ease. He plays for twenty minutes and cashes out exactly two thousand, netting five hundred profit for himself. Feeling on top of the world, he pockets the wad of cash, drinks two beers to ease his mind, then takes a cab to Mick's. He wonders what Mick's is like inside; whether the environment is grimy and the men are all creeps with spaghetti stains on their shirts. Reid hops out of the cab and struts to the entrance. *I've got this now. I'm a different man.*

"Have fun." The bouncer for Mick's opens the door.

Reid enters with wide eyes. He meanders through a large room with flashing disco lights, shaking breasts, and tongue-wagging men dressed business-casual. Although it doesn't appear disgusting, he notices judgments arise from his old point of view; he wonders how people could work here and how patrons would want to pay for attention. Then he recalls knowledge shared by Wish and rewords those thoughts: *Everyone here is seeking happiness in their own unique way. Support their quest.*

He continues through the room, which is filled with empty red chairs suitable for lap dances. He notices three stages, a large stage in the middle and two smaller stages on opposite sides. He stops at the bar, orders a bottle of beer, and sits in a leather chair next to a small stage.

He examines the stage closely, expecting to find a layer of filth caked on the surface, but the glossy platform appears clean. He looks down around his shoes, seeing clean carpet, then gazes across the room and observes that the booths appear well-kept too. He realizes the place isn't a grime hole at all; it's actually cleaner than most dive bars. He swallows a hefty swig of beer, feeling a sense of relief and excitement as he settles into the scene.

Then his jaw suddenly stiffens. A man walks past him, sporting a salt-and-pepper goatee. He resembles Youngblood — but it isn't him. Still, it's a reminder that Reid needs to look out for any sign of Youngblood, while remaining focused on the evening's assignment — saying "no" to twenty women.

"Hi, I'm Raven." A blond woman slides onto his lap. "Would you like a private dance?"

Reid freezes, caught off guard by her entering his space. "Umm." He searches for a polite response, but then he recalls Wish's instructions. "Umm, no. I don't want a dance."

"Ugh, whatever. You're missing out." She hurries off. Reid leans forward and runs both hands through his hair. *I hope I didn't hurt her feelings.* He reaches for his beer, but before he can grab it another dancer slides onto his lap.

"What brings you to Vegas?" she says.

"I'm just in town for fun. Where are you from?"

"I'm from Thailand. Would you like a dance? It's twenty dollars."

"No. But you are beautiful."

"Don't say that if you don't want me." She stomps away.

These women are gonna hate me. Reid stays true to the assignment, battling his guilt with each interaction. *Reps in the gym, reps in the gym.*

The parade of women continues. He speaks with more than twenty women, completing Wish's assignment, while noticing his comfort with the word "no" improve with each interaction. Now, he's working towards finding a dancer who seems authentically interested. He rejects the next three women who approach — each seems to be money-hungry; no flirting, touching, or questions that express authentic desire for creating a connection. *Are there any women here who care about my experience? Like Tasha the masseuse?*

"Hi," says a female voice. *Ugh, I just want a second to breathe and take a quick sip.* He lowers the beer, then turns and sees a brunette with Russian features. "Would you like a dance with me? I'll charge you twenty dollars."

"No, thanks." She leaves. Reid rolls his eyes and finishes his beer.

Two hands grip his shoulders from behind and squeeze. He looks back, seeing a woman who appears to be on the level of a supermodel. And something about her touch instantly signals to him that she's different. She massages for another thirty seconds, then walks around to face Reid, but doesn't sit on his lap. Instead, she pulls up a chair near him, sits, then locks her eyes onto his eyes with an adoring gaze.

"I have to know more about you," she says.

Wow, gorgeous. Reid straightens his posture. "What would you like to know?"

"I could ask you your name, what your job is, and if you are married. But I'm afraid to learn that you're more amazing than I already assume."

Reid laughs. "Now that's a helluva pick-up line."

"It's not a line. I just watched you turn down some of the prettiest women in this place. There must be something amazing inside you, but I'm hoping it isn't true, because I'd be embarrassed for you to have met me in a place like this."

"It's perfectly okay for us to have met here. I developed a curiosity recently to learn more about your occupation," says Reid. "What's your name?"

"My name is Mia. Normally, I just ask the losers who come here lame questions, but you seem different. You must have a unique career. What do you do for work?"

"I'm a college professor."

"Oh my God." Mia slides out of her chair and kneels in front of Reid. She digs her fingers into his chest. "I'd fuck your brains out if you were my professor."

"Is that so?" Reid gazes into her eyes comfortably. Her admiration ignites in him a sensation of strength. He takes her hands off his chest and lifts her onto his lap.

"Oh, you're so strong too. This isn't your first time here, is it?"

"Actually, this is my first time in any gentlemen's club."

"You just became ten times hotter to me. You're not one of those creepy mongers who always comes here. I knew there was something different about you." Mia's eyes study something at the back of the room, then return to Reid. "It's too loud out here. I have a comfortable area reserved in the back. Let's go there instead."

She abruptly rises, takes his hand, and leads him towards the back. Something about her urgency triggers a sense of caution within Reid. He doesn't feel as if she's guiding him; more like she's pulling him to the back room. He recalls Henry's teaching that he should always lead the woman or she'll lose interest. *But Mia seems to like me a lot. Maybe she's just excited.* Plus, Wish said to open himself up to a dancer who seemed authentically interested. Reid's relaxed demeanor suddenly tightens as they approach a hallway guarded by a large bouncer.

"Three hundred to go any further," says the bouncer.

Reid's brow furrows. "I didn't think this involved me paying you?"

"You're not paying me, silly. You're paying for us to have fun without the cameras on. I'll feel more comfortable with you back there. Think of it like us getting a hotel room."

"I already have a hotel room."

"My shift just started. You don't want to wait twelve hours for me," says Mia. She pulls his head forward, then presses her plump lips to his cheek. "I can't kiss you any further out here, and I'm dying to know what your lips taste like."

The sultriness he feels from her kiss causes him to ignore his slight suspicion. He reaches into his pocket and peels off three large bills for the bouncer.

He and Mia stroll down the hallway and enter a dimly lit room that only has space for a two-seater leather couch, a glass coffee table, and a curtain to cover the doorway for privacy. Mia guides Reid to sit on the couch, then slides the curtain shut. As Mia sits next to Reid, the curtain flies open and a waitress enters. She places two napkins on the small table in front of the couch.

"It's a two-drink minimum in here, hun."

"Two shots of Patron," says Mia.

The server nods, then exits. Reid's face burns. *Mia didn't even ask me what I wanted.*

The bouncer sticks his head into the room. "Five minutes left."

"What? We just barely got here," says Reid. "I thought this was like our hotel room?"

Mia whispers in Reid's ear, "Give him a hundie and he'll leave us alone."

She pops off her bra and dumps her breasts in Reid's face. His mind gets lost among the doughy mounds for a few seconds, then he pulls a bill from his pocket for the bouncer. The bouncer shuts the curtain. Mia's hands caress the back of Reid's head, then pull it forward, centering his face in her cleavage. He can't ignore his arousal as she slides her warm, soft breasts up and down his cheeks.

The server comes back with the shots. Mia hops off Reid and hands him a shot, then they tap glasses and swallow. Reid sets the glass down, then looks at the bill. His jaw drops.

"The shots were forty dollars apiece. That's gotta be illegal."

"Don't be a cheapo, Professor. I know you've got money. Hurry and pay it so you can play with your favorite student."

Reid feels a tightness go up through his neck and into his brain. He can't shake off the sense that he really shouldn't be here. He hands a hundred-dollar bill to the server, who then exits. Mia leaps onto his lap and grinds her underwear-covered core on his pant-covered member. Such movement makes it hard for him to think about anything other than how good she feels.

"Somebody is excited to see me," she says, centering her core on his stiffness.

A few minutes pass. Mia continues to grind. The once excitable tease has shifted into pain from his clothes being rubbed on his loins, taking his mind out of his erotic trance and back into logical thinking. Reid looks to catch her eyes and notices they are wandering about the room. He wonders if she was ever excited to be with him. Wish's Sexmysts would never do such a thing. He recalls how he felt Tasha's sense of caring channeled through everything she did. He glances across the room, seeing their reflection in a glass-framed movie poster. Mia continues her careless grind, leaning forward, resting her chin on his shoulder, with an arm across his chest. Unable to gaze up at her, he continues to study their reflection in the framed movie poster and sees a small bright light suddenly illuminate. His blood heats to boiling point. He recognizes that her free hand is holding a phone, and she appears to be texting someone while she grinds away. He nudges her back slightly just as she finishes the text.

Knowing she got caught, Mia leans forward and dumps her breasts in his face. "I was just checking the time."

Though he is steaming, Reid smiles and shrugs playfully. He tries to think of what to say, but then the bouncer pokes his head into the room.

"Okay, time's up."

Reid glares at Mia, knowing he got hustled. "That was wonderful, thank you." He slides Mia off his lap, stands, then looks at the bouncer with a flustered expression.

"Don't give me that look," the bouncer says to Reid. "You spent thirty minutes in here."

Reid looks at his cell phone clock — *it's barely been fifteen minutes, you prick* — but hesitates to speak. The man is twice his size.

"That was fun. Bye, honey." Mia kisses Reid on the cheek, snaps her bra into place, then hurries off.

Reid adjusts his suit, then steps into the hallway. He glances into the distance and sees the bouncer and the server hand Mia cash. He figures it's her cut in the scam. He keeps his gaze on the carpet as he walks past them and into the main room. He questions how he manages to keep getting duped by women, even after doing so well with Wish's training. How could he have failed to sniff out Mia's scam, thinking she was genuine? Though he feels angry and embarrassed, something inside tells him he'll learn a valuable lesson from this experience.

He feels nature calling, and strolls towards the bathroom at the other end of the club. He enters and locks himself in a stall to gather his thoughts. Never again will he be hustled by a woman. He takes mental snapshots, remembering the sense of shame he felt, making sure he reviews this experience and learns from it. He rises, unlocks the stall, and goes to the sink to wash his hands.

"I warned you about spending time with that man," says a man with a southern drawl.

The tone startles Reid. He looks in the mirror and sees Youngblood at the neighboring faucet. Reid nods but says nothing. He reaches for a paper towel, feeling the weight of Wish's cash in his breast pocket, triggering his already increased heart rate to jump to light speed.

"You've got your whole life ahead of you. This is your last warning. I highly recommend you leave town," says Youngblood.

Feeling less threatened, Reid considers the advice, but Wish's teachings are too valuable to pass on. He looks the detective in the eyes. "I'm just here for a good time. Excuse me."

Reid hastily exits the restroom and shuffles towards the front door. He glances back every few steps, but doesn't see Youngblood follow. He feels his phone vibrate, and slips it out of his pocket while pushing open the front doors. He reads the text from Wish.

I have some people I want you to meet. Where are you?

Reid types: **I'm leaving Mick's right now. This place blows.**

Wish responds: **Stand near the main entrance. We'll be there shortly to pick you up.**

Reid types: **YB is here.**

Wish responds: **Perfect. The plan is working.**

What plan? To get me busted in a strip club bathroom? Reid slides his phone into his pocket, moves a few steps away from the entrance, then glances back to see the doors open. His neck tenses, but luckily, Youngblood isn't there. Instead, it's just another patron. Reid sighs, then stares at the pavement below his feet. *Youngblood should arrest that thief Mia, not me.*

Reid notices a Hummer limousine pull into the parking lot. The bouncer hurries over to greet the limo and opens the rear door, allowing Wish to step out.

"You gentlemen have come to the perfect place to party," says the bouncer.

Wish tips his hat to the bouncer, then waves Reid into the limo. Reid hurries over and slides into the rear seat. He sees a stout middle-aged man sitting at the opposite end, wearing a Hawaiian shirt, khaki shorts, and sneakers. On either side of that man are two square-jawed men in black suits, who appear to be security. The man in the Hawaiian shirt is fumbling with the radio. Reid nods to each of the men in suits, but they ignore his gesture and keep neutral expressions.

"All the radio stations are playing fucking commercials. Can't we get some god-damned rock and roll playing?" says the stout man.

Wish leans towards Reid. "He's an old friend named Cherry. He improves the lives of millions of people every day. He comes to us to get dark twice a year."

"Get dark?" says Reid. He glances across the limo. Cherry is engaging in small talk with his security.

Wish lowers his voice. "'Get dark' means to let his dark side out. If a man is solely focused on doing good all of the time, and the dark side isn't allowed expression, it builds into a strong force like a pressure cooker, capable of exploding at an unpredictable and unwelcome time. It's always safer to make a conscious decision about the dark side and let it roam free in a controlled environment. I provide that environment."

Reid nods, then studies Cherry, curious as to how this man helps millions of people every day.

"Do you have the fifteen hundred from those chips I gave you?" asks Wish. Reid digs the cash out of his pocket and hands it to him. "Did you make any extra cash from blackjack?"

"Yes," says Reid. Then he lowers his head.

"You got hustled in there, didn't you?" says Wish.

"Five hundred," says Reid.

Wish laughs as he slides the cash into his breast pocket. "Glad to hear that place hasn't changed. We never go there. The women are scam artists. Add that cost to your student loan debt. The five hundred spent was a quality education in Hustling 101."

"Good point." Reid feels a sense of relief at knowing Wish isn't disappointed. He stares out the window and squeezes his hands into fists, reaffirming his commitment to never be hustled again.

"We're not born knowing our boundaries," says Wish. "Experiences such as yours help clarify and establish your boundaries; they build the wall to guard your self-respect. You've never been in a strip club, so it's okay to mess up. The key is to not let it happen again."

Reid releases his fists, then notices Cherry, appearing frustrated, lift his hands overhead.

"I need some god-damned rock and roll."

Reid looks at Wish. "Is there an auxiliary jack?"

"A Hillary what?" says Wish. "I don't know any of that technology shit."

"I've got you." Reid smirks. "Old man." Reid crouches and walks to the stereo, which is centrally located in the limo. He grips a small auxiliary cord, plugs it into his phone, then selects his classic rock playlist. The speakers blast the opening guitar riff to AC/DC's "Back in Black."

Cherry leaps up. "Who-hoo! Where'd you find this kid? I love him already." He moves his hands to play air guitar. Reid joins in. They sing along to a few lyrics.

The limo makes a sharp turn. Cherry falls on top of Reid. They both burst into laughter.

"Now I'm ready to party," says Cherry. He crawls off Reid, lowers the volume of the music, and returns to his seat. Reid stumbles back to the rear of the limo.

Cherry turns to his guards. "Lance, give me some."

Lance takes out a small vial and hands it to Cherry. He twists open the vial and dumps a small amount of white powder on the top of his hand. Reid shoots a cautious look at his mentor. Wish nods slowly, as if to signal that everything is okay. Reid stares out the window with wide eyes. He's lectured about the dangers of cocaine at work, but he's never seen it in person.

"It's go time, boys." Cherry snorts the powder, then tosses the vial to Wish.

Oh no. Is Wish gonna make me snort coke? Reid watches Wish open the vial and tap it on the top part of his thumb, but no powder comes out. Wish snorts his empty hand. Reid looks at the other end of the limo; Cherry is far enough away to have a distorted view. Wish then grabs Reid's wrist and pretends to tap some powder between his thumb and index finger. Reid catches on and also performs a fake snort. Wish winks, then tosses the vial back to Lance.

Reid exhales with relief, then examines the bright sign

illuminating the parking lot they've just entered: *Vixen Gentlemen's Club*. He wonders if he can handle another strip club, but feels comforted that Wish will be there as a safety net.

"I like you, kid." Cherry grabs Reid's phone, releases it from the auxiliary cord, and tosses it at Reid. Cherry exits the limo, with his security following behind. As Reid steps out, he witnesses Cherry remove a large stack of hundred-dollar bills from his back pocket. He instantly wonders just how wealthy Cherry is, recalling how Wish stated earlier that he'd be entertaining his wealthiest client.

The group of men are escorted into the club by a large bouncer. Vixen is double the size of Mick's with double the number of beautiful women. The men continue through the club. Cherry hands a hundred-dollar bill to each person who comes near. Cocktail servers, dancers, bouncers, and even a few patrons end up with a bit more money. Reid tilts his head to the side; he's never seen so much money given out. He can't help but wonder why Cherry's doing it. He doubts Wish would support a guy whose actions are about getting his ego stroked. Reid's thought is interrupted by Wish gripping his forearm, stopping their momentum as Cherry and his security continue forward.

"Cherry is gonna do his thing for a bit. For now, we observe," says Wish.

Before Reid has a chance to take in the scene, a woman in lingerie wraps her arms around Wish.

"Yoga was amazing today. You're the best teacher. I can't believe you led me to orgasm in a room full of women without even touching me."

Wish releases himself from the hug, then places his hands in the prayer position. "Namaste, Chanel. I was honored to serve. Thank you for being open to receiving."

Chanel gives Wish a kiss on the cheek and strolls off.

Reid's jaw drops. "You teach yoga also? Is there anything you don't do?"

Wish grins, then two women latch onto him, forming a group hug. Both express gratitude for their experience in the yoga class, then walk away.

"Why are these women responding to you that way? Are you

doing some kind of erotic yoga with them?" asks Reid.

"Yes. The yoga I teach is a sequence of movements designed to activate their female sexual-response system. They experience what modern science has labeled a 'coregasm,' heightened sensations channeled into their sexual organs through fitness, and some may go on to have a full orgasm. The result of the yoga session is a heightened sense of feminine energy. A university study concluded that exotic dancers earn more money while ovulating. My aim is to ignite a woman's sexuality through yoga, triggering her body to respond similarly to ovulation. I teach the class a few times a month, and it's for women only."

Reid's mouth falls open as he listens intently.

"I'll typically have the class before these dancers get ready for their work shift that night. The dancers with enhanced feminine prowess now serve the men better by using that to boost the men's masculinity. The men who come here will gladly pay for the experience of having their masculine energy heightened, because many are treated like shit by their wives at home."

Reid's mind flashes to his last relationship. "Jasmine always complained about me when I got home from work. She'd call me lazy and useless. I'd be exhausted, but she knew those words would get me to do whatever she wanted."

"I'm not surprised. Your lack of masculinity had her confused about her femininity. It's my hope that these yoga-inspired dancers can help their male clients discover the hidden pieces of masculinity. Understandably, it's a tricky goal to achieve through a few lap dances."

"How can they help a man find his missing masculinity?"

"Each man is different, but the frisky female has a heightened sense of how to crack the man's code. The woman should start by showing appreciation for the man's career choice while touching him. A woman can never go wrong with a compliment followed by physical touch."

"But not every woman can help every guy, correct?"

"Correct, just as you and I cannot help every woman we erotically stimulate. Some people aren't wired to understand. And others will understand, but they won't allow themselves to receive, because they've been taught to repress erotic stimulation. I take comfort from knowing that the women who attend my class learn to authentically care for their clients. It becomes a win–win, because the men get better service and the women experience profound happiness through providing worthwhile service. Plus, they earn more money than the average dancer. You got hustled at Mick's, probably by someone who uses her sexuality to abuse others. These yogi women are honored to serve and improve lives."

"Do any of these women work for you? Like as a Sexmyst?"

"No, the erotic yoga class is my way of providing community service. The women develop some basic Sexmyst skills, but they aren't trained to become a fully formed Sexmyst. However, these women do help society become a safer place through providing enhanced tactile experiences. Our agreement requires that they give me feedback from their work, which serves my research for our mission."

Wish and Reid shift their focus to the interactions of the dancers and patrons. Wish points out how his yogi women have men smiling while giving money; in contrast to the non-yogi dancers, who deal with men who appear to be hesitant. Reid notices a yogi woman sit on a man's lap, then touch the man in a unique pattern while engaging in a seemingly flirtatious conversation.

"Your yogi girls touch the men differently than the other dancers. They appear to touch the men more often and with longer strokes."

Wish turns to Reid. "The skin is the largest sex organ in the body. Most of these men just want to be touched by an admiring female. I mentioned to you before that lack of human touch is the most common characteristic amongst violent criminals. It's safe to assume that none of the men you see here with the yogi women will be committing a violent crime anytime soon."

A bouncer approaches Reid and Wish. Reid narrows his eyes, looking at Wish and expressing concern.

"Follow me," says the bouncer.

"Relax, kid," says Wish. "We're just going to Cherry's private party room."

The bouncer leads them towards the back of the club.

While walking, Reid speaks to Wish. "How do you know Cherry?"

"He was one of my first clients. He is a multi-millionaire whose work is all about saving lives and helping others. He specializes in neuroscience. Cherry knows as well as I do that the brain is a duality mechanism that learns through contrasts, such as the duality of good and bad. Therefore, Cherry comes to me to express his dark side twice a year."

"But he just snorted cocaine. Surely he knows that will mess up his brain."

"He's not afraid to use his body as a science experiment. The first thing Cherry will do when he returns home is jump in an fMRI machine and scan his brain. He and I can talk for hours about that stuff."

Reid now has an answer as to why Wish knows so much about neuroscience — *Cherry.*

The men enter the private party room, which is the size of a standard living room. Cherry's security men stand by the door. Cherry is plopped in the center of a half-circle couch. In front of the couch is a low table with four bottles of vodka, four bottles of champagne, and a handful of mixers.

"Bring the titties," says Cherry. He shakes his hands in front of his body, as if squeezing a set of invisible breasts.

The door opens and a stampede of women enter. Two of them run straight to Cherry and slide onto his lap. He stuffs their bras with hundred-dollar bills.

"Why hello, ladies. Thank you for joining me on this special occasion." Cherry looks up. He points to two other large-breasted women who've entered the room.

"You two. Tits in his face, now." Cherry points the girls over to Reid. "My man is too stiff. Make sure you take his mind off life stuff."

Within seconds, Reid's head is buried in a sea of silicone that swishes from side to side. A minute passes, then the women release him, leaving him flushed and with messed-up hair. He looks at his crotch and notices his erection bulging from his trousers. He quickly pulls the flaps of his suit jacket together, covering the tent-like protuberance on his pants.

"Ladies, do it again. He's too damned shy." Cherry hands the dancers two bills each. "Reid, do as you wish. We all see the happiness in your pants. Who cares?"

Cherry's right. I am being shy. Reid's nose and cheek suddenly sting as he recalls Wish's multiple slaps when he urged Reid to take ownership of his desire. He then looks at Wish, and sees he's sitting in a chair across the room with a woman on his lap. She's cooing as he gives her a neck massage. Her mouth falls agape, then her eyes roll to the back of her head as she melts from his touch. Reid studies the technique, shakes his head, and smiles. *The master is at work, and I can't believe his wife is totally cool with that. She must be a special woman.*

Reid's view of Wish is suddenly obstructed by four breasts shoved in his face. Refusing to be the shy guy, he wraps an arm around each woman's back and pulls them closer.

"There you go," says Cherry. "Now I see a man who is honest about his desires."

Minutes pass, then the boob parade on Reid's face comes to a stop and the women exit the room. Reid rests on the couch, his hair frazzled, looking dazed but grinning, enjoying the reminder that life is more rewarding when he dares to let loose.

Cherry asks the women on his lap to fix themselves a drink, then he leans towards Reid. "What do you want with your life, kid? Money, sex, freedom?"

Reid tilts his head back and takes a few seconds to think. "I love that you ask a personal development question while being surrounded by women in a strip club."

"Ha!" Cherry slaps Reid on the back. "It's the yayo, my man. But still, Wish has big plans for you. I'm curious to know if they're in line with what you want."

"Right now, the goal is to learn about myself and become comfortable around women." *Be brutally honest. Don't bullshit him.* "I want to be the greatest sexual experience a woman has ever had. And I fully believe in Wish's mission. I intend to serve others as best I can after learning from him."

Reid studies Wish, across the room with the same woman. Wish glides one hand along her neck and shoulders, stopping at various points to apply deep pressure. His free hand dances along her inner thigh with a feather-light touch. The woman's head falls backwards with a look of euphoric bliss. Reid shakes his head in awe.

Reid feels Cherry's hand grip his forearm, drawing his attention. "You can have anything you want in your life, so long as your focus is on providing a service to others. A man is one of two things: he's either a manipulator or a man of service. A manipulator always runs out of people to manipulate, but a man of service will never run out of people to serve." Both men glance at Wish. "Wish is a man of service. Follow his guidance, remain focused on serving others, and you'll be rich with all that you desire."

A dancer crawls onto Cherry's lap, giddy as she touches his round belly, distracting Cherry from the conversation. Reid meditates on the advice, reflecting on how Wish is constantly talking about serving others, but serving from a place of authenticity, not approval-seeking.

Reid's attention is suddenly captured by a beautiful blond entering the room. She stands near the door, wearing an elegant and form-fitting white dress. Reid leans back in his seat, hoping to appear calm, but inside his chest, his heart is fluttering.

Since each man is occupied, he has no choice but to take the initiative. Surprised by his lack of fear, he stands and signals to the blond woman to come his way. She walks towards him. *Damn, that was easy. Don't screw it up, Reid.* His brain fumbles for something witty to say. Henry's voice comes to mind: *Be brutally honest, express the truth of what you observe, and care about her experience.*

As she nears, Reid speaks. "I waved you over based on the guidance of my erection. My apologies, it's not something I can just force away." *I can't believe that just came out of my mouth.*

She laughs, sits on his lap, and puts her palm on Reid's chest. "I noticed. I'm glad I don't have to wonder if you're excited to see me. Thank you for being so honest."

"What's your name?" asks Reid. "First tell me your stripper name, then your real name."

"My stripper name is Jessica, and my real name is Diamond."

They both giggle. She shakes her head and her expression signals sarcasm. "I'm just kidding. My stripper name is Dani and my real name is Dani."

"Dani, I'm very much enjoying your charms." Reid's stomach tingles with the sensations of a giddy teenager. "I can't believe I told you about my erection. I don't know what it is, but something has me feeling instantly comfortable with you."

"You just spent a few minutes with your head stuffed in four boobs. Perhaps that gave you a sense of clarity."

"You saw that, huh? It was pretty awesome."

"It looked awesome," says Dani. "I might pay those girls to do the same thing to me."

Reid leans back, finding Dani even more attractive now that he knows she's sexually drawn to women as well. He glances up at the ceiling and smirks. *Jasmine got with a woman and that freaked me out. Now a threesome seems like the sexiest thing ever.* Reid can't resist his desire to create a real connection with Dani. He leans towards her. "Do you live in Vegas? Or fly here to work on weekends?"

"I just moved here."

"I'd love to hang with you sometime," says Reid.

Wish steps up to Reid and interrupts. "The Sexmysts are coming to Cherry's suite soon."

"Really? Why'd you bother bringing him here in the first place?"

"Contrasts. I bring Cherry here to experience the behavior of the uninitiated woman. His brain is then primed to appreciate the Erotic Sensory Experience from the Sexmysts." Wish nods his head sideways at Cherry, signaling that it's time to leave. Wish walks away, stops near the door, and waits.

Dani turns to Reid. "What's a Sexmyst?"

"Umm." Reid pauses. "I can't really explain right now. I must go. I'd love to invite you to come with us, but unfortunately, I can't. I'm so sorry."

Reid sees the frown that Dani quickly tries to hide. He wonders if she's a clever hustler like Mia, but he can't deny the sense of clarity he feels within. There's something about Dani, something powerful that suggests this is more than a random meeting.

Cherry stands. "Ladies, our party is over. Nice knowing ya." He tosses the rest of his cash into the air, creating a rainfall of hundred-dollar bills. Reid tilts his head back in awe. Then he sees Wish cross his arms, nostrils flaring at Cherry's action. Wish then abruptly leaves the room. Reid tenses with concern, but quickly becomes distracted by the chaos occurring on the floor. Aside from Dani, all of the women are crawling to gather the bills. Reid shakes his head in astonishment, then notices Dani roll her eyes at the ridiculousness as well — more proof of her seeming authentic. He feels a tingle in his heart, similar to what he used to feel as a boy around a schoolyard crush.

Dani slides off his lap, then carefully steps around the scavenging dancers. Reid moistens his lips, studying her behind while she walks to leave — plump from genetics, yet firm from the gym. He stands, realizing the tingle has caused his mind to forget a crucial action. *Shit, I should have gotten her phone number.*

Cherry, Reid, and the two security men make their way through the club. Reid sighs, then canvasses the club for Dani, sick with regret from not getting her phone number. He scans the main room one last time — no sign of Dani. They meander out of the club where Wish is waiting, but he appears to be less disgruntled. They all hop into the limo, which drives towards Cherry's hotel.

Wish glances out the rear window of the limo, then looks back at Reid. "I'll need you to come up with us to Cherry's suite and leave with the payment." He looks out the window again. "I think we're being followed."

A sudden coldness hits Reid. "Youngblood?" *And now you want me to leave with Cherry's payment?* He twists his neck and looks out the rear window, seeing many cars. He struggles to identify one that's following, because the limo is staying in one lane, going straight.

"The girls ready?" Cherry yells to Wish.

"Yes, set to arrive in thirty minutes. Your smelly ass needs a shower," says Wish.

Cherry's security men give Wish a stern look.

Cherry shakes his head and speaks to Reid. "Wish is the only man I allow to talk to me that way. He's right; I don't want to be smelly for his girls. They are the fucking best fifty grand I'll ever spend."

Fifty grand for sex? Who are the girls? Will Molly be there? Reid can't help but notice that Cherry's become a different person now he's talking about Wish's Sexmysts. Cherry could have had any of those strippers come with them, but now he's sitting quietly, with his fingers folded together.

Reid's weight shifts to the side as the limo makes a turn. He quickly looks out the rear window and spies a white sedan following behind. The limo makes another turn, as does the white sedan. Reid's throat tightens, his analytical mind filling with questions. He wonders about the risk involved if he were to get arrested for being connected to this. Would it be a misdemeanor, or something that could ruin his career? Is this a test of his boundaries? Should he refuse to follow Wish's instructions to leave with the money?

They pull up at the Carnival Hotel and Casino, located a few blocks away from the Strip. Reid looks around — no sign of the white sedan, but he remains on high alert. Reid suddenly feels an arm wrap around his shoulders. The touch seems to settle his scattered thoughts; it's almost how he'd imagine his father would comfort him. It's Wish's arm, and it's pulling him towards the hotel, and it feels natural. Wish doesn't say anything, and he doesn't need to. Reid straightens his spine. He's committed to this path into the dark world, and there's no boundary that's being violated. *I'm doing this because it feels like the right thing to do.*

The men enter the hotel and ride the elevator to the penthouse. The elevator doors open onto a massive suite. Reid's eyes widen as he enters and sees two full-length bowling alleys and a pool table. In the center of the room is a circular bar, stocked with various bottles of high-end liquor. He hears the faint sounds of a rock song playing through the speakers.

"Turn that shit up." Cherry jumps on the bar and plays his air guitar. One of his bodyguards turns up the volume on the stereo. "I'm gonna fuck some bitches tonight!"

Wish shoots Cherry a chilling gaze, then reaches for the stereo plug and yanks it out of the wall socket. The room goes quiet.

Cherry lifts both hands in the air. "What the hell, man? Why'd you do that?"

"If you just want to fuck, you can grab one of the hookers from the lobby," says Wish. "You know I don't deal with childish behavior. We're leaving." Wish walks towards the front door.

Reid sees the security guards look at Cherry, like hungry wolves waiting for a signal to attack Wish. Having seen Wish take down men before, Reid knows he shouldn't be worried, but these square-chinned guards come off as trained protectors, capable of inflicting more damage than the average street thug. Reid steps towards the front door slowly, but looks back to keep an eye on the guards.

"No, please, don't leave. I'm sorry," says Cherry. "I'll throw in an extra ten grand."

Wish stops and speaks over his shoulder. "Our money is earned from service, not from you throwing money at your mistakes." Wish walks towards the door. Reid follows, walking quickly to get closer to Wish. Though the room is tense, Reid admires Wish's commitment to his boundaries, walking away from fifty grand.

"Wish. Wait. Please," says Cherry. He runs in front of Wish, extending both arms outward to stop him in his stride. Like trained dogs, Cherry's security men hurry to stand near, a man on each side of Wish. "I'm sorry. Forgive me. I got lost in the dark side and became selfish. A momentary slip, I promise."

Wish exhales a long breath. "A momentary slip? Are you going to momentarily slip when the Sexmysts are serving you and they trigger an insecurity?"

"No, I won't. I promise," says Cherry.

"I've dealt with too many of you god-dammed millionaires, surrounding yourself with money to mask your fucking self-hatred. You threw your cash in the air at Vixen because you wanted to see women crawl before you. I should have left your ass at the club, but I ignored my instincts. I'm not making that same mistake again."

Reid recognizes that Wish is battling a boundary dilemma. Wish said that he and Cherry are old friends; surely he knows whether Cherry is a good man.

Cherry stares at the floor. Wish continues: "Before we met, your desire to earn wealth was motivated from fear — fear of people not respecting you. You were a little boy trapped in a grown man's body, desperately wanting the admiration of others. And you won their admiration by controlling them with your money. Your behavior this entire night has reminded me of the insecure little shit you used to be."

Reid thinks back to the first moments at Vixen, when Cherry handed out cash to each person he saw. Was that approval-seeking? Why didn't Wish say anything then?

Wish places his hands in the prayer position, and lowers his forehead to the tips of his fingers. "Do you remember what happened to you during the months after your first experience with a Sexmyst?"

Reid sees fire in Cherry's eyes as Cherry speaks smugly. "I quadrupled my net worth."

Before Reid can blink, Wish throws a punch that connects on Cherry's face, causing him to fall backwards to the floor. The security men lunge towards Wish, attacking from each side. Wish dodges a punch from one guard and it connects with the other guard's chin, knocking him to the floor. Wish then grabs the standing guard's wrist, twisting until the guard is hunched over, unable to free himself. Reid steps forward to help his mentor, but it's not needed; the guard on the floor is knocked out cold.

Wish puts his free hand on the man's elbow, further twisting as the guard groans. Wish yells to Cherry, "Call off your dogs or you're gonna end up with a one-armed guard. I know these guards are new, but you gotta get them in check."

Reid clenches his sweaty palms into fists, leaning forward on his toes, ready to handle any sudden moves.

Cherry gathers himself and returns to standing, then speaks while rubbing his jaw. "Relax, guys, we're cool. Wish and I are like brothers who bicker. His punch has gotten weaker over the years. You didn't let me finish my response, dumbass. After my first Sexmyst experience, I quadrupled my income because I learned what authentic service to others can do. It changed my life, and my business changed to match what I was feeling inside. I got out of using neuroscience to predict economic changes in the stock market and into using neuroscience to heal suffering. I give all the credit to you and the Sexmysts; I haven't forgotten."

Reid narrows his eyes. He wonders if Wish believes there's sincerity behind Cherry's words. Cherry seemed to have a kind heart when Reid spoke with him at Vixen.

Wish releases his grip of the guard, who goes to help his now conscious associate over to a nearby chair. Wish then stares at Cherry, as if studying him. Several seconds pass, then Wish shakes his head, looks at Reid, and nods at the door. "Come on, we're leaving. He's talking from his penis, not his heart."

Reid watches Wish walk towards the door, then darts his eyes to Cherry and sees that the grown man is sulking. Reid had felt the kindness in Cherry's heart an hour before, when he offered words of wisdom about being a man of service and said how much he respects Wish. He'd sensed authenticity in Cherry at that time, and wonders how he got off track and how Wish doesn't sense it now. Perhaps it was the cocaine. Regardless, Reid feels grateful to Cherry for helping him snap out of his shyness, which led to his confident interaction with Dani.

"Wait," Reid says to Wish, feeling the air escape his lungs. The pimp halts his step but doesn't turn around. "Cherry gave me good advice at the Vixen Club. He said a manipulator always runs out of people to manipulate, but a man of service will never run out of people to serve."

Wish talks over his shoulder. "I taught him that expression, but he's forgotten."

Reid sees Cherry glance at him with a look of hopefulness. He says to Wish, "Cherry hasn't forgotten. Tonight he went out of his way to make sure I understood. And he also sought to help me out of my shyness. His heart is in the right place. I think he got a bit carried away in the dark side, that's all."

Wish turns around, glaring at Cherry. "Is Reid telling the truth?"

Cherry nods. "I saw the potential you see in this kid, and I saw him holding back. He's got something special in him, and I, just as much as you, don't want him to fail at being himself."

Though his pulse is beating in his throat, Reid senses a shift in the tension. He notices Wish's glare soften. Then Wish walks towards Cherry.

"You're a good man. This is why we are friends." Wish and Cherry embrace in a hug. "Take a hot shower. But make it cold during the last minute to prep your senses. Two Sexmysts will be serving you tonight. Remember, you have permission to selfishly focus on receiving their touch. Have them be a reminder of what it's like to be in the presence of someone who cares about you, Cherry the human being, not Cherry the millionaire."

Reid bends over, resting his hands on his knees to settle himself from the shock of standing up for Cherry. He slowly rises, seeing Cherry skip down the long hallway to the master bedroom. He moves his gaze to Wish, and notices him extend his hand to shake a truce with the once-wrist-gripped security guard, who obliges. Wish and the guard walk to the other end of the suite, and Wish waves for Reid to follow. All three men enter another bedroom.

Reid is promptly handed a black backpack by the guard. He sees the zippers are locked by a thin chain. Reid feels what's inside the bag — loose stacks shaped like bricks — and figures it's the fifty grand. The weight of the backpack reminds him of his college days lugging around textbooks. Most of those books focused on life skills, sex, and relationships. *Not one of those books could even begin to describe all that I have experienced and learned from Wish.* The guard leaves the room, leaving Wish and Reid to talk.

"I need you to take this backpack to my place right now," says Wish. "Youngblood might be waiting for us downstairs in the casino, so take the emergency stairs down to the street and find a cab."

Reid's face tightens. "But what if Youngblood is circling the building, anticipating us leaving through the fire exit?"

"You'll be fine, kid. Youngblood is after me, not you. But if you do get pinched, don't say anything except that you need your lawyer present before you'll speak. I have a lawyer who can fix most problems we would encounter." Wish looks at his phone, reads a text, then looks back at Reid. "The Sexmysts have arrived in the lobby. You need to leave now. I don't want them seeing you just yet."

"I'm dying to know what they look like," says Reid.

"You will someday. But it's best they not see you until you're fully developed."

Reid smirks, exits the suite, and finds the stairway. Upon opening the stairway door, he notices a sign that reads "35th floor." He begins the trek down while analyzing worst-case scenarios. *If Youngblood is at the bottom, I'll just not allow him to open the bag. He would need a search warrant to go through my stuff — I think?*

He finally sets foot on the first floor and bends over while gasping for air. After a minute passes, he cracks open the exit to the back alley of the hotel. *No one in sight.* Reid starts his walk around the building. A black SUV with the hotel logo on the side pulls in front of him. He clenches the straps on the backpack as the driver's tinted window glides downward.

"You're a guest of Mr. C's?" says the driver.

Reid furrows his brow and shakes his head to say "no."

"I'm Max, a driver for the casino. We're not allowed to address our high rollers by their full name. His name starts with a C. I saw you enter the hotel with him. Do you need a ride somewhere?"

"C" must be for Cherry. Reid weighs his options, figuring it might be safer to ride with this guy because Youngblood might be waiting out front near the cabs. But then again, this guy might be up to no good. Yet the hotel logo on the side of the SUV seems reason enough to take the leap.

Max hops out of his car and opens the rear door for Reid. The driver reaches for Reid's backpack.

"No, thanks," says Reid. "I'll keep this with me."

Reid looks beyond the car, considering which direction he should sprint, if necessary.

"I remember you from a few weeks back," says Max. "Your suit was all ripped up when I picked up our mutual friend."

Reid darts his eyes back to Max, then remembers the night he was tossed from the club after the women called him creepy. Wish had found him out by the trash; they'd talked briefly, then Wish was picked up by a black SUV. But Reid doesn't recall noticing a hotel logo on the door. Reid stares at the logo and scratches his chin.

Max continues. "I was a private driver for him that night, with my own car," says Max. "I also work for the hotel."

Reid hears sirens in the distance, which startle him into making a quick decision. He slides into the SUV, sits behind Max, and instructs him to drive to Wish's building. The drive goes smoothly. Reid glances out the rear window a few times and doesn't see anything suspicious. He relaxes into the seat and closes his eyes.

"Dammit," says the driver. Reid jolts up and sees a bright red light shining from behind into the SUV. They're being pulled over.

"We should be fine," says the driver. "I haven't been drinking and I wasn't driving fast."

You're gonna be fine. I'm the one with a backpack containing fifty grand in cash. Reid slides the bag under Max's seat, but the bag is too thick to be out of sight. Max presses the button to roll down his window. A man — not Youngblood, and not dressed like an officer — flashes a badge, then instructs Max to roll down Reid's window.

The man looks to be in his fifties, with silver hair cut short. He's lean, appearing fit to work in law enforcement. Reid wonders if this man works directly with Youngblood.

"Step out of the car, young man," says the officer to Reid.

"Yes, sir." Reid slowly opens the door, while using his foot to further press the backpack under the front seat, then stands face to face with the officer.

"Can you tell me why I pulled you over, young man?"

"No, sir." Reid's voice crackles. He's quivering to the point that he almost urinates.

"We have reason to believe that you are involved in illegal activity. If you admit guilt right now, I can make things a lot easier for you."

Although he's overcome with fear, Reid remembers that Wish advised him to say nothing and assured him that a lawyer could clean up any mess.

The officer sticks his head through the car window, then turns back to Reid. "What's in the bag?"

Reid stares at the small pebbles in the gravel, remaining silent.

The cop steps closer to Reid, so close Reid can feel his hot breath. "What is in the bag, young man?"

Reid tightens his lips and keeps his gaze on the ground.

"Look at me," commands the cop. Reid looks up, seeing the officer's eyes dart left and right as if he's studying Reid.

"You selling drugs, kid?" The cop grabs Reid's elbows, pins his arms behind his back, turns him around, and slams his face into the hood of the SUV. The officer starts to search Reid's pockets. Reid feels blood trickle from his nose.

The officer's voice increases in volume. "Of course you ain't got shit on you. Tell me what's in the bag."

Reid sniffs the blood back into his nose. *He hasn't told me why I'm being searched. I think that's against the law. Plus, the officer would have opened the bag by now if he could.* Reid figures the best option is to continue with silence.

"I'm going to ask you one more time. What's in the bag?" The officer shoves his billy-club across the rear of Reid's neck, pressing his face onto the hood. Reid looks through the windshield and sees Max filming the interaction with a cell phone.

Reid's sniffs up more blood, feeling a hint of relief. "I'll only speak with my lawyer present."

The officer notices the camera and backs away. He talks into a microphone on his shirt, communicating with his headquarters. "No threats here. Everything is clean."

The officer gets into his car and drives away. Reid slides into the backseat of the SUV. Max hands him a napkin for his nose. As Reid blows into the napkin, he notices Max sending the video to someone.

"Did you film that entire thing?" says Reid.

"Yes, and I just sent it to the boss." Max starts the car and drives it towards Wish's building.

"That's smart. You can protect yourself and protect the hotel."

"This ride isn't a service from the hotel."

"What boss are you talking about?"

"Madam Dalia."

"Who's that?"

"The sexiest woman in the world." Max parks the SUV in front of Wish's tower. "She's Wish's wife and she's upstairs waiting for you."

Chapter 21

While riding in the elevator to the penthouse, Reid's mind spins from all that has occurred. He should be exhausted, but the thrill of meeting Wish's wife, the woman who captured his mentor's heart, energizes him.

The elevator doors slide open. Reid straightens his suit, uses the tissue to wipe away any remaining blood from his nose, and steps into Wish's penthouse. Every light is off, leaving the glow of the Las Vegas Strip to dimly light the space. He carefully steps into the living room, then hears a soft voice speak. "Your movement suggests you are more sensual than Wish has described," says the female voice. "I'm Dalia, Wish's wife."

As Reid's eyes adjust to the darkness, he notices the gorgeous matriarch resting on the couch. She's wearing a black silk robe and her legs are crossed. Dalia rises from the couch and the robe flaps open as she moves slowly towards him, exposing her sculpted body and black lace lingerie. Max wasn't exaggerating: each step she takes is like sex in motion. She stands before him, and his body freezes in pleasure-soaked paralysis. She takes the bag from him and tosses it onto the couch.

"Professor Reid Bradley." Her voice seeps into the pleasure center of his brain, like a gentle stroke of his member. She slides off his suit jacket and draws her finger down his chest. "You did well tonight."

"Thank you." Reid's mind fills with all the positions he'd love to put her in. He recalls his last visit here, when he learned to be honest about his desires. *But this is Wish's wife.* He catches his naughty thoughts, puts his hands in his pockets, and glances downward. He doubts Wish wants him to see his wife in lingerie. *This can't be good. I swear I'd never mess with another man's wife.*

Dalia lowers her head to catch Reid's eyes. She puckers her lips and squints at him.

"Max sent me the video." She draws her finger down Reid's chest again. "You handled Detective Jones quite well."

"Detective Jones? Wait, he's Wish's friend, right?" says Reid. Dalia nods in agreement. Reid lifts his eyebrows. "That was staged?"

"We needed to see how you'd handle yourself. You passed our little test."

"I was just doing what Wish taught me."

"You're a fast learner. Let's keep that in mind for what I'll be teaching you tonight." Dalia caresses Reid's hand and leads him towards the room with the cage.

Reid stops just before entering. "I don't think it would be appropriate for me to go in there with you."

Dalia grins at his hesitancy. "You have a thoughtful heart, a highly conscientious heart — very rare." She unbuttons his shirt. "You're not breaking rules, Professor Bradley. Wish knows you're with me. This is the only way you'll learn the techniques of a Sexmyst."

She places her warm palm on Reid's bare chest. "This heart is meant to serve; it's too large for you to worry about protecting it all the time. You're safe here. Release all guards protecting this heart, and open it to serve."

Dalia lowers herself to her knees. Reid's chest rises and falls with each breath. Her fingers brush his stomach, igniting sparks of pleasure throughout his body. She undoes his belt, then glances up at him while moistening her sensual lips. Reid's lips begin to part. He can't help but feel the urge to ravish Dalia, but still he feels unsure.

"Are you ready to enter?" asks Dalia.

Reid nods, struggling to swallow his next gulp amidst the euphoric tingle spreading through his body.

Dalia opens the door to the cage and they enter. Unlike the last time he was in the cage, the window blinds have been lifted, and he can see the Las Vegas Strip in the distance. He observes four candles spread throughout the room, lit wicks flickering.

Dalia leads him to the massage table and instructs him to remove all of his clothes. He obliges, then stands naked with his hands covering his erection. Dalia frowns, as if instructing him to release his guard. He drops his hands to his sides, then feels cool air crawl up his spine, causing his skin to ripple with nervous goosebumps.

Dalia walks to the display of erotic items and grabs a thin bamboo stick.

"Turn around, place your hands on the edge of the table, and close your eyes," says Dalia.

Reid obeys, then flinches as his back is touched with a cold bamboo stick. Then the bamboo lifts off his skin. He squeezes his bum cheeks tight, hoping his thoughts about what will come next are incorrect.

The bamboo whacks his right butt cheek with force. A sharp sting vibrates through his bum and up his spine. The sting quickly shifts into pleasure as he feels the softness of Dalia's hands caressing the punished cheek.

"This is to ignite the sensory response system in your body," says Dalia. "Never forget the power of contrasting sensations. Are we clear?"

Reid nods.

"There are ten major points of stimulation on the female genitalia," says Dalia. "You'll be learning about all ten tonight."

She slaps the bamboo on his left butt check. Reid clenches his teeth, absorbing the pain. *Fuck, that hurts.* His breath shortens.

"Everyone must feel pain at some point in the life. It's a requirement for the brain to be able to recognize pleasure. I'm sure you are familiar with the concept by now."

Reid nods and braces himself for another whack. A bead of sweat crawls down his forehead. *Molly found a way to experience pleasure from me whacking her with the paddle. I'm sure I can do the same.*

"Open your eyes and turn around," says Dalia. Reid turns and sees her leave the room. A minute passes and Dalia returns holding the hand of a naked, blindfolded woman. Reid instantly recognizes the scar from the stab wound below her stomach. *It's Molly. And she looks even more tantalizing. Her brown hair is cut differently; it's now chin length.* Reid studies Molly's backside as she walks past, again observing the tattoo that reads, "Acceptance." Dalia guides the blindfolded Molly to lie backside-down on the massage table.

"Professor Bradley, your training starts now," says Dalia. She grabs the bamboo and looks at Reid. "I want to see you please her."

Reid furrows his eyebrows. *Seriously? I don't even know where to begin.* He glances at the wall of hanging erotic objects, debating if he should use the fur glove again. Dalia swings the bamboo and hits Reid's thigh; a loud *thwap* echoes throughout the cage. The sting shoots from his hamstring to the front of his knee. *Ouch! Okay, so Dalia doesn't want me to use any items.* Reid walks to the edge of the table where Molly's feet rest. He places his hands on her inner thigh, pulls her legs slightly apart, licks his lips, and leans in to kiss Molly's private jewel.

"Fail," says Dalia. She launches a mighty strike across his back.

Reid jumps up, then paces in circles while rubbing his back, short of breath. He glares back at the seductive Dalia. Her beauty quickly makes the sting go away. She signals for him to return.

"There are three phases of the Erotic Sensory Experience. Phase one is foreplay. This can start outside the bedroom and continue building once inside the bedroom. Explore the skin with the purpose of activating her senses, but don't touch her pussy. Activate her dormant sensory response system with your palms and fingers. I'll tell you when she's ready, then you'll go into phase two: coreplay, channeling sexual energy released from phase one into her vagina. Phase three is penetration while maintaining your focus on the contrasts."

Dalia waves the stick, signaling for Reid to follow her to the end of the table where Molly's head rests.

"Tell me what you see," says Dalia.

Reid examines Molly. Fearing another whack, he struggles to find the right words. *Wish would want me to be honest about my desires.*

"I see a beautiful woman who I want to have sex with," says Reid. He looks at Molly's lips, hoping they'll form a smile, but they stay neutral.

"That's what your penis sees," replies Dalia.

But I thought Wish wanted me to speak from the desire of my penis?

"Let's look at her more closely," says Dalia. They both lean towards Molly's forehead. "There are trillions of cells that make up this body, each playing a specific role in her life. Our senses dictate the world we perceive. If you enhance her senses, you enhance the world she experiences."

Reid nods. "A person with limited sensory experiences will have a limited perception of the world."

"Precisely. Look at her. Go deeper than the basic surface level your eyes have become accustomed to seeing. This human in front of you, like all humans, has layer upon layer of sensory receptors throughout her body. When providing an Erotic Sensory Experience, your focus must go beyond that which only your eyes can see."

Reid studies Molly's forehead, noticing the thousands of pores on her skin. He then examines her more closely, and sees her hair at the roots, knowing they rest on top of a skull that protects the brain. He scans her facial cheeks, then cracks a smile as he gazes down the lines of perfectly sculpted body. Reid's awareness suddenly shifts into a deeper sense of understanding. He begins to appreciate the skin as more than something that covers the body.

Molly's thick strawberry lips curl into a smile.

"She can sense the energy of your admiration. Touch her skin now, consciously feeling her skin connect with your fingertips. Pay attention to the way your touch will stimulate the many facets of her body below the skin."

He rolls his fingers along the skin behind her ears, feeling its silk-like texture, then he glides his hands down to massage her neck. Dalia stands behind Reid's naked body, reaches forward, and places her hands on top of his. She shows Reid a rhythm to the touching, guiding his hands across Molly's body — hard, soft, scratch, pinch — then allowing time for no touch.

"Periods of non-touch are as important as touch," says Dalia. "The brain needs time to absorb the sensations, or it can become overwhelmed." Dalia's palms leave Reid's hands. He halts his touching pattern, then starts back in the same rhythm set forth by Dalia.

His palms brush Molly's stomach, then glide along the curves of her sides. He rubs her shoulders, arms, and neck once more, consciously connecting with the various sensory response mechanisms under her skin.

My goodness, this body is perfect. Touching her gives me more pleasure than I think I'm giving her. Molly lifts her chin and gasps lightly.

"She isn't moaning because you're touching her," says Dalia. "It's because she can sense your appreciation through your touch."

Reid smiles, knowing Dalia is correct. He felt the same thing with Tasha.

"Her breasts are ready for stimulation." Dalia points the edge of the bamboo at Molly's erect nipples. "With your lips, gently kiss her there. Taste her skin, but only for a few seconds, then move your lips away and gently blow cool air on them. That will release oxytocin into her brain, adding more pleasure hormones to the experience."

Reid feels his desire erupt from his loins into his brain. He launches his head down towards Molly's succulent breasts, wrapping his lips around her nipples, then sucking like a baby until his bum gets struck with a swift whack from the bamboo stick. He springs up, sucking in air through his teeth.

"You boys watch too much porn," says Dalia. "Don't kiss her to please your penis; such energy will take away from her experience. You must move past your selfish sexual desires and derive your pleasure from serving her. Kiss with the purpose of stimulating her brain. Touch with the purpose of enhancing her body awareness."

But Wish taught me to be brutally honest about my sexual desires. Reid hesitates to verbalize his question, fearing another bamboo strike. Instead, he follows her instructions, returning to a service mindset, ignoring the sensations from his stiffness, concentrating only on applying tender kisses and varying touches to Molly's nipples.

Soon, Reid recognizes how the disconnection from his own penis pleasure allows his own senses to be enhanced. He tastes the sweetness of Molly's skin and absorbs her floral scent, and the feminine sounds of her moans enter his ears and vibrate through his body. *I could do this all day long; this tastes better than any dessert I've had in my life. No wonder Henry said people often use food to replace the sexual experience they never knew they could have.*

He continues for a few more minutes, then Dalia caresses Reid's shoulder and pulls him to stand straight. Reid examines Molly's chest, seeing it rise and fall from the intensity of her arousal. *I've kissed nipples before, but no one ever responded this way.*

Dalia caresses his hand and places it on the skin just below Molly's belly button, where her upper pelvic bone and stomach meet. "This area is where people store the aspects of themselves they are afraid to express," says Dalia.

"The shadow-self," says Reid.

"Correct." Dalia uses her finger to draw a triangle from Molly's belly button, to the crevice where the thigh and groin connect, then across the pelvis to the opposite crevice. "Touch this area with great care. You must maintain an awareness of the human spirit that rests inside this body."

He recognizes the technique; Amber and Tasha did the same to him. Dalia places her hand on top of Reid's, then guides his palm along the triangular path, stopping to apply pressure at various points.

"This is called the Shadow Palm Technique."

Yes, finally. He recalls how stimulating it was to have it done to him.

"The Shadow Palm Technique is used to help free a person from their repression. We humans take action based on what our senses signal to our brain. If the senses are repressed or numbed, then we can be stunted in actions, limiting personal growth. This technique is a reboot for the sensory response system, waking the dormant senses with the intention of freeing the receiver from the sexual binds of the Collective Shadow. If performed correctly, she'll feel as though something inside her is being unearthed, like floodgates are becoming unlocked."

Dalia removes her hand, allowing Reid to continue on his own. Reid can't help but notice a change in Molly's body. "Her skin feels like it's getting a lot warmer."

"You are creating a great deal of blood flow towards her most erogenous sensory response zones." Dalia puts her hand on top of his again. "Remember to provide contrasts. Move your palm in small circles on each spot you touch. Change the intensity from deep pressure to soft touch to no touch." She guides Reid for a few seconds, then releases him, allowing him to continue on his own. Dalia signals to Reid to add his other hand to the mix. Molly's hips start to lift slightly and twist from side to side.

"The movement of her hips indicates pleasure. Keep going. You're waking up the erotic ghost that's sleeping within her."

As Reid continues with the Shadow Palm Technique, Molly's hips begin to twitch. Her moans echo throughout the cage. His eyes expand; he's shocked that he's the one stimulating her.

Dalia reaches towards Reid and carefully takes his hands off Molly. "Wish says you will respect the power of the Shadow Palm Technique."

"I swear I will."

"I trust that you will as well." Dalia studies Reid's eyes. "But there's an unhealed part of yourself that I worry about. I see it in your eyes — you still have wounds that you haven't healed. You must find a way to accept all experiences in your life, otherwise these skills will serve as a well-disguised form of escapism. Like placing a Band-Aid over the wound but not healing anything. Acts of escapism are acts of avoidance — of not accepting reality."

Reid nods, but internally he disagrees. *I think I've put in the work to heal my wounds. I've made peace with my father. I almost never think about Jasmine. In fact, I'm glad we aren't together anymore.*

Dalia guides Molly to rest on her hands and knees on top of the massage table, in the doggy-style position.

"When providing an erotic experience for a woman, you must change the positioning of her body. This is not intended to be kinky; the purpose is to alter the direction of blood flow and create fresh sensations. Everything you do must have a purpose for erotic sensory stimulation." Dalia presses Molly's head downward, causing her bottom to rise, exposing her rear entry and vaginal center.

"There are ten points of stimulation around the woman's vagina." Dalia extends a finger and points to each zone. She then grabs Reid's hand, and guides him through another pattern of touching, focusing on specific points around the inner thigh, lower pelvis, anus, and edges of the labia.

"You must first perform contrasting stimulations on the other nine points before touching her queen, the clitoris."

Molly coos as Dalia's hand leads Reid's fingers through a specific stroking pattern for ten minutes. This is a technique he never knew existed when he attempted to please the women in his past. Molly's hips begin to twitch again. She lifts her hand to cover her mouth, then runs the hand through her hair, gasping breathless moans.

"She's close to orgasm." Dalia lifts Reid's hand away. "Back off for now; it's not time yet."

"But isn't that the goal?"

"If you bring her to orgasm right now, it will be mediocre — like masturbation — because your masculine expression is low. You must provide something better. She needs to feel your innermost animalistic male."

Dalia guides Molly to return to lying on her back, except now with her legs slightly spread, ankles dangling off the edges of the table.

"How do I build my masculine energy?"

"For the rest of tonight, you're no longer the student. This is your cage. This is your world. And we are your women. It's time to channel the dominant man who is hidden within. Lead us."

Reid stares at the floor, his eyebrows squishing together. *Wish tells me to act from what my penis wants, and Dalia tells me to ignore what my penis wants and serve. I'm confused.*

He sees Dalia's robe fall to the floor, then feels her warm fingers lift his chin. His eyes take in every inch of her goddess figure, until their eyes meet.

"Undress me," she says.

Reid leans closer to Dalia, then backs off slightly, but keeps a proper distance to reach around her petite frame and grip her rear bra straps. His quivering hands struggle to unhook the straps. Dalia puts her hands on Reid's shoulders, then shoves him back. *Oh no. Was I too aggressive?* Before Reid can expand on the thought, Dalia slaps him across the face. Reid's head launches to the side. He rubs his stinging cheek while looking blankly at Dalia.

"Don't touch me like a scared boy," says Dalia. "You're not a child."

A sense of rage rises from his stomach into his brain. Jasmine would call him a boy to hurt him at his lowest point. She'd tease him when he couldn't fix something around the house, saying he was pathetic and she'd have to hire a real man to do the dirty work.

Reid shakes his head, then looks away from Dalia. *I'm not a boy. I'm just really confused. I'm not going to be an asshole who dominates, and I'm not going to be a kiss-ass who just serves all the time. That's what got me cheated on.*

Dalia moves close to Reid and speaks in a distinctive tone, a tone of caring femininity. "You're a man. You're a male human-animal. You have permission to behave like one. Lead us from the desire of your loin and serve us from the awareness inside your heart. Those two ingredients are the duality within masculinity."

Reid's heated mind begins to cool. Her words seep into his brain. He comes to a realization. *This might be the answer to the question I have been asking my entire life. Lead women as the dominant male that I am, while simultaneously serving women with my conscientious heart. Henry said I'm being trained to be a male Sexmyst, but more specifically, a conscious dominant. Holy shit. I think I get it now.*

Reid gazes at his feet, recalling his first night in the cage with Wish. A flood of warm masculine energy enters his toes and fills his body. His eyes return to Dalia, and he beams with an aura of confidence. Dalia dips her head slightly, as if to say, *Take me, I'm yours.* Without hesitation, he grips the back of Dalia's neck with his fingers expanded wide, ensuring she recognizes that she's a slight female captured in his large grip. He then leads her to the edge of the table where Molly's feet rest.

"Close your eyes. Then don't move anything else," Reid commands Dalia. She obeys. He sees her curved lips begin to open, a sign of arousal. He then goes to Molly's side, grabs her hips, keeping her legs wide apart, and slides her closer to Dalia. Then he bends Dalia forward and places her hands on Molly's inner thighs. He grabs a handful of hair on the back of Dalia's head and leans close to her ear. "Open your eyes and please her."

Reid holds Dalia's hair as she licks and strokes Molly's glistening slit. Within seconds, Molly's breathing becomes heavy. He releases his grip of Dalia's hair, then stands behind her with the bamboo in his hand, appearing dominant while also studying her technique. He glances at a mirror across the room, viewing the reflection of the three of them. Reid stands in awe, chest lifted, while two stunning women share an Erotic Sensory Experience in his presence.

He notices Dalia slide her hand up her own back to unhook her bra. Reid swiftly strikes her butt with the bamboo. "I'll decide when I want you naked. Ignore your needs and focus only on serving Molly."

She twists her neck, smirking at Reid with lips that are glossy with Molly's dew. "Yes, master." Reid winks. Dalia then returns to serving Molly.

Reid makes mental notes so he'll remember how Dalia uses both hands to apply pressure to the stimulation points, then follows with feathery strokes. Molly's breathing gradually shifts into panting, then her hips undulate and her extremities start to shake. Molly's panting transitions into uncontrollable cries of orgasmic pleasure.

Molly soon goes silent as she melts into a relaxed position on the table. Reid steps towards Dalia, snaps off her bra, and rips off her G-string underwear. Reid lifts Dalia onto the table, setting her into the doggy-style position with Molly remaining underneath on her back. Dalia lowers her head to kiss Molly's erect nipples. Reid then uses his fingers to stimulate Dalia's shiny entrance, mimicking what he just observed. Dalia looks back at Reid with fluttering eyes as she bites her lower lip.

Reid continues for a few moments, then steps back. *The act of no touch is just as important as touch.* Once more, he takes a gander at their reflection in the mirror. *This is so fucking sexy. How did I end up here? Things like this don't typically happen to nice guys like me.*

Reid darts his gaze to Dalia's plump rear end. He's not that nice guy anymore. This is his world and he's ready to take ownership of it. A potent force sweeps through his body. He grips Dalia by the back of her neck. "Follow me."

"Yes, master," she says, smiling in her submissive role.

He leads her to the edge of the cage near the window. He places her hands up high on the glass and spreads her legs. He kisses a trail down her backside, then kneels and swirls his tongue on the back of her knees — remembering how amazing he felt when Tasha did the same to him. He looks upward. Dalia's head is tilted back and her chest is pressing forward. *This is working beautifully, but I'm running out of ideas of what to do.*

Reid looks across the room, hoping for creative inspiration. He sees Molly, still blindfolded, resting on the table and using her fingers to pleasure herself. He leans near to Dalia's ear. "Don't move."

Reid walks over to the table, grabs Molly's glistening hand, then leads her to the window next to Dalia. He has her stand in the same position — legs apart, hands overhead and pressed against the window. Reid leaves to grab the bamboo stick, then returns.

He lightly whacks Dalia's bum, then leans towards her ear. "Touch her how you want to be touched."

Dalia removes Molly's hands from the window and leads her two steps away. She lifts Molly's hands overhead to grip an iron bar, which is fastened to the ceiling. Dalia's hands slowly move up and down Molly's breasts, rolling her nipples into tight points. Dalia then strokes the sides of Molly's hips and kisses her spine, leaving a slick trail of saliva.

Dalia's hands return to Molly's entrance. *Not so fast.* Reid reaches back with the bamboo and swiftly cracks Dalia's behind. She gasps, then inhales deeply with a slight cry. *Oh crap, was that too hard?* Dalia looks back at Reid with a devilish yet satisfied expression. *Good girl.*

"I'll tell you when you can please her there," says Reid. He smacks the bamboo on her cheek. Dalia's breasts squeeze into Molly's back as she hugs her tightly, cooing through the sting from the bamboo.

Reid steps away to note the beauty of the moment, the lights of the Las Vegas Strip serving as a backdrop for two gorgeous women sensually exploring each other. He feels another rush of masculine energy ripple through his body. *I think I'm going to love this new version of myself.*

Reid grabs the back of Dalia's neck. He has her turn and kneel, then does the same for the blindfolded Molly.

Dalia looks at Reid, her eyes dancing as she studies him. "Wish was right about you. I'm so happy he was right about you."

Reid glances back at the view of the Strip, then feels the warm touch of four hands as both women begin to caress his legs. Dalia guides the blindfolded Molly as their hands work their way up to his hardness. His heartbeat accelerates. *I'm happy Wish was right about me as well.*

The sensations come to an abrupt halt. Reid sees Dalia's hands return to her sides. *Wait, don't stop.* She pulls Molly's hands away too, then lifts her and they both stand.

"Your lesson is over. I'm impressed. The women in this world will be fortunate to have you serve them."

Dalia takes Molly's hand, then walks to the exit. She stops near the door and turns back to Reid. "I should warn you: living with this knowledge will be the greatest challenge of your life — use it to serve, not escape. Wish will be in contact with you. You may find your way out now."

Reid puts his pants on, then leans on the edge of the table to gather himself. He senses he's crossed a major threshold tonight, and he's eager to practice what he has learned. He rests for a few more seconds, then puts on the rest of his clothes, heads down in the elevator, and catches a taxi back to his hotel to sleep.

I hope Wish was okay with what I just did.

Chapter 22

Reid wakes to the sound of his phone vibrating on the nightstand. He grabs it and sees that Wish is calling. *I hope I'm not in trouble.*

"Where the hell have you been? I've been calling all day," says Wish.

Reid sits up. "I've been in my room at the Lexi Hotel. I just woke up. What time is it?"

"It's half past three in the afternoon," says Wish. "We got arrested after leaving Cherry's suite this morning."

"What? Really? How? What happened?"

"We'll discuss it in person — can't trust our phones anymore. In an hour, meet me at the place where I first met Goddess Mindy. You remember, right?"

Reid thinks back to Mindy's story of how they met at the UNLV library. "Yes, I remember."

The call ends. Reid hurries to get ready for the day. Flashbacks of his experience with Dalia and Molly play through his mind. He tastes the sweetness of Molly's skin on his lips, and feels the softness of Dalia's skin on his fingertips. But his erotic memories also heighten his fear about how Wish might react.

Reid catches a taxi over to the UNLV campus. He examines the campus map and locates the library. He checks the clock on his phone; he has fifteen minutes before the scheduled meeting. He strolls through the campus, enjoying the clean air, feeling a sense of peace. There is something comforting about being back in this environment. The sight of students hustling around with heavy backpacks and eyes looking down at their phones reminds him of the other world that occupies most of his time.

He yearns for the safety of that world, but then grins, enjoying the taboo, as more flashes of his erotic experience with Dalia and Molly pulse through his mind. He can't deny that it felt so right to take charge. He reflects on the countless women he's walked past in Las Vegas, many of whom he never thought he'd have a chance of attracting; the hot bartenders, bikini blackjack dealers, bachelorette parties, strippers, and go-go dancers. Reid finds himself walking light-footed, filled with a sense of excitement for the future. He's finally been trained to know what to do with women — and he has the courage to do it.

As Reid proceeds to the library, his thoughts shift from reflecting on his own growth to future plans, service-oriented plans. *I'm a college professor, but I'm also a man who'll provide Erotic Sensory Experiences for research and to promote personal growth. The ultimate plan is to share my discoveries worldwide with the hope of saving a world that doesn't yet understand the depth of its suffering.* He stops just before the library and studies the energy of the campus that surrounds him. *I'll always be a professor. But soon my class size is going to be significantly bigger.*

Reid enters the library and meanders towards the back. His muscles are tense. Though Wish didn't seem disgruntled on the phone, Reid still fears what may come of Wish knowing about Dalia and himself. He arrives to find Wish sitting at a table with a young male student. Reid nods at Wish, then stands silently as his mentor tutors the young man. Wish appears to be pointing at a specific section in a textbook.

"The most important takeaway from this chapter is that the brain is a computer, and you must understand key components of its operating system and then program it to work in your favor. If the most you've challenged yourself is a three out of ten, then the most joy or pleasure your brain is capable of feeling is a three out of ten. Therefore, happiness comes from constantly increasing the challenges and conquering them. Experience a ten-out-of-ten challenge, so your brain will expand to be able to experience ten-out-of-ten pleasure. Make sense?"

The young man nods. He then packs up his book, shakes Wish's hand, and walks away.

Reid sits across the table from Wish. "Did you know him?"

"No, we just met. I walked by him and saw that he was studying a shitty psychological neuroscience textbook. I couldn't resist the chat."

Once again, you've redefined "pimp." Reid sits up in his chair. "So what happened with Youngblood?"

"He was the one following us when we were in the limo. He waited in the casino lobby and pinched me and the girls when we were leaving the hotel. He cuffed us on the spot, took us to the station, and made up a story about how he saw me soliciting hotel patrons with the girls. Obviously, it's not true, because we all went straight up to the suite, then through the lobby to the exit. Max, the driver, reached out to a friend at the casino, who sent the surveillance video to the police station, and we were released in a few hours."

"Youngblood seems slimy."

"I think last night was just an act on his part. He needed to bust us to get the names of last night's Sexmysts. I'm sensing Youngblood actually wants us out there working so he can build enough evidence for a big bust that will lead to his promotion."

Reid nods. "Your friend, Detective Jones, did a number on me yesterday."

"He called me this morning, said you handled yourself well. Jones also mentioned that Youngblood's actions last night got him suspended for four weeks — making a false arrest."

"Really? No way," says Reid. "That's a good thing, right?"

"Yes, Jones and I agreed we're both going to retire four weeks from now. That way we avoid any more Youngblood garbage. Youngblood being suspended allows me and the Sexmysts some freedom to work extra-hard without looking over our shoulders. This means you will be busy handling any casino chips that accumulate over the next four weeks."

"Makes sense," says Reid. He taps his finger on the table, and his mind flashes to his experience with Dalia and Molly. He debates whether he should initiate a conversation about that experience. His tapping shifts into him pressing two fingers firmly on the table, mimicking a pressure-point massage technique.

Wish notices, leans back, and smiles. "Dalia said you passed her tests last night. You don't need to tell me what she did to you. She said you're trained and ready, and that's all I need to know."

Reid drops his hands to his sides, sighing with relief.

Wish slides a cell phone across the table. "You and I will communicate through prepaid phones. They aren't traceable and they expire in four weeks. I don't know the full extent of what Youngblood's capable of, but it's best we proceed with caution."

Reid examines the prepaid phone. "Women are going to love seeing me use this old-school phone. It doesn't even have apps for social media."

"The phone will do the job for now." Wish leans back. "Each night, your job will be to check in at the Adult Megastore around eight o'clock. Goddess Mindy will have a package for you with instructions for that evening. The instructions will include the casino chips to exchange, and an assignment to provide an ESE. Each night when you arrive, bring the cash from the previous evening to Goddess Mindy. Understand?"

"Yes. What will the ESE assignments entail?"

"Most assignments will involve finding a specific type of woman who is seeking the Erotic Sensory Experience that you now know how to offer. But remember, you're not allowed to bring women back to your room at the Lexi Hotel, and the women must only know minimal information about you. When you find a date, text Andrew, and he'll have a room ready for you at the Largo Hotel. Once you've provided the sensory experience, wait for the woman to fall asleep, then leave."

"But what if I want to see her again?"

"You'll be experiencing plenty of women in your life. I can't have you falling in love during the next four weeks. It's important that you care about the women, but you must maintain your boundaries and understand that this is your research. Through experiences, you'll be learning about to provide ESE's for a variety of women, because they are each wired in a unique way. Women have varying sensory response systems, sexual preferences, and personalities. This is the most crucial stage in becoming a Sexmyst. You must remain focused on serving, making sure the experience guides the woman into understanding a part of herself she didn't know existed."

Wish reaches into his pocket and hands Reid a stack of chips.

"These are from Harrah's — four thousand. I need you to cash these out tonight. For each stack that I give you, I expect four hundred less than the stack to be returned in cash. So out of the four grand, I expect thirty-six hundred. You keep the difference based on whether you win or lose at blackjack. Play fifty-dollar hands conservatively, and you'll often leave with a few extra hundred bucks."

"Are you sure I won't get in trouble for exchanging these chips?"

"Your face is new; they won't suspect you. The exchanges will occur in different casinos each night, so you don't become familiar to casino staff."

"What do I do about clothes? My suit stinks from last night."

"There are two new suits being delivered to your room as we speak." Wish leans in. "Tonight will be your first assignment as an entry-level Sexmyst."

Reid smiles, eager to hear more, but a hesitant thought arises. "Wait, does being a Sexmyst mean I charge for the experience?"

"No, you're not a gigolo." Wish looks around the library, then at Reid. "The experiences you provide for women will be free. You are conducting research on the power of tactile experiences, while simultaneously serving others. Never lose sight of that. Your purpose is to build upon the knowledge that I've shared with you, furthering the research with the hope of us succeeding in our mission. Once you feel that you fully understand what it means to be a Sexmyst, then it will be time for you to get that knowledge out into the world."

"I look forward to helping many people, just as you have helped me."

"I know you will," says Wish. "Your assignment tonight will be to provide an Erotic Sensory Experience for a woman you meet on your own. This town is filled with women, but you must be able to spot the one who's seeking what you offer. Unfortunately, many women don't believe that men like us exist."

"Is there something specific I should be looking for? How will I spot one?"

"Over time, you'll be able to spot the women who are seeking an experience quite easily. But you're correct, your radar for spotting a seeker isn't developed just yet. That's why your mission for tonight is to find a bachelorette party and provide an experience for one of the women in the group."

Reid feels a tightness in his throat as he reflects on how Jasmine visited Las Vegas for her friend's bachelorette party the week prior to him catching her cheating. He explains the bachelorette story to Wish.

"When Jasmine got home, she talked about how all of the girls took advantage of every man they could. She said they even got a guy to pay for their hotel rooms. She said the group referred to the men as 'toys' all weekend."

Wish leans back in his chair and folds his arms. His relaxed expression shifts into a look of concern. "You know I hate hearing stories of abuse. And what you just shared is no different. Granted, it's on the males for letting that shit happen. Not all, but many bachelorette parties are little cluster-fucks of repressed shadows, creating a mini Collective Shadow for that weekend, each participant agreeing to repress her sexual desires while abusing men. It's like a way to initiate the bride into her Collective-Shadow-based marriage, where the husband is addicted to porn and she's addicted to food. She'll wonder why he struggles to get an erection and he'll wonder why she's gained weight."

"That seems to be what marriage is for most people. I used to want marriage, but now it doesn't feel right." Reid glances down at his ring finger. *Thank God I never married Jasmine.*

"For some, marriage can be a wonderful thing. But the truth is, modern marriage, especially in America, is vastly different from how and why it was originally created. Research conducted by evolutionary psychologists and anthropologists has led to a new understanding of the origins and original purpose of marriage."

"How so?"

"Back in the early times of humanity, everybody was fucking everybody. Villages had a bunch of kids running all over the place, but struggled to identify which child belonged to which father. So, the concept of marriage was created, with those first marriages being arranged. Two people were paired together, had children, and made an agreement to raise those children. But rarely did those people love each other; they were more like friends. True love often occurred through infidelity, when the husband or wife found desirable sexual partners outside of the marriage. It was acceptable for the arranged couple to be involved with outside partners, as long as they stuck to the goal of raising the children."

"So, the creation of a marital agreement was purely in order to make a structured environment in which to raise children, not because of love?"

"Precisely. The arranged couple may have loved each other, but they were able to handle infidelity because the children were always the main focus. There are tribal communities and long-established cultures that still follow the original intention of marriage. To them, it's considered normal for a husband and wife to have additional lovers on the side. I'm not saying every person should view marriage like this, but at least there is now academic research to support that not everyone is wired for monogamy."

"I had heard about cultures like that existing. It wasn't something that I could wrap my head around, but hearing your explanation about marriage being mostly about the children, it makes sense." Reid looks at Wish's wedding ring. "So how would you describe your marriage? What do you and Dalia do for fun?"

"We fuck other people." Reid's jaw drops. Wish smirks. "I'm kidding. That's a small part of it. We actually do normal couple things, like go to the movies or hike. However, we also have a clear understanding of our sexuality. Neither of us thought we'd be with someone who understands how we're wired, but it works for us."

"Why are you married then? I haven't noticed any children."

Wish leans back in his chair, appearing hesitant to speak. He huffs a short breath, then leans forward. "We have a teenage son."

Reid smiles at his mentor. He can sense that sharing this information is not something Wish does often.

"My boy's name is Juel, and from what I have heard, he's a helluva basketball player." Wish's face glows like a proud father's, then his expression switches to a look of concern. "He lives with Dalia's mother in Miami. We raised him here until he was ten, but then we had to make the difficult decision to let him grow up in Miami. It wouldn't have been right to have him grow up around our business. Plus, raising

Juel here would have taken us away from the mission and the research. It was the hardest decision of our lives."

Wish's eyes begin to water. He lifts his head upward to prevent the tears from coming out. "I just hope —" He looks at Reid. "I just hope he'll accept us and understand why we had to make that decision."

Reid leans forward, nodding empathetically while piecing the information together. *Wish's mission is focused on saving the next young generation on our planet. He always talks about the ten-year-old, technology-addicted boys and the dangerous society they will be living in. The mission is not only about saving society; it's about protecting Juel.*

"You're an amazing father," says Reid. "Your decision came from wanting to protect your next of kin, not escapism. I have no doubt that Juel will come to accept the decision that you and Dalia had to make." Reid shifts his voice to a playful tone. "C'mon, man, you're the master of teaching acceptance. That's all you've been preaching to me this whole damn time."

Wish wipes his eyes and straightens himself. "Give me your word you won't share that with anyone. The only other person in our circle who knows about Juel is Henry. We clear?"

"Yes, sir," says Reid. "So my mission tonight is to fuck an entire bachelorette party?"

"Smartass." Wish rolls his eyes. "You are to provide an experience for one woman. I want you to focus on a bachelorette party because your ideal woman in that group will be easier to spot. These groups usually consist of the bride, six of her best friends from childhood, and one or two co-workers. The friends from childhood feel too much social pressure from each other to leave the group and have an experience with a man. They remain committed to the group's collective repression. But the co-workers are usually annoyed and eager to separate from the group. They don't give a rat's ass about judgment from the rest of the party, because they'll never see the bride's friends again."

"It will be fun for that co-worker to have a steamy story to share with the bride when they return to work on Monday."

The fatherly glow returns to Wish's face. "Look at you. You're speaking the erotic lines you'll need to be saying to her during phase one — foreplay."

"I've noticed there's a theme when interacting with women. Things typically go well as long as I'm honest, playful, masculine, and comfortable expressing sexual desire. Sean Connery's James Bond was a master of that."

"You're correct. Henry taught me the same thing, years ago. He'd say, 'People don't pay attention to what you say, as much as they pay attention to how comfortable you are expressing yourself. If you're comfortable, then she will be too.'"

"Henry was your teacher?"

"Yes," says Wish quickly. He rises from his chair. "I've got to get going. Just to be safe, wait five minutes, then leave. Have fun tonight, but stay focused on the assignment. Remember to take the cash to Goddess Mindy tomorrow."

"I will." Reid watches Wish walk away. He wonders what it must have been like for Henry to mentor a younger Wish, and why Wish is so guarded about discussing his past.

He waits for five minutes, then takes a cab back to his hotel and settles in his room for a nap, eager to be rested for the ESE he aims to provide later tonight.

Chapter 23

His new suits are exactly the same as the one he already owns. Reid grins slyly as he slides the jacket over his white dress shirt. *Superheroes wear the same outfit every night too.* He adjusts the jacket, then speaks confidently to himself in the mirror.

"Your mission, should you accept it, is to rescue a damsel in distress from the ridiculousness of a bachelorette party. Provide her with an Erotic Sensory Experience that leaves her with a better understanding of herself, which will ultimately improve her life."

Reid exits, excited about what the night has in store for him. He arrives at the Harrah's Casino, plays blackjack for thirty minutes, and leaves with thirty-six hundred in cash for Wish and an extra two hundred for himself. With added pep in his stride, he heads to the Largo Hotel, itching with excitement as he walks into the vibrant nightlife scene at the Diamond Bar.

"Hey, Professor, great to see you. What-a-ya have?" says Ronald, the bartender.

"Mescal. Chilled," says Reid.

"Coming right up." Ronald whips up a drink and slides it in front of Reid.

Reid holds the drink up to honor Ronald. "Thanks. Our mutual friend has changed my life for the better."

Ronald bows his head, then steps away to serve a customer. Reid turns around slowly, intending to assess the scene, but is intercepted by a girl in a black dress.

"Hi, I'm Cheryl. I'm with that bachelorette party over there." Cheryl points at a booth full of eight women dressed in black and a bride wearing white.

Reid expresses a courteous smile, while feeling surprised at how quickly he's come into contact with a bachelorette party. "Nice to meet you, Cheryl."

"We have a list of tasks to check off before our night is over. The girls sent me to you hoping you could help us check something off the list."

He sips his mescal, then gazes at her. "What task are you hoping to complete?"

Although she is friendly, something about her forwardness reminds him of the non-genuine strippers who just wanted money.

"We need to get a hot guy to buy shots for all of us, then have the bride drink her shot off the hot guy's belly."

Reid instantly feels the discomfort of a potential boundary violation; the abuse Wish warned him about. He glances at the party. "Is that so?" With narrowed eyes, he observes them laughing while sloppily leaning on each other. They're louder than any other group at the bar.

"Come introduce yourself to the girls. You're the hot guy we all chose." Cheryl grabs Reid's forearm, turns towards her friends, and tugs for him to follow.

Reid's body fills with a filthy sensation, reminding him of the years of mistreatment he's tolerated from women. *No way I'm doing that again.* Reid pulls his tugged arm back towards his body, yanking Cheryl's light frame back to him. He grins as she furrows her brow and glares at him.

He calmly takes another sip of mescal, then peels her fingers off his forearm. "I'm going to have to politely decline your offer, Cheryl."

"Why? Do you have a girlfriend or something? All those women want to have some fun with you."

Reid curls his lips into a friendly half-smile, knowing he's keeping his self-esteem intact by committing to his boundary. "I'm sure they're amazing women. But I'll have to respectfully decline your offer."

"You're an asshole," says Cheryl. She stomps back to her group.

Reid rotates to face the bar, savoring the taste of the smoky mescal. He snickers quietly, knowing his old self would have done anything for those women's approval. *Being called an asshole didn't even sting. It actually felt good. Nicely done, man. Wish would be proud.*

Ronald returns. "What'd that girl want?"

"She wanted me to buy a bunch of shots for that bachelorette party in the booth behind me. There are nine girls over there."

Ronald looks beyond Reid. "They seem to have found a sucker. You're off the hook, man."

Reid twists his neck to re-examine the group. A man in a suit is chatting with the girls. The bride puts her necklace of small penises around the man's neck. The friends whip out their phones and snap a few pictures of the guy. The man rises and walks towards the bar, still wearing the penis necklace. Reid spins back to face Ronald and rolls his eyes.

The man in the suit steps up to the bar. "Ten shots of tequila, fine sir."

"Any choice of tequila?" says Ronald as he sets ten shot glasses on a tray.

"Top shelf. Money is not an issue. Gotta look good in front of the ladies; can't be cheap."

Reid turns his head away, struggling to keep a straight face, but then wonders if he should offer this guy some guidance — just as Wish did for him in this exact seat.

The man continues: "I'm sure I'll bang one of them tonight."

Reid's face goes warm; he's angry that this pathetic man is part of the male gender. However, he realizes that a man who is seeking to use a woman is also a perfect target for a woman who is seeking to use a man.

"The girl on the far right is smoking hot," says the man. "She's a co-worker of the bride's."

The information catches Reid's attention. *Hmm, the co-worker?* He watches Ronald finish pouring the ten shots, scoffing internally as he hears Ronald charge the man two hundred and fifty dollars. The man drops three large bills and carries the tray towards the bachelorette party. *Glad I stood by my boundary. The shots would have sucked up all my winnings and then some.*

Reid watches the girls celebrate as the shots are handed to them. He fixates his gaze on the woman identified as the co-worker. She's the most attractive in the group. She's sitting on the far-right side of the booth and appears bored with the festivities. Recalling Wish's guidance, Reid wonders if she's looking for something more stimulating.

As Reid observes, the man slides next to the co-worker and they exchange a few words. He hopes she's wise enough to sniff out the man's poor intentions. Before their conversation can go any further, the man is pulled onto the table by Cheryl and the other women. Cheryl lifts his tucked shirt, then unbuttons it to expose his stomach. One of the girls drips a bit of tequila onto the man's belly. The women all cheer as the bride sucks the liquor off him. Reid sees the co-worker roll her eyes and walk off in the direction of the restrooms, located in the casino, just outside the bar.

It's now or never. Time to make the move.

Reid turns back to Ronald. "That girl in red deserves better."

"Looks like she went to the restroom," says Ronald.

"Yup. And that's where I need to go too."

"You're gonna bathroom-stalk her? Good luck."

Will this be considered stalker behavior? Reid finishes his drink and heads into the casino. *As long as I'm comfortable with the situation, she will be too.* He stands in the hallway near the entrance of the women's bathroom, appearing as someone who is just waiting for his wife or girlfriend.

Reid's mind fills with doubts. *What the hell am I going to say? I'm standing here like a god-damned creep.* He takes a deep breath. *You're different now. Remember, Henry said a woman calls a man creepy when she senses he's not being authentic about his intentions. What are my intentions here? I want to know if she's seeking what I now know how to offer. Right?*

The restroom door opens and the co-worker steps into the hallway. Reid's body stiffens, and his brain signals to him to stay silent, safe. But deep down he knows that's just a safety mechanism he's got to force himself through.

His toes are shaking, but he steps into her path, pauses, then speaks. "I ... I have to say hi to you or else I'll be kicking myself all night long." Reid braces himself for rejection, then feels a cooling sensation roll through his body. *At least I said something. The hard part is over.*

"Were you waiting here for me?"

"Yes. I was being extra-creepy. This is the most uncomfortable I've ever felt in my life. But I'd rather be uncomfortable for a few seconds than wonder for the rest of my life what could have been."

Her mouth forms into a friendly smile.

Reid continues: "I noticed you with that bachelorette party and figured this would be the only chance I had to talk when you'd be away from that group."

"I actually think it's sexy that you had the balls to do that. Most of these men just try to buy me drinks. My name is Candace."

Reid introduces himself. "Let's go sit at a different casino bar. I promise I won't buy you a drink."

"I don't think I can leave my group," says Candace. She lowers her head. "Ugh, but those girls are so annoying. They grew up with the bride. I'm just a friend from her work. Trust me, I'd love to leave them. But the bride would be so pissed."

"I promise that the bride won't be pissed when you two are back at work on Monday."

"What makes you so sure?"

"Imagine the two of you sitting there, bored from reviewing a predictable bachelorette party weekend. But then you reveal your secret adventure from tonight."

"Secret adventure?" She moistens her lips. "I like how you think."

"There's something about you. I feel the urge to know more," says Reid. "I'm going to sit at the casino bar near the craps tables for fifteen minutes. I trust you can find a way to meet me there."

"I'll see what I can do." Candace squeezes his palms, then releases him and leaves, walking in the direction of the Diamond Bar.

A flood of elation pulses through Reid's body. He's aware that she may not return, but the way she squeezed his hand suggests that he'd better get a room from Andrew, just in case. Regardless, he knows this experience has increased his confidence because he walked through his fear. He slides his newly acquired phone out of his pocket. He takes notice of the time and starts the fifteen-minute timer in his head, then types a text to Andrew.

Wish said to contact you if I need a room at the Largo. There's a chance I'll need a room in a bit. I'll let you know. Might be

meeting a woman at the casino bar near the craps tables.

Andrew responds: **Just saw your "bathroom move" through the eye in the sky. Well done, compadre.**

Reid glances at the ceiling; it's littered with security cameras. He stares into the nearest camera and smirks while subtly waving his hand. *Looks like I have an audience now. Henry loved having an audience. He'd say it makes conquering fears even more worthwhile.*

Reid struts to the bar near the craps tables. He slides onto a tall chair, orders a beer, and sips it for several minutes. He glances at his cell phone clock: six minutes remain. Reid swigs more beer, nervous about how he'll handle things if she does show. He can't tell her he's been training to provide possibly the greatest sexual experience of her life — that would kill the mysteriousness and come off as insecure.

He finishes his beer and nods to the bartender while pointing at the empty bottle. The bartender switches in a new beer and Reid takes a long sip. *Hold on, cowboy. Don't wanna get sloppy for Candace. Remember, you're a man of service.* He sets the bottle back on the bar, closes his eyes, and breathes through his anxiety.

He reflects on Cherry's words: *"A man is one of two things: he's a manipulator or a man of service. Manipulators run out of people to manipulate, but men of service never run out of people to serve."*

Reid reopens his eyes, feeling a sense of peace with whatever outcome may occur from the experience. If it doesn't work out, he knows there are plenty of other women he can seek to serve tonight.

A small hand caresses his shoulder. He turns to see the freshly dolled-up face of Candace. His heart races with excitement as he pulls her in for a hug. He reminds himself to remain in charge, to lead her while remaining conscious of creating a valuable experience.

"Looks like I made it in time," says Candace. She sits on the high chair next to Reid.

Reid looks at his cell phone clock. "You had one minute left." He reaches for her chair and pulls it closer. "Why are you sitting so far away from me?" She releases a high-pitched feminine yelp — his favorite sound on earth.

She orders a drink, mentions that she's from Dallas, and explains her job to Reid. "I do billing in a medical office. It's not the most exciting job, but at least it's a steady income."

"What's been your favorite experience so far this summer?" asks Reid.

"To be honest, it hasn't been that great of a summer. I broke up with my boyfriend a few weeks back. He was awful. We were together for two years, and I should have ended things after the first month."

Reid tilts his head back, not expecting that kind of answer. But he knows he'll find such conversation interesting. "How was he awful?"

"He was jealous and controlling. He'd always look at my phone and would freak out over the smallest issues."

A knot forms in his belly. *Another asshole male who has no clue.* Reid stares at his beer, half-smiling at the irony as he recognizes that he's starting to see the world like Wish — feeling disgruntled when he hears about men treating women so poorly. He reminds himself that he was once a clueless man as well, and that his part of the mission will be to help guide men like her ex to be better partners.

"I'm sorry," says Candace. Her head remains tilted down. "Probably not the best topic for sexy bar banter."

Reid lifts her chin so their eyes can meet. "I find you-being-you fascinating. Thank you for feeling comfortable enough to share this with me. Please continue."

He catches her gaze; she appears mesmerized by his words. He touches her forearm to break her trance.

Candace continues: "He told me that he wanted to keep taking me out to dinner to get me fat so other men wouldn't be attracted to me. I finally realized he was crazy and broke up with him that moment."

Reid's senses his anger increasing. *Calm down. This is about her. You two met for a reason. Be the man of service.* He takes a calming breath.

"On behalf of the male gender, I apologize." He places his hand on her thigh. Candace slides her palm on top of his — a sign that she's open to further touching. He leans closer to her. "Soon, men will learn to be better. I promise."

"Oh really? How so?"

"It wouldn't be appropriate for me to go into great detail about that right now." Reid moves his hand on her thigh, knowing he has to activate her senses. "All I know is that I admire the courage you had to walk away from a bad situation. Because that's exactly what needed to happen for this moment to occur."

He squeezes her thigh, then slowly releases it while studying her expression to gauge her sensory response system. *Can she handle deep pressure into the muscle?*

Candace bites her lower lip, then smiles. *Yes, she can.*

"There's something I have been dying to try," says Reid. "It involves touching you. Nothing creepy, I promise."

"I've already noticed something different about your touch. Please, feel free."

Reid lifts his hand from her thigh, then grips her wrist and turns it so her palm is upward. He then uses both of his thumbs to massage the connecting point between her wrist and palm.

"My God, that feels amazing," says Candace.

"Just for a few minutes, shut off your thoughts and focus on receiving my touch." Reid continues to massage her hand, wrist, and forearm. "You've impressed me with your openness and femininity. Forgive me, but I yearn to help you relax."

Candace smiles and tilts her head back slightly.

Reid recalls the various contrasts of touch that Dalia emphasized, and slides his fingers up her arm, applying pressure-point stimulation to her forearm, bicep, and the back of her shoulder.

Candace then rolls her neck forward. "I want you to do this all over my body."

I gotta get that room key from Andrew. Reid stands, steps to be behind her, then uses both hands to massage her neck and shoulders.

He takes a hand off Candace and reaches into his pocket to fetch his phone to text Andrew. Before he can fish the phone out, he feels a tap on his shoulder. He turns and sees Andrew. He keeps one hand actively massaging Candace's neck, ensuring her head remains down so she's unable to notice Andrew.

Andrew hands Reid a plastic key-card and whispers in his ear: "Room ten-forty-one, and hidden under the bathroom sink is a gift from Wish."

Reid nods to say thank you. As Andrew walks away, he wonders

233

what the gift is; perhaps condoms or an erotic item? Sensing it's time to lead Candace to the room, he grips the back of her neck and carefully twists so she faces him. Her look is one of appreciation and awe, different from the women of his past. In this moment, he realizes he's no longer wired to beg for approval. He's in control — not seeking to give flowers or gifts, but instead giving the gifts of his masculine essence and his understanding of her body, all while being honored to serve. He notices her lips begin to separate.

"Your lips look like a gift that should be treasured," says Reid. He leans forward, gently resting his lips on hers, moving into a tender kiss.

Reid carefully pulls his lips away; her eyes are glistening. "Follow me." He grips her hand and leads her to the bank of elevators.

"Where are we going?" she asks as they enter the elevator.

Reid answers her question by kissing her softly as the elevator flies up the shaft. The ping of the doors opening pauses their lip-locked passion. He then leads her, arm in arm, to the room located a few steps from the elevator.

While walking, he recalls the rules for being serviced by a Sexmyst, and expresses them to Candace. "Once we enter this room, you are only to focus on yourself. No thoughts of pleasing me or wondering if I'll be impressed by your sexual expression. I want you to focus on you, paying attention to the sensations your body feels."

Candace grins, then puckers her lips. Reid kisses her once more. Then leans back to gaze at her. He sees her blinking eyes settle into a submissive stare. He grins, then slides the key into the electric lock, opens the door, and they enter.

The room is a standard Las Vegas hotel-sized room with a king bed in the center. He walks towards the window, leading Candace by the hand.

"The view is amazing," says Candace. "You can see the entire Strip."

Reid stands behind Candace and kisses her cheek. "Enjoy the view. I'll be right back." *Gotta find that gift box.*

Reid goes to the front door and clicks off the master light switch, leaving the space to be lit by the dim glow of the Las Vegas Strip. He steps into the bathroom and grabs the gift box from under the sink. A small note is attached.

Her mind will dance all over the place. Provide the experience with patience. The greatest challenge for your generation is to relax and simply feel. Remind her to focus on feeling the experience moment to moment. The item in this box will serve to block one of her senses, which will enhance the others. Serve her as best as you can. You have proven to us that you understand the human body and the importance of erotic tactile interaction. Relax, have fun, and trust your creative expression. She is your blank canvas, go paint a masterpiece. — Wish

Reid slowly opens the box, fearing it may contain a butt plug or an electrical shock unit. He moves the tissues away, and feels slight relief when he sees it only contains a blindfold. *Okay. I can handle this. I hope Candace doesn't freak out. Molly was blindfolded. I've been around this before. As long as I'm comfortable, Candace will be comfortable.* Reid straightens his posture, slides the blindfold into his rear pocket, and returns to the bedroom, seeing Candace in the same position.

"This town never ceases to amaze me," says Candace. "So many giant hotels. It's like one big fantasy land."

"I agree. Vegas is a land of fantasies." *I hope to be able to fulfill yours.* He lifts her hands over her head and presses her palms on the window. "Take in as much of the view as you can."

"Your hands are so much bigger than mine," she says.

"I like that you observe the differences between you as the female and me as the male." His hands slither down her forearms to her shoulders. "Do not remove your hands from the window until I say."

"I love how take-charge you are." Candace lowers her head. "Why does your touch feel different to that of any man I've been around?"

He chooses to remain silent, appreciating the softness of her skin, while simultaneously focusing on the layers of sensory transmitters below her skin. Her body begins to sway slightly, then she drops her chest a few inches to press her bum into his groin. Reid steps back, knowing it's not time for her core to be actively stimulated just yet.

He reaches into his pocket and pulls out the blindfold. "One last view of the Strip. Take it all in."

"Why do you say that? Are you kicking me out?" she says. He

extends his arm around her, dangling the blindfold in front of her face. "Oh my, you are a kinky one. I knew something was different about you."

He laughs internally, recalling a statement Wish made. *This ain't kinky. It's neuroscience.*

He slides the blindfold over her eyes. "Blocking your vision will enhance your other four senses." He presses his lips against her cheek, feeling the edge of her lip curl upward. He pulls back, connecting to the dominant energy that vibrates through his core. He also remains aware that they've just met and she may also be a bit scared. He chuckles to himself, recognizing that his thought pattern is in line with conscious dominance. He grips the back of her hair and speaks softly. "Tell me to stop if it goes too far for you. Your safety and comfort are most important to me. Understood?"

Candace nods. He touches her skin carefully, allowing his thoughts to sync with his sensual actions, ensuring she feels his care. *I'm honored to serve you. I find you fascinating. Your courage, your femininity, your delicious scent, your thirst for adventure.* He slides the zipper of her dress down slowly, then peels it off her hourglass-shaped frame. *Her body is perfect, my goodness.* She keeps her hands on the window, breathing deeply, then presses her bum back into his core.

He grips her waist and gently pushes it forward. "We'll get there eventually. Your body has so many areas I'd like to explore first."

"I'm not going to stop you doing anything," Candace releases a soft moan. "This feels amazing."

He continues to dance his fingers across her body, changing the intensity of his touch, adding in scratches and kisses. His palm brushes across her breasts, and he feels her nipples tighten at his playful stroke. His hand rests on the skin over her heart, and he notices her accelerated pulse. *Perfect.*

"We haven't even fucked and this is the deepest pleasure I've ever felt in my life," she says.

I'm honored to teach you about your unknown self. Reid turns her to face him. He carefully glides his lips across hers, drawing them in for a sensual kiss. He squeezes her cool bum cheeks, lifts her naked body, and lays her across the bed — face up, head resting near the side edge.

"What I'm about to do may feel different, but I promise it's with the intention of serving you." Reid draws his fingernail across her chest, seeing her grin with teeth clenched. He removes all of his clothes and stands where her head rests. He moves his hands across her chest, around her breasts, then down towards her pelvis to perform the Shadow Palm Technique.

"Oh my God. Amazing." Her hips lift. "How are you so good at doing this? Oh my God. Oh my God. Oh. Ohhh. You are gonna make me…"

He continues the Shadow Palm Technique. He adds in slight touches around the lips of her fold, with his fingers dancing around the area but not inserting. Candace's moan shifts into several elated, orgasmic gasps. He feels her core muscles tighten as she jerks her hips from side to side. Her high-pitched moans settle into choppy breaths — shocked with hits of post-orgasm sparks. Soon, her lifted hips fall to a relaxed position.

He steps away from her and studies her satisfied expression. He runs his hand through his hair, feeling awe and slight disbelief. *I can't believe I just did that.* He scans the curves of the blindfolded beauty who rests before him for a few more seconds. *The foreplay phase was downstairs. I just finished the coreplay stage, focusing on stimulating her external body. And now she's primed to feel joy from the internal body.* He digs in his pants for a condom, tears the wrapper open, and slides it into place. He takes the blindfold off Candace, enjoying the sight of her eyes dancing as they adjust to being freed from the blindfold.

"You are so fucking beautiful." Reid climbs on top of her into the missionary position. He locks his eyes onto hers, then slips his member inside her warm opening, hearing her breathy moan. He thrusts slowly, feeling her dew surround his hardness. He places her in various positions throughout the room, as Dalia taught him, not to be kinky, but to channel blood flow in different directions and activate additional sensory centers within the body. Eventually, Reid brings her to her bliss twice, then experiences his own release.

He cleans himself in the bathroom, then returns to the bed. They relax in each other's arms while lying naked on top of the duvet.

"I've never been touched like that before. How did you learn do that?" Candace draws her index finger across Reid's chest.

"It's a long story," says Reid. He chooses not to share his relationship with Wish. However, he does explain the value of providing Erotic Sensory Experiences for a partner and the power of contrasts.

"Amazing," she says. "How come nobody knows about this stuff? It should be taught in school. I've learned so much from you, Professor. Will I be seeing you again? I have a feeling this will be it."

Reid feels lifted from the admiration. He could see himself spending time with her and possibly taking things further, but his heart remains connected to the mission. "I'd love to be able to spend more time with you, but I'm committed to a special project this summer that allows me very minimal free time. And I don't know that I'll be able to visit Dallas anytime soon."

"I understand. Well, maybe our paths will cross again in the future. Thank you for educating me about my body, Professor. I'll be sure to try the techniques on the next man I'm with."

"Please, spread the word, or I should say, spread the experience."

They rise from the bed. Candace dresses and Reid does the same. He smiles, knowing growth occurred from the experience, and perhaps Candace will recognize how to avoid the low-quality males like her ex-boyfriend. They engage in one last passionate kiss. Reid opens the door and Candace steps into the hallway, then turns back to him.

"There is no need to walk me down. I'm staying one floor below." She takes one last look at him. "You were right, I will have a steamy story to tell the bride at work on Monday."

Reid winks, then quietly shuts the door. He walks to the window, then stares at the Strip. He smiles as he feels connected to a sense of certainty, a sense of finally being comfortable in his own skin.

He slides his phone out of his pocket and types a text to Wish. **Mission accomplished.**

A few moments pass, then he receives a response from Wish: **Well done. Andrew said you performed quite well. Your routine will be as follows: take Sunday through Wednesday off to get away from the intensity of this research (trust me, I made the mistake of not taking enough nights off in my past; rest is important). During**

that time, remain committed to working on your fitness and mental health. Connect with Goddess Mindy on Thursday, Friday, and Saturday nights for your assignments.

Reid responds: **Understood.**

Reid stuffs the blindfold into his back pocket and exits the room. He's walking down the hallway when he suddenly halts. All of the excitement with Candace has distracted him from his job for Wish — the cash. He quickly pats his pockets, then sighs as he feels the envelope stuffed in the inner lining of the jacket. He hurries out of the Largo and takes a cab back to the Lexi Hotel. He enters his room and stuffs the $3,600 in the safe. *Tomorrow is Sunday. Damn, I've gotta wait four days until I get to experience this again? No way. I'm sure Wish won't mind if I put in more work on the research.*

Chapter 24

Although Wish told Reid to lie low until his next assignment on Thursday, he can't help but continue his skill development and research on Sunday, Monday, Tuesday, and Wednesday nights. Each day becomes routine for Reid, as if he's at a sexual summer camp. He wakes up around noon, eats a healthy meal, then works out with Andrew. Then he returns to his room and dives into various books that cover erotic massage, dominant/submissive play, body language, and the science of touching. Each night he practices what he's read when providing an Erotic Sensory Experience for a tourist. At times, he feels fatigue from information overload and going out each night, and recognizes the value in Wish's warning to have nights off. But the warning is easy to look past once he feels the rush from providing an ESE. He loves seeing a woman's eyes roll back mid-orgasm, then melt with post-coital gratitude as they lie in the sheets of a Largo Hotel room.

Come Thursday, Reid enters Goddess Mindy's office to give the thirty-six hundred in cash earned the previous Saturday night. He observes her using tweezers on the Ghost Piranha, the cone-shaped vaginal insert with small slits lining the interior. He then stares at Goddess Mindy's friendly face, feeling giddy when he sees her thick glasses magnify her milk-chocolate-colored retinas.

"Hi, Reid. You look great compared to when I saw you last." They embrace in a hug. "I don't have time for chitchat. I have a big purchaser coming Saturday for the Ghost Piranha and I need to make sure its design is flawless. Turns out there may be a market for it."

"That's the thing that cut up Wish's penis, correct?"

She giggles. "Yup. I'll tell you more about it later when the new version's complete. No time to chat today."

Goddess Mindy and Reid exchange packages. They hug again, then

Reid exits to his car while reading his assignment from Wish. He must cash out casino chips at the M Resort, an off-Strip casino in the south part of town. Then he needs to set up a date with a cocktail server for later that night, and provide an ESE.

Reid completes the twenty-minute drive to the M Resort. He plays blackjack, but finds himself staring at every cocktail waitress who walks past. They're all drop-dead gorgeous. As he gathers his chips, he silently thanks Wish for choosing a casino that's well-stocked with beauties. He walks away from the table with Wish's money, plus four hundred in winnings for himself, which makes him feel this night is off to a great start. As he slides the cash into his breast pocket, he's captivated by the sight of a brunette strolling by with a tray full of drinks. He reads her nametag: *Nadia.* Reid observes her walk away, identifying which section of the casino she's cocktailing, then he makes his way over and sits at a slot machine.

Minutes later, Nadia approaches him, pen in hand, pad on the tray, with her other hand securing the tray on her hip. "Hi, hun. What can I get you to drink?"

"I'm only betting twenty-five cents a pull," says Reid. "Is that enough for a free drink?"

"Yup, if you're playing a machine, you get as many drinks as you want."

"If I up my bet to fifty cents a pull, will you see me as a high-roller and beg to hang out with me tonight?"

Nadia steps back, laughing as she rolls her eyes. "Well, aren't you cute."

"I bet I'm the eightieth guy who has said that to you today."

"No, you're number seventy-six. Close guess, though."

"Oh, you must be slacking with your flirt-game tonight," he says. She grips the tray with both hands and giggles. "Just so we're clear, I'm not interested in sex with you."

"Excuse me?" Her brow furrows.

Reid stays grounded, relaxed. He used to be afraid of saying something so bold, but now he loves it when a woman challenges his emotional comfort. "I might be wrong, but I think you had a specific thought immediately after I asked for a date with you tonight. The thought was something like, 'Here we go again — another dopey tourist who wants to try to fuck me.'"

"Yes. You read my mind almost perfectly, except I didn't call you dopey." She winks.

"I'm not a tourist," says Reid. "Nor do I ... just fuck."

"So why did you ask me out on a date? I doubt you just want to get together and hold hands."

Reid stands and gazes down at her confidently. He notices her eyes enlarge as she takes in his tall frame. She breaks eye contact and canvasses the area, but remains standing before him. He figures she's checking for a manager or boss who would want her to move along to other customers. *Clock is ticking. I've gotta move faster.*

"I want your phone number," says Reid. "I'm highly curious as to what your response will be when I text you a specific question."

She curls her lower lip, then sets her writing pad on the tray and clicks her pen. "I'm sorry but I can't give you my number. There are cameras all over this place. But I can get you a drink."

"I know you can't give your number out here. I'm curious to see your rebellious side, the side of you that enjoys the thrill of bending the rules." Reid pauses to study her response; her smile doesn't move as she glances to her left and right. She's on the fence and needs a little nudge. "I would like a bottle of Bud Light, and when you go in the backroom where there aren't cameras, write your number down on a cocktail napkin, then wrap it around the beer when you hand to me."

"Are you some kind of a spy? You know all the tricks. How about you just ask the question you plan on texting me, since I'm standing here right now?"

Reid huffs a short breath. He can sense her limitations and fears. "Never mind," he says while maintaining eye contact and giving her a coy smile. He nods once, then turns to leave.

"Wait," says Nadia. Reid manoeuvres to face her. She scribbles on her notepad, rips the paper off the pad, and hands it to him.

Reid examines the first three digits written on the sheet. *702, the Vegas area code.* "So you can't write your number down in the casino, huh?"

"That was just a line. You got me to change my mind."

"Is that so?" says Reid. "When does your shift end? Do you have plans tonight?"

"At ten o'clock, in an hour. No plans. Why?"

Reid tears the paper into little pieces, drops them in a trash bin, then gazes at Nadia with a sly grin.

She looks shocked. "Why'd you do that?"

"Your interest is based on seduction."

"Aren't you trying to seduce me?"

"I have no interest in seducing you. Seduction is grounded in manipulation. And using manipulation would mean I'm seeking companionship for escapism or validation."

"So you're not trying to seduce me? What are you interested in then?"

"Companionship that leads to personal growth. A potent way to expand personal growth is to take risks, stepping into the unknown."

Nadia squints while looking at Reid, studying him.

Reid continues: "Are you the type of person who likes to face challenges and take risks, knowing it will lead to a better understanding of yourself? My guess is that you're a risk taker, but something happened recently to create hesitancy."

"What makes you so sure?" She cocks her head slightly, then whips her hair off her shoulder.

"Because you've been standing here talking to me for a while. Your manager is probably pissed, but you don't care because you're enjoying the thrill of taking a risk. Your body is releasing dopamine and adrenaline, giving you a rush of pleasure, something it doesn't typically do at work."

Nadia stands quietly, appearing to analyze his words.

Reid moves closer to her and lowers his voice. "I'm looking forward to the self-growth rewards we will experience from taking the risk of meeting each other tonight."

Her eyes narrow, then a naughty smile forms on her face.

"Come midnight, I'll be at the Diamond Bar," says Reid. "I'll wait twenty minutes."

"Are you sure you don't want my number?"

"I'll see you at midnight."

Reid walks off, gets into his car, and drives back to his hotel. He has three hours to kill before midnight.

Inside his room, he sees the stack of books he has devoured on his desk. Reid's never read so much, so fast — he wonders why his brain has been primed to absorb all the information. He cracks open a book on mastering first introductions with people. His mind wanders into a reflection on his interaction with Nadia as he reads. He slams the book shut, realizing he has a strong grasp of the tools prescribed within the text, and he's taking those tools to another level by adding erotic themes to his social interactions with women. Reid freshens up in the bathroom for a few minutes, texts Andrew to secure a room at the Largo, then walks to the Diamond Bar for a drink.

"Back again?" says Ronald. "Mescal, chilled?"

"Yes, sir," says Reid. He unbuttons his suit jacket and slides onto a seat at the bar. He glances to his left and immediately drops his lower lip. *Oh, my goodness.*

Reid's noticed a seductive yet girl-next-door blonde woman wearing a slim white dress. He watches her slowly sip a green martini, allowing the liquid to graze her glossy, thin lips. Without hesitation, he collects his drink and moves to the seat next to hers.

"If I don't say hello, I'll be kicking myself all night long."

She giggles, then extends her hand to shake. "Hi. We've met before."

Reid's mind goes blank. He tilts his head back, scrambling for something to spark his memory. He wonders if he got her phone number but never contacted her. Or maybe she was a dancer from Mick's that he rejected due to Wish's assignment? *So many women in so many days, dammit. I'd surely remember a beauty like this.* He watches her take another sip and wonders if she's joking with him, but he can't ignore the feeling that they have met before. The lack of memory triggers a sense of caution in Reid. He gazes at the liquor bottles across the bar. *Maybe Wish was correct in his warning. I shouldn't be going out so often.*

"The Vixen Gentlemen's Club," says the woman.

His brain flashes through all of the memories of the Vixen Club, meeting some of Wish's yogi women and how Cherry paid for his face to be swallowed by breasts. But none of those women looked like this one. He thinks for a few more seconds, then realizes there was one that night. He glances at her suddenly. "You didn't dive onto the floor for the money like all the other girls did." He pauses as his mind fills in the blanks. "Your name is Dani."

She nods. "Impressive. Yes, I am. And you are Reid. I've never met a man who seemed interested but then left me so abruptly."

"I was hoping to run into you again. Are you still working there?"

"No. I've found a new business. Dancing felt too fake."

Reid swallows a long sip of mescal. He knows the type of employment a beautiful woman sitting at a bar by herself might be into. "I think we might work in the same business, although my role is slightly different than yours."

"What business do you think I'm talking about?"

"We both like to serve others."

"You're cute. You must do well."

"I was thinking the same about you," says Reid. "What's your story?"

"I've recently moved here. I worked in tech and hated it. I've always been sexual, but never gave myself permission to fully explore it. For some reason, I kept craving an adventure in Las Vegas. And now here I am, two months in."

She sounds like the female version of me. She might have the gene that Wish talks about. And she's willing to explore her dark side.

"How do you feel about your experiences thus far?" asks Reid.

"Each night is a thrill, although I'm not making as much money as I expected." She looks around the room, then returns her gaze to Reid. "You seem to have a way with women. I've noticed you here a few nights this week with someone different."

"Are you stalking me?" says Reid. Dani winks. "It's totally fine, because you'd win an award for being the sexiest stalker of the year."

Dani chuckles, then playfully punches Reid on the shoulder.

"I'm a bit of a nerd when it comes to the skill development within our chosen occupation," says Reid. "I like researching this stuff. How would you describe your strategy for getting a client?"

"I can't say that I have a strategy. I just show up, look pretty, and laugh at their dumb jokes."

Reid finishes the remainder of his drink, giving himself time to process his response. He suddenly feels a strange uplifting sensation — as if he's back to being a professor interacting with a student.

"You're in a unique position to improve the lives of the people you encounter. Respectfully, nothing you just mentioned was about serving a client."

"What do you mean, serving?"

"Serving means that their lives will improve from time spent with you. They will learn something about themselves. Otherwise, it's just sex for escapism, used like a drug to temporarily hide from their problems."

Dani pauses, appearing to think in depth. "I love that you're saying all this. I want clients to feel better about themselves, then I'll feel happier about my job. So, how should I interact with a potential client then?"

"There are several areas of focus, but I'll give you two standard desires of men who are looking for an experience. The first desire is feminine admiration. They want admiration for who they are, and to be accepted for the life they've chosen to live. The male animal is wired to seek admiration from a beautiful woman, even to the point that they'd pay for it."

"What's the best way to offer validation?"

Reid sits up straight, feeling a rush of excitement from her curiosity. *It's crazy. She's the female version of me.* "Be fascinated. Fascinated by his job, his humor, his style. Find the things in him that fascinate you. Men will go to great extremes to be around a woman who boosts their masculinity with admiration."

"And what is the second thing they seek?"

"A sensory experience. You're surrounded by people who've lived their lives experiencing the bare minimum of what their bodies are capable of feeling. This is something they won't believe exists until they experience it with you."

"You're different. You seem to see this world differently than most." Dani rests her head on Reid's shoulder for a few seconds, then returns to sitting straight. "I like you — you give me hope. I always thought men were assholes who wanted to get off."

"Sadly, your description is accurate. Most people settle for mundane sexual expression because they haven't been taught to provide something better. I believe the world will be a happier place if we all seek to provide life-altering Erotic Sensory Experiences." Reid pauses, then grins. "By the way, you just expressed admiration to me."

"I did?" Dani draws her tongue along her lower lip. "Oh, yes I did. How would you go about providing a sensory experience for someone?"

Reid is loving this conversation. He begins to feel how dry his lips have become. *Good God, I'm dying to kiss this woman.*

"Actually ..." He takes her hand. They slide off their chairs and stand. "Leave your drink here for a second; there's something I have to show you." He leads her towards the escalator.

They ride to the second floor, an area that only has conference rooms. Reid figures this floor will likely be empty at this time of night. He leads her down the hallway, then pulls her into a dark conference room, leaving the door open a crack to provide a hint of light. He grips her thin arms below the shoulder, then pins her against the wall. He reaches to grab the hair behind her neck, but she quickly pulls his hand away before he can touch a strand. He looks at her with a befuddled expression.

She giggles. "Sorry, forgot to warn you about my hair extensions."

Reid winks as if to say, *No big deal.* He places both hands under her jaw line and pulls her in for a kiss. Her lips brush his, then she turns her head slightly away.

"Hookers aren't supposed to kiss."

"You're not a hooker with me," says Reid. He maintains his gentle grip of her jaw and twists her head to face his. "You're a student who's eager to learn. I'm honored to serve as your professor."

Her lips begin to part.

"Close your eyes," says Reid. She obliges. He grazes his finger along the curves of her top lip and speaks slowly. "You're not my entertainment right now. Just for this moment, turn that part of your brain off. You are an incredible woman. You deserve to be touched by a man who adores and appreciates every part of who you are."

He moves his hands along her body, focused on authentically appreciating her full being. He kisses her neck, tasting the sweetness of her skin. *Why does my attraction for Dani feel deeper than for any other woman I've met?* He lifts his lips off her neck and rolls his head back, studying her relaxed yet erotic expression. *Do not fall in love. The mission is too important. Stay focused on teaching.*

He whispers in her ear: "The brain recognizes sensations best by comparing opposites. You will feel slight pain with my touch, but trust that its purpose is to add depth to the experience of pleasure that will follow."

"I love what you're teaching me, Professor."

He kisses down her neck, placing each index finger on the rear of her shoulders, finding the pressure points he discovered earlier that week while reading his erotic massage book. He digs his fingers into the nerve centers.

"The way you touch me ... feels better than sex." Dani exhales a breathy moan while lowering her head to rest it on his chest.

Reid continues to stimulate her pressure points while smothering her neck with kisses. He then lifts her chin, bringing her lips to meet his, and they connect. Her mouth is tense, a sign that she's battling her "not kissing" rule. He understands that creating an intimate connection would be bad for her business, and it's just as risky for his mission as well. But he can't deny there's a connection here worth exploring.

He draws his fingernails down her spine to her rear end. With his thumbs, he applies deep pressure to the area where her lower back and butt connect, then gently releases. He moves out of the kiss while remaining locked on her gaze. She has the same look he's become accustomed to seeing on all women he now shares experiences with, a look that combines gratitude, overwhelming intrigue, and submissiveness.

"How are you doing this to me?" says Dani.

"I care about you, and express my sexual art to demonstrate my appreciation for all that you are. You are quite the muse."

Her head falls onto his chest. He lifts his arms to wrap her in a bear hug. He speaks softly near her ear.

"I believe you're a sexual artist as well," says Reid. "Take what you are experiencing now and create that experience for someone else. You have a very important natural gift — the power to make someone feel alive in a world that is making them utterly dull."

He pulls out of the hug, reaches into his pocket for his phone, and has Dani type her number. As he slips the phone back into his pocket, she launches towards him. Their lips connect for another passionate kiss. *I could kiss these lips all night. I could see us having fun talking about providing erotic experiences, then exploring each other's bodies.* He moves his hands across her back, then draws his fingernail down her spine. Her hands suddenly mimic his touch; he feels her pointy nail drag down his spine. Strangely, he senses some type of future between them. He knows he can't fall in love, but he realizes that combining their experiences could be a much more productive form of research. He could even serve as her coach.

He feels his phone vibrate with a text. "Excuse me." He slides his phone out, then a reads a text from Andrew informing him the room is ready. The text reminds him of Nadia and tonight's assignment. He stares at the carpet. His temptation to remain with Dani is strong, but he knows he must remain true to the evening's assignment.

He slides his phone back into his pocket, kisses Dani briefly, then pulls her close for a hug. "It's time we go back out there and find you a client."

"I don't want a client," she says. "I want you."

"Unfortunately, that can't happen right now." Reid steps back and straightens the collar of his dress shirt. "It's clear our connection is quite potent, but further physical expression wouldn't be good for our businesses."

Dani nods in agreement, then glances away.

Reid continues: "I go out just about every night. If I come across a man who is worthy of your service, I'll definitely reach out to you."

"Yes, sir," says Dani.

They return to the Diamond Bar. Their drinks have been cleared away, and now a man is sitting where they were. His head is down and he appears to be sucking a fruity drink through a straw. Reid senses this guy may want company.

"He looks worthy of you," says Reid.

"If it works out with him, I'll give you commission," says Dani.

"Sounds like a deal."

"I want to learn more from you."

"Don't worry. I'll be in touch."

Reid kisses her on the cheek, then shuffles out of the bar. He reflects while walking along the Strip. *Did I just agree to be her pimp?* He shakes his head. *I'm just helping someone become better at providing Erotic Sensory Experiences. Maybe if she's worthy, I'll tell Wish about her.*

He continues for a few minutes, then stops to watch the fountain show. He can't deny that he felt something with Dani — her scent, her vibrant sexual energy, her desire to learn. He runs his tongue along his upper lip, tasting her leftover sweetness. Then he reminds himself to stay focused and get back to tonight's mission. Nadia the cocktail server will be here soon.

Chapter 25

"How many women have you been with so far?" asks Goddess Mindy.

"Well, it's been two weeks since that first Saturday." Reid counts with his fingers. "Twelve. I've been on a hot streak. I've been with a woman every night of this week so far."

Goddess Mindy frowns like a disappointed sister.

Reid continues: "The wildest experience so far was that cocktail server named Nadia from last Thursday. She was quite a screamer during the ESE. She loved the paddle you gave me. Andrew still teases me about how much the neighbors were complaining."

Goddess Mindy puts her hands on her hips, her frown not budging.

Reid grabs the candle that contains a hidden video camera from her desk. He lifts it to his nose for a smell. "I love this scent. I'll definitely have to use this thing at some point."

"There are only two of those in existence. One belongs to Andrew, and that one has already been sold to someone else." Goddess Mindy grins slightly, appearing to enjoy his admiration of her hard work.

Reid shrugs his shoulders. "Last night Wish wanted me to find a woman who wasn't from the United States. So I found Cassie, a gorgeous Australian. I've never heard someone beg for my penis with an accent."

"Your penis might fall off soon," says Goddess Mindy. "I can't believe you've been with twelve women in fourteen nights. You're using protection, right?"

"Yes, always." He sets the candle back on the desk. "By the way, I'm also sort of training this girl-next-door prostitute named Dani. She's smoking hot, witty, and fascinated to learn about Erotic Sensory Experiences. We have an agreement that our friendship is purely business, though."

"You're becoming a mini-Wish," says Goddess Mindy fondly.

"It's not like I'm her pimp. I'm just spreading the word about providing life-improving Erotic Sensory Experiences."

Goddess Mindy rolls her magnified eyes. Reid pulls thirty-six hundred in cash, from the previous night's blackjack assignment, out of his suit pocket and hands it to her. She then gives him a small brown paper bag. It contains four thousand in chips to be cashed out at Treasure Island, and a note from Wish with his next assignment. Reid opens the note.

Tonight you'll need to provide an experience for an exotic dancer. You may go to any gentlemen's club that you prefer. This will be your greatest challenge yet. Saturday night is their biggest night for earning tips, and you will not be spending any money on dances. You must demonstrate to her that an Erotic Sensory Experience with you will be more valuable than the money she'd earn hustling someone else. Your skillset needs to be extra-tight to pull this off. Good luck. Plan on meeting tomorrow for lunch to discuss your weekend.

"Service an erotic dancer? Why does Wish keep upping the challenge of the women I need to service?" asks Reid.

"To sharpen your sword," says Goddess Mindy. "Tonight you're going after a woman who works in the sex industry. Men offer them money for sex on a daily basis; therefore, their sexual expression and attraction will be vastly different than someone like your bachelorette girl from last Saturday. You cannot be a typical guy around strippers. They hustle men for a living."

Reid stuffs the cash into his breast pocket. "I'm certainly not gonna be played by a woman." His mind flashes images of that dancer from Mick's Cabaret, Mia, hustling him for five hundred dollars. A conniving grin forms on his face. "I know exactly who I'll be spending time with tonight — and the special experience she deserves."

"Don't get out of control."

"I'm always in control. You know that by now."

Reid exits and heads to Treasure Island, the exact place he gambled a few weeks ago before getting scammed by the dancer Mia at Mick's Cabaret. While driving, he imagines how he's going to handle

Mia tonight, convinced he won't fall for her scam this time. He parks in the Treasure Island garage, knowing he'll leave his car there and use cabs for the rest of the night.

"Where ya from?" says a forty-something man sitting to the right of Reid at a Treasure Island blackjack table — fifty dollar minimum bet.

They engage in small talk. His name is Tom, he's from Texas, and he's recently separated. He caught his wife cheating on him with her co-worker.

"We were married for eighteen years. No issues. We never fought. I did all I could to please her. I've got more money than I know what to do with and I still failed."

Reid feels a yearning to help this man, noticing the man's heart seems to be in the right place.

"What if I were to tell you that catching your wife cheating will go down as the greatest moment of your life? It could be the death of the old you, and the birth of a version of you that you've always hoped to become."

"Are you going to get all woo-woo on me? I could do without the positive psychology crud right now."

The dealer tosses the next round of cards. Reid gets an ace and a nine. He then feels his phone vibrate. Tom is dealt a blackjack and he throws his arms up in the air and cheers. Reid signals to the dealer that he'd like to stay on his hand. The dealer loses his hand and gives Reid his winnings. Reid steps away from the table to check his phone. It's a text from Dani.

Where are you? Meet anyone interesting tonight? I'm at the Mirage. It's dead here.

Perfect timing. The Mirage Hotel is next door.

Reid responds: **Treasure Island, BJ tables, man to my right in black dress shirt. Just caught his wife cheating. Money not an issue. Deserves an experience.**

Reid slides his phone into his pocket, places a bet, then continues the conversation with Tom. "I'm definitely not going to get woo-woo. I went through the exact same thing you did a few months ago."

"You seem pretty happy. How'd you get over it?"

"I thought about all the things I wanted to do in my life, but never had the courage to actually do. In short, I started coming to Vegas often and doing those things, conquering fears. What's something you've always wanted to do in this town?"

Tom thinks for a moment. "I keep having dreams of winning a bunch of money and having a young, beautiful woman next to me to enjoy the ride. I'll even pay for that, I don't care."

Bingo. The men play through the remainder of the deck, and win often. Reid is up a thousand and Tom has mounds of chips as well. Reid sees Dani enter the playing area, wearing a blue tank-top and a grey cotton skirt that reaches to the floor — sexy yet casual. Reid lifts his hand, intending to wave her over, then quickly runs his fingers through his hair, remembering he needs to pretend he doesn't know her. Eventually, she drifts to the table and slides onto the seat between them.

"Hi, boys," she says. "This looks like a lucky table." She pulls a fifty-dollar bill from her purse and places it in her betting circle. "Money play."

Reid quickly glances as her, raising an eyebrow. "Money play" is a casino term, meaning that there is no need to exchange the bill for a chip; the player intends to play one hand, then leave — unless the player wins.

"Golly, I hope you win," says Tom. "You're too beautiful to only stay here for a single hand."

"Awe, you're sweet. I have a feeling you'll be my good luck charm," says Dani. "I love your accent by the way. You must be from Texas."

Reid grins as he sees Tom blush. The dealer tosses each player their cards. Reid is dealt a twenty, Dani an eleven, and Tom receives a king and an eight for eighteen. Before Dani has a chance to signal her move, Tom places two green twenty-five-dollar chips next to hers.

"The lady will double down on her bet," says Tom.

The dealer flips an eight on top of Dani's cards — totaling nineteen.

"Oh, gosh. I hope I win. You've been too kind to share your money with me," says Dani.

"Those are words my ex-wife would never have said," says Tom. "I can't help but be nice, though."

Reid hears those words as confirmation to his early liking Tom, appreciating the man's kind heart. *He definitely deserves something special, a special experience.*

The dealer's cards total twenty-two, meaning he busts his hand and they win. They all high-five and continue to play the hot table for another hour. Reid keeps his small talk to a minimum, instead silently observing Dani work her magic on Tom. She's doing exactly what he taught and more, expressing deep admiration for his career choice and physical presence, touching his arm, back, or shoulder as she compliments him. He feels a sense of pride. *All of her actions are tied into boosting his sense of masculinity.*

Dani seals the deal after hearing Tom's sob-story. She even uses Reid's line. "On behalf of the female gender, I apologize for what you have been through. You're an amazing man." She leans over and kisses his cheek. "Let's get out of here and grab a drink at the Largo. It's important to walk away from blackjack when you're ahead."

They stand, grab their winnings, and leave. Reid places one last bet, then pauses as he notices the irony of how he's feeling — like a proud professor who just witnessed a student blossom into their potential. He knows Dani is leading Tom to Largo because her room is there. Reid admires that she pays for her own room, which ensures she's safer with clients by controlling her environment. Also, that way she can better serve her clients with an environment set up to provide Erotic Sensory Experiences — candles that melt into massage oil, ice, clean linens and towels, and a few erotic toys.

Reid loses his last bet and figures it's a good time to leave. He stands and grabs all of his chips. Then a sudden sting crawls up his spine, and he notices a man staring at him from another blackjack table thirty feet away. Reid instantly recognizes the man's bone-chilling gaze. It's Youngblood.

Reid's mind races, wondering if Youngblood saw the entire transaction between himself, Dani, and Tom. *But I barely talked to Dani. There's no way he'd put us together from that interaction.* He takes a deep breath and walks towards the cashier cage. *Stay calm. I'm just a normal blackjack player and now I'm going to go to a strip club.*

Youngblood can't do anything to me right now anyway; he's suspended.

Reid arrives at the casino cage and cashes out forty-six hundred, which is Wish's cut, plus a thousand for himself. *Not bad for a night's work.* He slides the cash into his breast pocket, exits the hotel, and jumps into a cab to go to Mick's Cabaret. During the ride, his mind wanders into reflecting on his last experience at Mick's, when he got hustled by Mia. He feels a rumbling in his stomach, but then remembers that Wish assured him it was a good lesson. *The key with boundary control is to not let the same mistake happen twice.* Reid rolls back his slouching shoulders and wipes his sweaty palms on his pants. He holds his chin up high as the cab arrives at Mick's, knowing Mia will now get to experience the new and improved Reid. He strides, wide-legged, towards the entrance, shows the bouncer his ID, then continues into the club.

He stops a few feet into the main room and scans for his target, Mia. He focuses his gaze directly on the eyes of each dancer who passes, causing many to blush and walk away, appearing shy. He recognizes the stark contrast with a month ago, when the dancers approached him with ease, identifying him as a sucker.

Reid cruises to the rear of the club and slides into a large chair near the small stage. Within seconds, he feels a cold hand grip the back of his neck, then hears the sound of a familiar voice.

"Well hello, Professor. I'm so glad you've come back to see me."

Reid turns his head and sees Mia, wearing a red-lace bra and matching bottoms. He huffs a short breath, smirks, then twists his head back to face the stage.

"Whatever," she says.

Through his peripheral vision, he sees her start to walk away. He quickly grabs her wrist and yanks her back to him. Mia's body glides across the chair and settles on his lap. He studies her perplexed expression, savoring it, then winks to put her at ease.

"I'll take that as a yes, you are excited to see me. Shall we go straight to the backroom?"

He stares into her eyes fiercely, as if to say, *We play by my rules now.* He lifts her tiny frame, then turns her to rest her back on his chest. He grasps the area between her shoulders and neck and squeezes, then moves his fingers to the pressure points behind her shoulders and proceeds to squeeze and release, noticing her chin falling towards her chest.

"Mmmm, that feels so good. Are you going to give me a massage?"

"Yes. Effective massage requires two participants; one person gives and one person receives. In order to receive the full benefit, you must turn your brain off and focus on ... receiving."

He slides his hands down to her hip, pressing his thumbs deep into a pressure point, causing her to release a breathless gasp and melt onto his chest. He then draws small circles, with a feather-light touch, from her hip down to her knee.

"O.M.G., that feels amazing. But security might yell at me if they see me getting a massage."

"Close your eyes," says Reid. "I'll keep an eye out for security. If they come near, I'll touch your sciatic nerve, cueing you to move your hips like you are giving a lap dance. Let's practice for a second."

Reid caresses the skin of her back with his hands, then glides them down towards the upper portion of her butt cheek and presses his thumbs firmly into the sciatic nerve. Obeying the cue, she grinds her hips on his lap slowly, continuing for a minute, then two. Reid anticipates her stopping, but then notices she can't help but continue her movement.

"You can stop now. It's important that you relax and feel the massage." Reid grips her waist, forcefully holding it steady as a signal for her to stop, but she continues.

"I don't wanna stop. You know you like me rocking my thang on you. Let me turn you on now."

The disobedience flusters Reid. He tightens his grip on her sides. "I'm not a client." Her movements halt. She lies on his chest. He begins to massage again. She coos, appearing to be enjoying his take-control attitude and erotic massage techniques. His daytime reading combined with nightly practice has drastically expanded his techniques from the basics taught by Wish and Dalia.

Mia reaches back and caresses his hair, staring at him with her mouth agape. He notices her legs begin to separate, her knees lifting slightly, while she presses the tips of her shoes into the floor. The slight gyration of her pelvis signals to Reid that she's receiving jolts of erotic energy in her jewel.

He grips her hand, pulls it away from his hair, and places it on her lap. "Close your eyes, and only focus on what your body feels."

He presses her spine forward, then unhooks her bra, exposing her breasts. He then pulls her in, resting her back on his chest. He brushes his fingers across her nipples, feeling them become erect. He playfully flicks and pinches, then wets his fingers to rub small circles on each areola. Her head rolls back and her shoulders shake subtly, signaling that a surge of oxytocin has been released into her brain. Reid looks around, noticing a few of the patrons are observing his experience with Mia. Reid returns his attention to Mia, smiling within.

She leans to the side, turns her head, and looks up at Reid with glossy eyes. "My God, you've changed, Professor. I wasn't even sure it was you when you walked in, but then I saw the scar." She shifts her body around to straddle him, face to face. She places her hands behind his head, then rolls her hips along his pant-covered stiffness. "I want to take you home and ride you all night. You didn't come here to go in the backroom with me, did you?"

Reid glares at her, knowing his silence will convey his lack of interest in going to the backroom. He moistens his lips, savoring the dramatic pause.

"I came here to provide a service to someone who deserves it," says Reid. "You work hard. Nothing wrong with a little rest and relaxation."

"You even know the perfect thing to say," she says. "I have to dance for these losers all night, but I'll be fantasizing that they're you."

"You're in a unique position to inspire the men here."

She rolls her eyes. "They're all the same — easy money in my pocket. But you're different." She leans closer Reid, then kisses his neck up to his ear. "I want more of you."

"What time does your shift end?" says Reid.

"Three."

"Perfect. Meet me at the Largo Hotel, Diamond Bar, at three forty-five. If you are a minute late, I'm gone."

She nods, then her eyes widen. "But what if I'm late? Don't you want my phone number?"

"Don't be late."

He reaches under her legs, places his other arm across her back, then lifts her with ease as he rises to stand. Her lightness is a reminder that all of his time in the gym has paid off. He then carefully sets her on the chair by herself, noticing her entranced expression. *The psychological work I've done on myself appears to be paying off as well.* He winks, then exits without looking back.

He steps outside, and nods to the valet to signal a cab.

"Did you have fun in there?" asks the valet man.

"Oh yeah," says Reid. "Something about this place brings out the best in me."

The valet man chuckles. "I can't say I've heard that response from other men who are leaving. Good on you. Your cab will be here in a few seconds."

Reid looks at his phone, and notices that it's half past two and there's a text from Dani.

What do you want your commission to be, Professor?

My commission? Silly girl must think I'm her pimp. Reid chooses not to respond, but the thought of commission reminds him that he needs to lock Wish's cash away in his room at the Lexi Hotel. He hops in a cab, arrives at the Lexi fifteen minutes later, and stuffs the cash in the safe. He then gathers a few erotic items for his date with Mia — a blindfold and bondage rope purchased earlier that week. Reid stuffs them into the breast pocket of his suit jacket. He then texts Andrew about opening a room for him at the Largo.

He jumps in a cab and instructs the driver to head to the Largo Hotel, then feels his phone vibrate. He pulls it out and reads a text from Andrew confirming his room key is available at the front desk. Then he receives a text from Dani.

Made good money tonight because of you. Can you teach me more? Please let me know what you want your cut to be. Tom left and I'm hanging in my room at the Largo.

Reid laughs, then types his response: **I'm open to any commission you feel I deserve. Can't talk much right now, busy for the night. Let's connect later.**

Dani responds: **I'm jealous she gets to experience what you are blessed to offer.**

Reid grins, then feels a sudden surge of excitement as he thinks about how Mia gets to experience what he's now blessed to offer. His fingers seem to tingle with a yearning to touch Mia's skin, to make her erupt with pleasure — proving that he's no longer an easy hustle.

The cab drops Reid at the valet section of the Largo Hotel. He strolls towards the front desk to get his room key, then heads over to the Diamond Bar. He settles on his usual seat, orders a chilled mescal, and swallows a large amount of the savory, smoky beverage.

A few minutes pass, then Reid feels a claw of fingernails scratch a line down his spine. He turns to see Mia wearing a body-hugging blue gown. His jaw begins to drop, but he catches it and smiles confidently, then lifts her onto the neighboring seat.

"Two shots of Patron," she says to the bartender.

Excuse me? Reid widens his eyes. "Are you buying?"

"Nope. You're buying," says Mia. "Women aren't supposed to pay for anything. And both shots are for me, since you have your drink."

He turns his head away, steaming with the discomfort of a boundary violation. His temptation to leave is strong, but he can't resist her beauty and his commitment to completing the assignment.

Mia takes out her phone and appears to open a camera app. She squints and perks her lips in front of the camera screen, pressing the button multiple times while tilting her neck around to different angles. Reid's eyes narrow. *Ugh, a selfie queen.* He shifts his gaze to the TV.

The bartender rests the two shots in front of Mia and a bill. She slides the bill to Reid. "Here ya go, sugar daddy." She quickly swallows each of the shots.

His gaze remains on the TV screen. Feeling heated, he slides the bar tab back to her. *This is the type of woman Wish and Henry warned me about — she uses her beauty to abuse men.*

"I told you, silly, women don't pay. I thought a professor would have known better. You bring the money. I bring the boobs." She grips each bosom and lifts them towards her lips for a smooch.

Reid maintains a thin-lipped smile as he explores his options. He could walk away and explain to Wish why he backed out of the assignment. Only that might disappoint Wish. He takes a long sip of mescal, wondering what would appease Wish. *The answer has to relate to service.* He considers using his skills to educate her on the value of serving others, but she's been unreceptive thus far. *Is it possible to teach someone who isn't seeking to learn? It doesn't usually go well in the classroom.*

Reid plops his glass on the bar. *I suppose I'll find out.* He reaches into his pocket, then throws down cash to cover the bill. He grips Mia's hand and leads her to the bank of elevators.

Shortly after he presses the call button, an elevator door opens. They step close to enter, then Reid halts their walk, seeing that a woman needs to exit first. His eyes bulge as he recognizes the woman: Dani.

Dani looks Mia up and down, smirking as if Mia is less than garbage. Reid stiffens. Dani then struts past with her eyes fixated on Reid. Dani wiggles her eyebrows, as if to say sarcastically, *Nice catch, Reid.* His face flushes; he hopes Dani doesn't think this is the type of girl he typically goes for.

Mia and Reid step into the elevator. Mia yells as the doors slide shut, "You better walk away — he's my man." Reid's mind goes blank. He stares at Mia incredulously. Mia doesn't seem to notice and pulls his head down for a kiss. "You're my man tonight."

Service, focus on serving her. He tries to center his mind on the kiss, but struggles to stop thinking about what Dani must think of him now. Dani didn't say a word to Mia, but appeared to sense something was off. He pulls away from Mia's lips, feeling strangely guilty, but keeps his expression neutral. *I don't need to care what Dani thinks of me.* He leans into Mia's neck, applying light kisses, aiming to distract her while he sorts through his approval-seeking thoughts. *Dani has probably had to service disgusting men; she'll understand me having to be with a disgusting woman.* The shift in self-talk settles his mind enough for him to continue. He kisses Mia's lips again, focusing on setting a rhythm while feeling the juiciness of her bottom lip. Mia ignores his attempt to lead the kiss and launches her tongue deep into his mouth, swirling it like a load of towels in a washing machine. *Ugh.*

The elevator "dings" and the doors slide apart. Mia pulls her tongue from his mouth, then hops into the hallway. Reid stands for a second, and considers staying in the elevator, riding it to the bottom floor, and then running away. He shrugs. *You've made it this far. Might as well see it through.* He uses the back of his hand to wipe Mia's saliva off his mouth, then steps into the hallway.

"I want more of what you were doing to me at the club tonight," Mia says, grabbing his hand and leading him down the hallway. A knot develops in his stomach — the feeling of being tugged along sparks the memory of when she pulled him towards the backroom at Mick's and scammed him. *Wish said to always remember the icky feeling from that night, and never let it happen again.*

Reid stops mid-step, then yanks Mia close to face him. He expects his masculine demonstration to make her coo, but instead she huffs with angst while standing with a pensive expression. Reid's mind races, searching for answers. All week long the women have enjoyed him leading the way, but from the time Mia arrived at the bar she hasn't seemed interested in that dynamic.

"Why'd you stop?" says Mia.

"Umm." Reid's mouth opens, but nothing more comes out. His face blanches as he looks at the floor. He begins to question if he's doing something wrong.

"What the hell — are you okay?" says Mia. "Did you forget the room number, Professor? You're one of those book-smart guys who's actually really dumb. All those years in school, and you don't know shit."

He stares at her with an empty gaze, puts his hands in his pockets, then walks towards the room.

"Awe, I'm just teasing, Professor. Don't worry, I've fucked plenty of dumb guys in my life. You're just as worthy as they were."

He cringes while continuing to walk, suddenly feeling overwhelmed by a familiar sensation, a sensation he thought he'd never feel again — he's retreating back to who he was with Jasmine. His shoulders fall forward as he walks, gaze locked onto the carpet, fearful of her spouting another insult, fearful of being told he's awful when he knows his intentions are good. He hears Mia's heels thump along the thin carpet as she approaches from behind, then feels her pointed toe playfully kick his bum. The kick causes his mind to flash back to when he and Jasmine were living together. She'd behave the same way: insult him, then tease him further for feeling disrespected, which made him feel worse. Then she'd playfully kick or punch him and say, "Toughen up, man." He didn't know how to toughen up. Instead, he strived to maintain an environment that left her little room to complain, *because I was always afraid of her wrath.* The memory helps him realize he's become afraid of Mia's wrath, afraid to take the lead, afraid to say "no," and now he is cowering — fearful of more abuse.

He approaches the room, hesitant to take the room key out of his pocket, eager to tell Mia to get lost. But something inside him senses such action would be cowardly. *I'd be giving her my power, and she'd win. Fuck that. I'm the one in control of my power.* He straightens his posture, slides the key-card into the slot, then pushes it open. He enters first, normally to ensure his partner's safety, but now to prove he's no kiss-ass to the princess. He sees the same type of room as usual, one king bed and floor-to-ceiling windows with a view of the Strip. A brush of wind hits the side of his head as Mia rushes past and leaps onto the bed.

"You were my biggest payment last month," she says while jumping up and down. "I've never gotten five hundred out of a guy that quickly. And you returned because you want my tight pussy, huh?"

The hairs on the back of his neck rise. He grins slyly, then brushes the back of his neck with a downward stroke, as if to signal "false alarm" to his ego. He didn't know how to have thick skin with Jasmine, but his new experiences, combined with the teachings of Wish and Henry, have taught him otherwise. He's been strong up until meeting Mia, but now he realizes he's being tested by his strongest obstacle yet, and failure is not an option.

He stands at the foot of the bed, wide-legged, staring at her, feeling as if he's babysitting someone's spoiled child. Mia continues jumping on the mattress, while peeling the top part of her dress down to her stomach and popping off her bra. Reid crosses his arms, watching her lush globes bounce freely with her motion — something he's always wanted to see in person, but in this context, he's hardly interested. She jumps one last time, then lands on her back. As her momentum settles, she grabs each bosom, then tilts her head forward, kissing the nipples.

Reid's arms remain crossed. "Is that your go-to move?"

"No, I've got way more moves." She moves to stand on the floor and peels off her dress, then her underwear, until she's standing naked in front of Reid. She sways her hips from side to side and moves her hands along her curves, dancing closer to Reid. Although the animal inside him enjoys the sight, he can't escape the feeling that she's using her sexuality to manipulate him. He continues to stand wide-legged, unmoved, certain she will not cross his boundary and abuse his masculinity.

"Walk to the window and face the Strip," says Reid. "Do not look back at me."

Mia rolls her eyes as she turns, then ambles to the window. He huffs a short breath, then unbuttons his suit jacket, but keeps it on — certain he won't get naked with her unless it feels right. *Maybe she'll buck at first, but once she starts to feel the ESE, she'll begin to value the experience I provide.* He approaches her from behind, gripping each of her hands and lifting them above her head, then pressing the palms on the window.

Mia begins to talk; Reid cuts her off. "Don't say a single word, and don't take your hands off the window." He reaches into his breast pocket, pulls out the blindfold, and secures it over her eyes.

"O.M.G., I had no idea you were like this," says Mia. "You seemed so innocent when we first met."

That old me is dead. Reid lifts his hand, pulsing with extra strength from his frustration, then spanks her right butt cheek — hard. She yelps, then gasps through the sting, lowering her forehead to the window.

With his fingers, he traces small circles around her bum, using a feather-light touch to soothe, hoping his actions will open her mind. *There's so much I could teach you.* He's tempted to explain the science behind his actions, but figures the logic will spark her out of the sensory trance. He continues the light touch for a few more seconds, seeing her pale skin darken with the flush of arousal. He then provides the contrast, extending his hand back and launching it into another powerful spanking. She releases a high-pitched moan. Reid glides his tongue down her spine, while gently dancing his fingers across the spanked area. He then drops to his knees and circles his tongue on the back of her thighs, while moving his hands up her inner thighs, pressing his thumbs into potent nerve centers, then drawing his thumbnails upward to release tingles into her core.

"My God, you are worth it. I thought you were just another douche at my club," she says. "During the cab ride here, I considered charging you for sex. But now, you are definitely getting my pussy for free."

Heat flushes through Reid's body. *She still sees this as rewarding me?* He abruptly rises to stand, then glances at the ceiling. *Maybe she's lost in the land of the Collective Shadow; clearly she's abusive to men.* He shifts his head downward slowly, unable to resist the view of her immaculate curves, searching for a reason to continue. *She does enjoy the foreplay phase. Maybe she's getting closer to seeing the value in this.* He extends his arm back, then fiercely smacks her bottom once more. She coos, then glares back at him, biting her lower lip. *She likes that too.*

He folds her hair to the side, brushes her neck with his lips, then nibbles upward to her ear. Recalling a teaching from Dalia, he backs away from Mia, allowing for a moment of zero touch, building anticipation and tension in Mia's mind. He reaches back and thunderously whacks her rear. She yelps, then rolls her head back. He leans close and briefly dances his tongue along the edge of her ear. He reaches around, brushing his hands across her nipples, down past her stomach, circling around her pelvic center.

"I had no idea you'd be this amazing," says Mia. Reid's hands move closer to her vulva. One finger grazes a warm, slick lip, then moves away. He continues that pattern several times.

"I'm so freaking horny," she says. "Please just fuck me. I can't wait anymore. I'm gonna explode."

Reid grabs a handful of hair behind her neck and pulls. "I told you not to speak."

"I give you permission to do whatever you want to me," says Mia. "And tomorrow you'll take me shopping."

Fuck you. He releases her hair, then steps back, steaming with anger. He tries to remind himself that this is a test, but he's being pushed to his limits. She's scammed him for five hundred dollars, forced his purchase of drinks tonight, and now she demands he take her shopping. It's become clear to Reid that this is bigger than testing his toughness around women; she's a member of the Collective Shadow, and just like Amber who robbed him and Drea from the gym, she's been sent to disrupt the mission. This sparks him to further wonder if Jasmine, his other exes, and the girl who got him thrown out of the club were also CS soldiers who attacked. Could they all be part of the same plot to steer him away from knowing himself?

Wish never explained how to handle a threat from the CS. Reid only saw how Wish handled Amber, her boyfriend, and the skinheads from the Collective Shadow; they were physical threats, so Wish had to be physical in return. *Mia is a psychological threat, so perhaps I need to combat her with psychology.*

He pulls the bondage rope from his pocket. Then he takes her hands off the window and uses the rope to bind her wrists together behind her back.

"Am I getting arrested and thrown in a kinky jail?" asks Mia. "Please ... can I just feel a bit of your penis inside me?"

"You're definitely being punished." He grips Mia's bound wrists and leads her to sit on the couch, then reaches to ensure the blindfold is securely covering her eyes. "Tell me something, Mia, what is your favorite part of your job?"

"Stop the stupid chitchat and just stick it in me." She bites her lower lip. "No man has ever made me wait like this. Take this blindfold off. I wanna see you."

Reid's fists curl in so tight his fingernails bite into his palms. "I'm not touching you again until you answer the question. When you're working, what gives you the greatest feeling of satisfaction? Is it providing a service to the man?"

"Service? Ha! All men are suckers," she says. "I tease fools like you for a living; get you all to want me so badly, then walk away with all of your money."

Reid smirks, then leans close to her ear. "Very interesting. I'm enjoying doing the same thing to you tonight. Except when I walk away, I won't take your money."

"Think you're gonna fuck me and leave? You're not walking away from me until we finish shopping tomorrow, honey baby love."

Reid moves away from her and buttons up his jacket while releasing a long sigh.

"Your teasing won't faze me," she says, while leaning back on the couch and extending her legs in the air. "You know you want to lick my tight snatch."

He grabs her small purse and carefully sets it on her lap, then, shaking his head, he stalks towards the exit. *I'm outta here.* He cracks the front door open, steps into the hallway, and hears her curse his name before the door slams shut.

He cruises down the hallway with a wily grin, typing a text to Andrew.

Need you to go to my room. I left a stripper in there. She's blindfolded and her hands are bound. She's the one who scammed me, and probably hundreds of other men. Hopefully, she's learned her lesson.

Andrew responds: **No freaking way. You wild man. Yeah, I'll handle that for you. And don't worry, I won't try to bang her. I don't mess around at work. I'll tell Wish that you completed the mission with style."**

Reid steps into the elevator, chin held high, knowing how much Wish is gonna love this story. He may have failed with Jasmine, the girls at the club, Drea, and Mia during their first meeting — but now he feels a sense of victory. He just defeated a threat from the Collective Shadow. As the elevator shoots down to the lobby, he leans against the wall, grinning from knowing he has taken control of his life. He will never again be a victim, giving himself away with such ease.

He steps out of the elevator and walks towards Las Vegas Boulevard en route to his room at the Lexi Hotel. His phone vibrates and he fishes it out, then stiffens as he reads a text from Wish.

YOU FUCKING CHILD! GET YOUR ASS TO MY PENTHOUSE ASAP.

Chapter 26

Reid steps into the dimly lit living room of the penthouse. It's darker than he's seen it before because the heavy blinds are drawn, blacking out the windows from the lights of the Strip. As he nears the sofa, he feels the skin along his jawline tingle, sensing the slap his face may soon experience. Perhaps he let his ego get the best of him. He figures Wish will probably lecture him about the dangers of using his sexual prowess for something other than growth-oriented intentions. He hopes Wish understands that Mia was clearly a solider sent by the Collective Shadow, and that he won the battle. Maybe he didn't do it in the classiest of ways, but he protected his boundaries.

Out of the corner of his eye, he notices a red glow briefly appear down the hallway, then disappear into the darkness. "Hello? Wish, I'm here." He steps cautiously towards the hallway, figuring the red glow came from the room with the cage. "Hello? Wish? Dalia? Anyone here? I know I was an idiot. I'm ready for my lecture on how leaving the stripper was a dumb idea."

He slides his phone out to see if Wish sent another text. Nothing. Maybe Wish is playing some kind of hide-and-seek game. "I know I screwed up the assignment. Can we talk like normal people?"

Reid approaches the door of the cage room and twists the knob. It's locked. He knocks lightly, then touches his ear to the heavy wood. Silence. Before he has another thought, he hears a loud *kerwack*. A split-second later, his brain receives the signal, a painful signal, that he's been struck by a whip from behind. He sucks in air, drops the phone, and crumbles to the floor, unable to make a sound because the sting has stolen his voice. Lying on his stomach, he cocks his head and gazes upward. The light from his phone illuminates the man who stands before him, holding a thin leather whip. It's Wish.

"I'm glad to hear you're ready for my lecture," says Wish, then he cracks the whip across Reid's back again. Reid groans, squeezing himself into the fetal position. Wish remains calm, standing wide-legged.

"Please, I was wrong. I get it. I don't need punishment to learn."

Wish cracks the whip across Reid's shoulder.

"Ahhhh." Reid vigorously rubs his shoulder, fighting back tears.

"The pain you feel now is nothing compared to the pain you'll feel if you keep living your life without accepting all experiences as gifts. Tying up that stripper and leaving her in the room was an act of revenge, not acceptance." Wish cracks the whip across Reid's leg. He curls tighter into a ball, hiding his tears in the sleeve of his suit jacket.

"She's an awful person," says Reid. "She tried to abuse me. I left her there to teach her a lesson."

"Don't you dare hide your selfish acts behind the goal of our mission. You felt the need to win back the pride that you believe she stole. You wanted her approval. It's the same story for you — more approval-seeking, except now you're masking it with slick moves and a fancy suit." Wish cracks the whip again, this time across his exposed ankle. Reid groans, banging his fist on the floor, then reaches to rub his ankle.

"Please, stop. No more with the whip. Tell me what you want."

"I want your brain to be ready."

"Ready for what?"

"Ready to remember everything it's about to learn." Wish cracks the whip on Reid's back.

Reid's gasps, then decides he's had enough — he doesn't have to take this. He rises and launches himself to tackle Wish. The pimp steps to the side, extends a leg, and trips Reid.

"Don't waste your energy, kid." Wish unlocks the door of the cage room, pulls it open, and enters. "Your brain won't absorb information if it's lacking oxygen."

Reid lies on his back. His body burns as if it fell down a tree that caught fire, hitting every branch before connecting with the ground.

"Do I have your full attention now, son?" asks Wish.

Reid nods while fuming inside. His mind questions why he's here, but then he remembers that everything Wish has done has been for Reid's benefit — even violence. Now he sees the red glow he noticed earlier. He picks himself up to stand, recalling that the room had red lighting before, but this hue is different, brighter.

"What I'm about to teach you must never be forgotten. And if something were to happen to me, I expect you to someday share this with my son, understand?"

Reid nods in agreement. Wish has confirmed Reid's thought that this is all part of a lesson, and his anger starts to calm as he steps into the cage. He widens his eyes as he notices that the red glow is coming from rope lights attached to the rods of the cage — rope lights that weren't there before. The lights outline the strange pattern these metal bars have been shaped to form.

"I don't remember seeing these rope lights on the metal rods," says Reid.

"Xavier installed them today," says Wish. "This has been our art project for months, and it's officially complete as of today."

"Who's Xavier?"

"Xavier is a good friend of mine. An artist in the greatest sense of the word, and deeply connected to masculine expression. Someday you'll meet him."

"Everyone you have in your circle seems to be amazing at something. I look forward to meeting him." Reid's thoughts about Xavier are quickly silenced as he studies the magnificence of the cage. There's a special aura to it now, something beyond erotica.

He originally believed that this dome-shaped cage was simply a bunch of metal bars molded in a random pattern. He lifts both hands to his forehead as he realizes his assumption was wrong, very wrong. The pattern made by the metal rods mirrors the lines of something familiar. He turns around, studying the design further, piecing together what he sees.

"This cage is designed so that we appear trapped inside a —"

"Human brain," says Wish.

"Absolutely amazing." Reid continues to look around, his eyes widening. "I'm blown away. This looks like a ton of work to create. Xavier must be something else. Why did you guys decide to create this?"

"This is a shrine. As much as I respect the spiritual symbols that have guided many individuals towards their bliss, I've never felt connected to those symbols. But the brain — seeking to understand the brain — has been my obsession since childhood. This shrine exists to remind us that our external reality is always created from within."

"But you do all of your kinky stuff in here?"

"I've told you before: what we do isn't kinky. It's neuroscience."

Reid studies the shapes of the metal rods again, surprised that he didn't notice the brain design on his previous visits; but then the cage was never lit this way. Now his attention is drawn to the rear portion of the brain-cage, where a smaller patch of woven rods is lit gold instead of red.

"Why is that area gold?" says Reid.

"Excellent question. The gold represents our desires. It could mean money, love, happiness, et cetera."

Wish walks over to the erotic items which dangle on hooks attached to the cage. Wish drops the whip on the floor, then grabs the thin bamboo stick. Reid sighs, knowing the bamboo doesn't sting nearly as much as the whip.

"Have you ever heard of the Reticular Activation System within the brain?" says Wish.

Reid lifts his hand to his forehead. "I know I've heard of it before, but I'm not remembering exactly what it does."

Wish nods for Reid to follow him. They walk towards the gold-lit portion of the cage. Wish uses the bamboo to tap on the back of Reid's head, signaling the section of the brain that corresponds to where they are standing, then points the bamboo to the gold-lit metal design.

"The Reticular Activation System is located here. It's the single greatest discovery by modern neuroscience researchers. Unfortunately, much of mainstream society is not aware of its powers. We designed the art piece specifically to draw attention to the Reticular Activation System, figuring the gold lighting would create a sense of curiosity."

"You've certainly sparked my curiosity."

"The Reticular Activation System, or RAS, is a filter for our brain. In any given moment, our brain is exposed to two million bits of information, which is too much to take in, so it needs a filtration system. The RAS is like a nightclub bouncer at the entry of our brain, only allowing in the most important information."

"So how does the RAS know what's important?"

"By the thoughts you focus on the most. And once the RAS knows what's important, it prioritizes based on the amount of emotion you have attached to that specific thought."

"Can you explain in simple terms? Like, give me an example?"

"Do you remember when you wanted a new car, and you choose the exact year, model, and color of that car you wanted?"

"Yes, absolutely."

"Once you had the specifics of what you wanted and you attached an emotion, such as excitement or anticipation that someday you'd get that car, you suddenly started seeing that car all over town."

"I've totally had that happen to me."

"Seeing that car all over town is the work of your Reticular Activation System. You were not walking around intentionally looking for that car. Your brain was taking you through normal daily activities, but when that car drove past, you stopped whatever you were doing and, without thinking, you turned your head and noticed the car, because your subconscious received the filtered information from the RAS, pointing out the opportunity for you to have what you desired. You programed your RAS to look for the car, because you had a strong emotion to support your desire for the car. Your RAS went to work pointing out opportunities to give you what you were seeking."

Reid shakes his head in amazement. He pieces together the puzzle of his past experiences and how he's now here with Wish, subtly seeing the dots connect. His entire life he wanted to be who he is now, but deep down he knew that he needed a mentor, a father figure, to show him the way. Could it have been his RAS that brought him to Wish?

He looks at Wish with narrowed eyes. "I think I get it. But why are you telling me this?"

"Your life will be the result of what you focus on the most. If you constantly worry about money, then the RAS will go to work and only allow in information that ensures you're always worried about money — leaving you broke. And this isn't some wishy-washy spiritual jargon. It's simply understanding how the brain filters the information it receives to match whatever you focus on and feel emotion towards."

"But nobody wants bad things to happen to them."

"Because the brain grows through contrasts, bad experiences must happen to all of us from time to time, and many of those experiences are simply random occurrences. But if a similar negative experience keeps occurring, forming a pattern, then the RAS must be examined. You've experienced unfaithful lovers multiple times. The issue isn't your cheating partners; the issue is you and your RAS being hooked on feeling the intense emotion of experiencing an unfaithful partner."

Reid shifts his gaze upward. He wonders how powerful the RAS can be. Was Jasmine's choice to be unfaithful more his fault than hers? "But I don't want to experience infidelity. Why would the RAS work to show me what I don't want?"

"The RAS doesn't know positive or negative. It only provides information to support the thoughts and emotions you have consistently. Unfortunately, we are wired to have stronger emotional responses to negative situations, because of our animalistic fight-or-flight response. But in modern society, there isn't the threat of being eaten by lions or bears. With conscious effort, we can minimize negative emotions."

Reid studies the design of the brain-dome as his mind sorts through what Wish has shared. Something about being inside the dome and grasping Wish's teaching brings him to a *eureka* moment. He's always been afraid experiencing the pain of infidelity, and that fear was the driving force behind all of his actions with Jasmine. He used that energy to get himself through college. No wonder it came back to bite him.

"I think I get it. So this goes back to us being told to always focus on what we want, instead of focusing on what we don't want."

"Yes. In order to consistently experience the positive outcomes that you want, you must cleanse the deep routed negative beliefs out of the RAS. Clean it so it becomes a blank canvas, ready to receive the paint of your positive desires. If repressed, our shadow-self prevents us from ever having a clean RAS, because the repression locks away negative emotions that need to be dealt with."

"So the next step is to clear negative beliefs. How do you suggest I do that?"

"First, you must learn to love all past experiences. Easier said than done. Your emotionally painful experiences must be worked through to the point that acceptance is present deep in your subconscious. Otherwise your RAS will make sure you continue to experience those awful things. Your desire to have revenge on the stripper was a sign — a sign that you're angry at women. As long is your anger is stuffed within you, the RAS will guide you towards women who will act in a manner that supports your angry beliefs."

"Angry at women?" Reid stares at the floor. He can see how Wish would make this assumption, but he knows he was initially trying to serve Mia. Her behavior knocked him slightly off track. And he doesn't feel any emotional pain from the break up with Jasmine; he's happy they aren't together, because it has led him to be here with Wish.

Reid looks at Wish and cracks a half-smile. "I think you are looking into this too deeply, Wish. I'm fine. I walked away from a stunning woman who was begging for me. She abuses men, and she was certainly attempting to abuse me. She was a member of the Collective Shadow, and I withstood her charms."

"You sought to get revenge. Revenge is the Collective Shadow's favorite recruitment tool. Revenge is blaming someone for the pain you can't deal with on your own — guaranteeing you'll never get to the place of acceptance."

"But I wasn't out for some kind of crazy revenge tonight. I was trying to serve her, and I just went off track. I left her there thinking it would be a funny story. I know myself well; I swear I've worked through my psychological wounds. And you have been a huge help in that."

"Your denial is concerning, a sign that your wounds are deeply lodged beyond your consciousness." Wish looks away.

Reid's mind flashes to Dalia saying the same thing to him when she studied his eyes. How can they see what he can't, or are they the ones who are blind to his growth?

Wish continues: "I've heard of your extra escapades these past two weeks. Those were not part of our plan."

"But I thought you'd be proud of me for seeking to serve others?"

"Your ego is eager for you to show off your new skills," says Wish.

"I'm eager to serve as many women as possible."

"Bullshit. You reek of approval-seeking."

Reid holds his tongue. *He hasn't even been there to see what I do. He hasn't seen how happy the women were after their experience. I swear this isn't approval-seeking.*

"I promise that I've only focused on making their lives better. I care deeply about the experience they have."

"You're forgetting about working on you. You're using the skills as a distraction from the wound inside you that must be healed."

"But I don't even know what that wound is. I swear I feel fine."

"The Collective Shadow knows exactly what your wound is. And it's going to create a shit-storm to attack your greatest weakness. Soon, you'll be facing bigger obstacles than that stripper. We have to take immediate action — you must cleanse the RAS before things get worse. I was hoping it wouldn't come to this, but it's clear to me now. You need to go back to Los Angeles and have a face-to-face conversation with your ex, Jasmine."

"What? I don't want anything to do with that crazy bitch." Reid quickly covers his mouth, realizing he's not supposed to use that word around Wish, or even have it in his head.

Wish crosses his arms and glares at Reid for several seconds before speaking. "Do you hear yourself? That gun-slinging response just erupted out of your wound. Never forget that it was her actions that sent you down the path of discovering who you really are."

Reid knows deep down that her actions were a blessing, but he can't repress the hot anger. "What am I supposed to do with her?"

"Do whatever is necessary to cleanse your Reticular Activation System. You'll have all week to figure that out. I don't want you back in Vegas until Saturday afternoon." Wish nods for Reid to leave.

Reid exhales a long sigh, then walks to exit. "Okay, I'll figure something out."

He leaves the penthouse, then takes a cab to the Lexi Hotel. During the cab ride, his mind processes what he's just learned about the RAS and how it relates to Jasmine. He thinks about how Wish and Dalia keep mentioning that there is a wound within him that needs to be addressed. He has always felt self-aware, but now he struggles to find the heart of the wound; it seems non-existent.

The cab pulls into the lot of the Lexi Hotel. He pays the driver, then steps towards the asphalt, but slips. He catches himself before falling, and looks down to see his foot is on a glossy flyer displaying a half-naked woman posing seductively. He reads the headline: "Hot bitches to your room 24/7." The word "bitch" creates a heavy feeling in his stomach. He remembers that he just called Jasmine a bitch in front of Wish, and it shot out of him like emotional vomit. Even though he feels he's forgiven her, he realizes that there might be more depth to his wound than he's aware of. He just can't pinpoint it yet.

He walks to his room and crawls into bed, reminding himself to get his car from Treasure Island when he wakes. He'll then spend this upcoming week in southern California, doing the right things to figure it all out — even if that means facing the pain and discomfort of seeing Jasmine.

Reid sighs, knowing he has his work cut out for him, but he's determined to clear his Reticular Activation System of any issues. He's going to create the reality he wants, even if it means he first has to find out how to stop creating the reality he's been stuck in.

Chapter 27

Reid is sitting at his desk in his bedroom at his mom's house, reading a guidebook on dominant and submissive erotica. His mind connects the dots as he delves deeper into the subject, realizing that dominant and submissive play is an exaggerated form of masculine and feminine dynamics. Studying this topic serves to distract him from constantly checking his phone. He's awaiting Jasmine's reply to his texted offer to meet up. Though he's determined to resolve the issue, he can't justify why Wish would want him to see her in person. *I can forgive her from this chair.* But if Jasmine does respond, he hopes she tells him to leave her alone and move on.

Minutes pass, then Reid's phone vibrates. He fishes it out and sees a message from Jasmine.

I've actually been wanting to meet with you for a while now. I'm glad you reached out to me. What kind of meet-up did you have in mind?

Reid struggles to swallow his next gulp. *I don't know what I have in mind. This is Wish's idea.* He stares at the ceiling, searching for the answer to what his hidden wound is. If it's anger from Jasmine cheating on him, he can forgive her from this chair — easily, because his life is awesome now. His head suddenly feels heavy. He lowers his forehead to rest on the desk. *What could Wish want me to uncover from this? Maybe something with contrasts for my brain? Perhaps I'll show her the man that I've become. I can show her that I'm no longer a pathetic boy who smothers her with flowers.* He turns the page of his book and notices a picture of a dominant man towering over a submissive woman. Each of her limbs is tied with rope to the corners of the bed. This image triggers an idea for his plan for the night. *But this can't be for revenge or approval-seeking — I must remain in a mindset of authenticity.*

He grips his phone and types: **Let's meet at that dive bar across the street from your home. The place we always talked about**

visiting but never did. Tonight, 9pm.

Jasmine responds: **Perfect. I can't wait to see you. Forgive me if I'm out of line for saying this, but I miss you.**

A tingle dances inside his chest, but it quickly shifts into tightness. A few months ago, he begged her to say those words, and now he wishes she didn't miss him. He suddenly realizes the comfort he's created by hating Jasmine. The hate serves to cover his heart with a protective shield. He wonders if he'll gain a better understanding of his wound by moving away from his hatred and opening his heart — finding a way to love all of his past experiences with her.

An uplifting energy rises in Reid. He feels like a detective who's discovered a major clue, and he's now eager to go back to the crime scene, back to Jasmine's home. He may discover something about himself, and if he serves her, she may also discover something about herself.

Reid leaves his bedroom and heads to the gym for a muscle-pumping workout. Once he's finished, he leaves the gym and stops at an erotic shop, where he purchases a few bedside bondage straps. At home, he decides not to wear a suit, instead dressing casually in a form-fitting black tee and slim jeans — maintaining the V-shape frame. He slides the bondage straps into his long socks, then gets in his car and completes the hour-long drive to the dive bar near the home that he and Jasmine used to share.

Reid enters the bar and spies Jasmine sitting at the far end, sipping a martini. She's wearing a low-cut black dress and high heels. As much as he tries, he can't deny that she looks good. She recognizes Reid and stands to face him.

"You look ... I don't know how to describe it," says Jasmine. "You look amazing."

"Thanks," says Reid. His mind races as he struggles between allowing his desire for her to surface and not forgetting her shameless actions in the past.

They embrace in a cold hug, then sit. His heart rate accelerates, yet he forces himself to appear calm. Seeing her, smelling her, simply being in her presence releases bits of anger that seem to be stored within. But he doesn't act on his anger, instead he smiles through the discomfort, hoping it will pass.

They order drinks, then engage in small talk. Reid doesn't tell Jasmine about Wish and his new adventures, figuring he may never see her again. He only discloses that he's been working on himself. Soon, the awkwardness and anger subside as he feels the buzz of alcohol, and Jasmine also becomes looser.

"I should tell you that I'm not seeing Daphne, the woman you saw me with, anymore," says Jasmine. "She was insane. I don't know how you men put up with us women. I certainly couldn't handle one."

Reid turns away to hide his expression. *Of course she's insane. You fell for a hooker you met online.* He turns back to Jasmine and smiles while sitting up straight, determined to be a brick wall, unaffected by her. "How come you never told me you were attracted to women?"

"You're so tightly wound and set in your beliefs. I didn't think you'd understand."

Tightly wound? He stares deeply into her eyes, silently talking himself away from denial and the desire to defend himself. He yearns to lash out, but the new man inside keeps that old self at bay. He squints slightly, catching her studying his lips, a sign that his unshakable strength may have sparked her feminine sexual response system. Her action causes Reid have an epiphany. *Could this be about healing the wound while being the new version of myself in an old environment? A contrast so that my brain can grow. It's too easy to be the "new me" around people I've never met. But to be face to face with the person I allowed to have the most power over me — that will be the ultimate test to see how much I've grown. She's challenging me to fall back into old behavior patterns.*

Reid's anxiety shifts into a sense of feeling grounded. "You're correct. I was tightly wound. Things have changed."

"I can tell. There's something different about you. It's like you have a darkness, something edgy about you that I can't grasp." Jasmine leans closer to him, and her sweet scent hits his nose. "There was an innocence that was always present with you. And now it's gone. Are you still the same man I fell in love with?"

Reid breaks eye contact and glances across the bar. *I'm not the scared little boy who begged for your approval every day.* He catches himself clenching his teeth, takes a long sip of his drink, and faces her once more.

She puts her hand on his thigh. "I've missed your infinite affection so much. I can't control this urge anymore." She leans forward to kiss Reid's lips.

Her quick move freezes Reid. His lips stay stiff and shut, but her soft, plump lips work slowly to pry them open. A whiff of her scent triggers his brain back into the old pattern, where he allowed her to do whatever she wanted. *I don't want her to feel bad. She's vulnerable and showing courage right now.* He slowly opens his lips, expanding the basic kiss into one of passion. His mind swirls with conflicted emotions. *What the hell are you doing, Reid? Worrying about her feelings is the same as seeking her approval. End this now.* He grabs the back of her neck and pulls her head back, disconnecting their kiss. Jasmine stares at him with glossy eyes.

"We will kiss on my terms," says Reid. He releases his grip of her neck, turns to the bar, and finishes the remainder of his drink.

Jasmine doesn't move; she just continues to stare at him. He senses that she's perplexed by this new man who sits before her. He returns to face her and sees her expression change — she looks awed as she bites her lower lip.

He grabs cash from his pocket and tosses down enough to cover the drinks and gratuity. Reid rises from the chair and heads towards the front door. "We're leaving."

Jasmine follows Reid. "Where are we going?"

"To your home," says Reid.

They stroll across the street towards Jasmine's place, their old home. As they near the front door, Reid's mind flashes back to the night of his twenty-ninth birthday. *I was standing right here with my keys in my hand, debating whether to enter and face my greatest fear.* Reid looks at the keyhole, feeling the discomfort of that night creep into his heart, but then he takes a deep breath and smiles. *That was the moment everything changed for the better.*

Jasmine slides the key into the lock and they enter. He sees the home looks the same, except it seems to have more space. As he walks further into the home, he remembers how it used to be filled with flower vases, and now there aren't any vases to be seen. *I can't believe I bought her flowers every damn day.* The thought causes him to lift his chest, knowing he's a different man now, a better man. He now understands he was buying her flowers to make up for the work he was afraid to do on himself.

"Can I get you something to drink?" says Jasmine. "I'm gonna make a martini in the kitchen."

"I'm good," says Reid.

"I'm gonna be a minute. I need to look up a martini recipe."

As he walks towards the bedroom, he feels a chill roll up his spine. The visual hits him harder than he anticipated; it's like that nightmare is happening all over again. Reid looks at the bed and his mind flashes to Jasmine moaning blissfully while being pleasured by a woman wearing a strap-on dildo. *Was I so bad that she needed to hire a prostitute? How could she not appreciate all that I did for her?* The painful images continue to bombard his brain one by one: the hooker thrusting in and out of his future wife; being told he's a terrible lover.

Overwhelmed, he feels dizzy. He bends over and drops his hands onto his knees. He slows his breath to regain clarity. *No, no, no. Remember how she looked at you at the bar? The truth is that this occurred because I didn't know how to accept who I really am. She's never been around the "real me."*

He hears a faint voice wanting to cry from within his soul. *I'm not that pathetic male who used to beg for her approval and manipulate her with kindness.* His mind flashes through images of his experiences with Dalia and Molly. *That's the man I am now. Jasmine courageously stuck with a shitty version of me. At least for tonight, she deserves to learn who I really am — not for revenge, but perhaps to give us both a sense of peace.*

Reid straightens himself, sticks his head out of the bedroom door, and looks to the kitchen. Jasmine is just getting started on the ingredients for her martini. He pulls up his pant legs where he hid two bondage straps. He quickly wraps each strap around the bottom of the headboard. Then he tucks the straps under the bed. His mind wanders to his experience with Mia, tying her hands together, then leaving her. *That was seeking revenge.* He reminds himself that if he ties Jasmine to the bed, it's to serve her.

Reid turns to leave the room, but then stops to observe the reflection in the body-length mirror hanging by the door. He's never felt comfortable looking in this mirror. He'd check it before heading off to lecture on topics that he now sees as bullshit. *No wonder I hated my reflection; I knew I was a fraud.* He squares his shoulders while reflecting on what he now stands for. *I'm Professor Reid Bradley. My mission is to save the world from the dangers of the Collective Shadow, a destructive force that thrives on individuals not accepting all that they are. The Erotic Sensory Experience will reconnect the recipient with an accurate sense of who they are as a human-animal — unaffected by numbing technologies and sexually repressive belief systems. All five senses must be stimulated with contrasts: hearing, tasting, smelling, touching, and —* Reid looks around the room, then looks back at the mirror — *seeing.*

He dims the bedroom lights, then strides towards the kitchen with a sense of certainty, knowing he'll authentically serve and not seek revenge.

Jasmine is taking a sip of the martini. She notices Reid and sets the martini on the counter. "It tastes good. Are you sure you don't want some? It's nice and cold." Jasmine's eyes expand as Reid nears; she appears to recognize the shift in Reid's energy. "Oh my — ahhhh!" Reid lifts Jasmine off her feet and sits her on the long kitchen counter.

"The last thing you're going to be thinking about for the rest of the night is the sensory experience created by that drink," says Reid.

She leans forward to kiss him. Reid reaches behind her neck and grips some hair to prevent her from going further. She gasps and looks shocked.

"We kiss on my terms," commands Reid. His grip of her hair is firm, but it's not about insecure dominance; it's about knowing how this will affect her sensory response system — serving her with his masculinity. He feels the hair on his fingertips, and is conscious of how his pulling her hair is activating the neurotransmitters in her brain. He smiles, noticing her gaze slowly shift into a look of submissive awe. "Do not talk. Do not make a sound. Do not touch me. Do not lick me. Do not attempt to please me in any way."

"Who are you? I'm loving this new Reid Bradley."

He steps back, then speaks in a caring tone, the tone of a conscious dominant. "If you say another word, I'll be gone forever."

Jasmine nods. With his fingers, he gently strokes her arms, feeling goosebumps prickle across her skin. He leans towards her ear and speaks slowly. "Only focus on the sensations that your body is about to feel. Commit to silencing your dancing mind, and just absorb the sensations."

He then presses his fingernails into her arms, scratching down from her shoulder to her elbow. His heart begins to flutter; he starts to sense that serving Jasmine is going to be different to serving the random women he's been with. But he cannot fall for her again. He's determined not to lose the progress he's made spending time with Wish.

He pulls the blindfold out of his back pocket and covers her eyes. "This is to enhance the other four senses."

Jasmine bites her lower lip.

He then drops to one knee and carefully peels off each high heel while massaging her feet. He studies her awestruck facial expression as he applies pressure in the exact spots that are tense from wearing the heels. She tilts her head back and her mouth falls agape. His hands slide up her calves, applying pressure to nerve zones just below the back of the knees; he knows her calves are also tense from wearing heels.

"Don't move," Reid says as he stands. He steps to the sink and turns the hot water on. He then goes to the bathroom and retrieves a long towel and a small washcloth. He spreads the long towel out on the counter, then guides Jasmine to lie on top. He pulls her dress over her head, taking it off and exposing her bra and underwear.

He moves two steps back and observes his one-time lover lying semi-naked on his old kitchen counter. *Her olive skin looks stunning with the matching white bra and panties. Why didn't I think of doing this before?*

He holds the small towel under the hot water, wrings it out, then carefully places it on her chest. She sucks in a breath as the heat touches her skin. He then reaches into the freezer for an ice cube and places it on her stomach.

"Ahhhh," says Jasmine through clenched teeth displayed through a smile.

"Do not make any sounds. This is your last warning."

Reid glides his fingers across her body, consciously channeling all of her sexual energy towards her navel. He continues to apply the hot towel and ice to various areas of her skin, seeing her lick her lips, a signal that she's eager for a kiss.

"A kiss will be earned with good behavior," says Reid.

He grabs one of Jasmine's arms and folds it around his neck, then he lifts her off the counter. Surprised by how light she feels, Reid recognizes that he's in a trance; he senses he's involved in something beyond an ESE. He carries her to the bedroom, feeling every step occur in slow motion, like an athlete in the zone experiencing the game on a higher level than anyone else. He sets her to stand in front of the bedroom mirror. The focus he's experiencing right now is deeper than any he has felt in his life before. He wants to question why this is happening, but knows that would take him out of this zone. He glides his hands along her back, noticing each millimeter of skin, consciously sending his erotic energy into her body. He then pops off her bra, removes her underwear, and places each of her hands on the wall at either side of the mirror.

Reid takes off his shirt and stands behind Jasmine. He studies them in the mirror. The sight of her petite frame in contrast to his muscular figure further confirms that he's no longer that man from the past. He slowly peels the blindfold away from Jasmine's eyes and off her head. *She deserves to see who I really am as well.* Jasmine immediately moistens her lips as she views his brawniness in contrast to her delicacy. She lifts her hand off the wall to touch his washboard stomach. He swiftly grabs her wrist and returns her hand to the wall. Jasmine dips her head, then slowly looks at Reid's reflection with an expression that says, *I'm loving this new Reid.*

He smiles within, becoming aware that he used to beg her to desire him. Wish said Reid wouldn't experience love until he loved himself. He wonders if the way he feels means he's now in a place of self-love.

He returns his focus to providing the ESE, allowing his hands to explore her smooth skin with a feather-light touch. "Your skin gives me so much pleasure."

Reid draws small circles around her rosy-tipped nipples, then pinches briefly. Jasmine coos as her head rolls back. He grips a handful of hair on the top of her head, squeezes firmly, then gently presses it forward until her eyes return to focusing on the reflection.

"Do not deny yourself the pleasure of seeing your perfect body in this mirror." Reid pulls her hair away from her neck. "You're irresistible." He bites her exposed neckline with just enough pressure to sting but not break the skin. He checks her reflection to ensure she's viewing his actions. *Perfect. Visual stimulation is intact.*

"You've proven that you can remain fully present. You've earned a kiss." Reid presses his lips onto her neck, then kisses a path up to her lips. They embrace in a passionate kiss. But the kiss shifts Reid's focus away from providing an ESE as a Sexmyst. He's now distracted by a sudden feeling of the love he once experienced with Jasmine, feeling butterflies in his stomach. *No, no, no. Provide the ESE. Ignore the love.* Reid's eyes begin to water. *Don't blow this moment. Focus on the ESE.* He notices his lips start to quiver in the kiss.

He quickly moves his lips away, then lifts her, carries her to the bed, and sets her into the doggy-style position, facing away from him. He wipes his eyes and goes to the corner of the bed. *Channel the dominant energy, Reid.* He reaches under the bed, grabs a strap, and secures it tightly around her right wrist, then does the same for her left wrist. He returns to the bottom of the bed, where she remains set up doggy-style. He grips her waist and pulls her towards him, so her arms are fully extended from the straps. Her bottom remains elevated. Reid uses his fingers and palms in a rhythmic pattern to stimulate the sensory zones around her vulva. Jasmine coos at his touch. Her moans increase in volume as each minute passes. He feels the lips of her vulva flood with warm dewiness. He sees her spine rise up and down as her heavy breathing increases. *She's nearing orgasm.* Reid lifts his hands away from her core just before she climaxes.

"N-no, no —" Jasmine catches herself attempting to speak and shifts to silence.

"In the kitchen, I told you not to speak. And that applies here as well. You broke the rule."

He raises his hand back and releases it towards her bum with maximal force. Jasmine lifts her chin forward and exhales loudly, cutting off her scream. He reaches into his back pocket and retrieves a small purple feather that he purchased earlier that day. He notices the skin of her bum become ripe with a red hue and draws the feather along the redness.

Jasmine continues to inhale and exhale deeply, as if he's providing her sting with an antidote. He steps back and releases a thunderous spanking onto her opposite cheek. Jasmine's groan seeps through her clenched teeth, but she cuts off the sound within a second. Reid thinks of punishing her further, but lets it slide, knowing it would be practically impossible for her to silence her natural sounds. He brushes the purple feather along the newly flushed redness of her bum. He stiffens his index and middle fingers and applies firm pressure to the skin on the outer edges of her slit.

Reid then stops and steps back. *My one-time lover is bound and submissive to my every desire. Good girl.*

He widens his stance, scanning the room that once housed his greatest nightmare. *Could it be that Wish wanted me to heal by flushing out that nightmare and replacing it with my ideal scene?* He recalls that this is about cleansing the canvas of his RAS. Experiencing a new scene like this could be the exact thing he needs.

He returns his focus to Jasmine. She's slowly pulling herself forward, attempting to minimize the tautness of her bound wrists. He launches a powerful whack onto her bum, then yanks her body backwards, returning her arms to the fully extended position.

"I didn't say you could move forward," says Reid. Jasmine gasps and sways her hips. "Stop moving. I'll decide when you will be penetrated. Begging will not serve you well."

Reid continues to stimulate her erogenous zones with his fingers, lips, and tongue. Jasmine shivers with goosebumps. Her panting increases. He reaches around her stomach to lift the skin of her pelvis, knowing it will cause the head of her clitoris to become exposed. He eases his free hand onto her vulva, then strokes her clitoris with soft, darting movements. Jasmine's hips gradually rise. She can't help but break the no-talking rule as she spirals into euphoria.

"Oh my God! Oh my God! Yes. Yes. Yes." She releases orgasmic screams, then melts into the mattress with her arms still bound.

Reid moves to stand a few feet from the bed and observes her while grinning. He knows her sounds were released with a sense of restraint, creating a more potent sensory experience, and this matters more than the no-talking rule. He realizes the rule was not about control, but about being a conscious dominant, about giving her this experience. He takes a mental snapshot of this scene he produced. Being with Jasmine, contrasting his old self versus the new one, is bringing a sense of confirmation. *I love who I am.*

Reid moves close to her and releases her wrists. Jasmine turns around to lie on her back. She stares at Reid with a satisfied, yet bewildered expression. Reid then moves to stand near the bedroom door, allowing himself to taking it all in, cleaning his RAS canvas. *This is the exact position where I caught you with that woman. You had a look of elation while being penetrated by that woman. But that was nothing like your gaze right now.* Reid watches her stroke her body, satisfied to see her experiencing the retroactive effects of the ESE.

Jasmine moves her hands towards her glistening vagina. She then glances up at the half-clothed Reid with an expression that tells him she's begging for penetration.

Reid feels tempted to talk, but instead chooses to stand in silence. *You're very tempting, but I can't. There was too much emotion behind that kiss. I still have feelings for you. I have to remain committed to Wish. I have to see that journey all the way through. Maybe one day we will reunite, but now isn't the time.*

He picks up his shirt and walks towards Jasmine. He leans close and kisses her forehead. "I'm glad we met up again."

Jasmine frowns as she realizes he is leaving. Her eyes begin to water. She opens her mouth to speak, but nothing comes out.

"I want you to know," says Reid, fighting his urge to comfort her, "I'm committed to something very important right now and it requires me to continue my journey alone."

"Are you running away from me because I hurt you before?" she asks apologetically. "I'm so sorry for causing you pain, lying, being unfaithful. The last thing I would ever want to do is hurt you."

Reid leans against the wall. Her apology is refreshing, but Reid knows this isn't what he's supposed to do, that he's not here in this moment to take her back.

"At first, I was hurt. But I've since learned that you were acting in a way that you felt would connect you to your happiness. You were exploring your dark side, and I respect the courage it took to do so. And the results of your courageous act forced me to explore parts of myself I was afraid to examine. I'm forever grateful for what you have done for me."

He watches a streak of mascara drip down her face. He feels tempted to stay, but realizes his temptation is a reflex inspired by her tears. It has become clear to him why he needed to see her: to cleanse the RAS — being his brand-new self around her, further disconnecting himself from the man he once was, and having a conversation to express his gratitude. Given all he's experienced since meeting Wish and the power of this moment, he now has clarity on what is most important: the mission, his mission. He's always known that if he can heal his own suffering, he must then share his methods with the world.

Reid slides his shirt on. He moves close to Jasmine, caresses her fingers, then kisses the top of her hand, hearing her sob. He feels a hint of curiosity about what their life might have been if he went back to her, but deep down he knows that he'll never be happy with anyone unless he remains true to his mission, even if it makes them cry. He takes a deep breath to gather his strength, mouths the word *goodbye,* then exits.

Reid gets into his car and tears up as he drives home. He turns on the radio. The station is playing the song he and Jasmine used to claim was their song. He mouths the lyrics. *I would do anything for you ... I would do anything for you.*

Reid hits the radio button to turn it off. *Enough of that sappy shit.* He smirks, observing the irony of hearing that song in this moment. *Perhaps the Collective Shadow has something to do with the timing of radio songs, wanting to take me away from the mission.*

Though he feels emotional, he anticipates his heart will settle by the morning and he'll be ready to head back to Vegas to reconnect with Wish. He digs his second phone out of the glove box. He sends Wish a text, confirming that his assignment has been completed and he'll return tomorrow. Wish quickly responds.

Meet me at the place where those skin-heads threatened us, tomorrow at 4pm.

Reid furrows an eyebrow, curious as to why Wish would want to go back there. He wonders if something is up. Then he hears the phone "ding" three times. He gazes at the screen, seeing three texts from Dani.

Your teachings have drastically improved my life.

I hope things are going well for you in LA.

We would make a great team, just like we did with Tom from Texas. I've got 2k waiting for you. Tell me you have more secrets to teach, Professor?

Reid sets the phone back on the passenger seat. He just experienced major victory of self-improvement and he has zero time to enjoy it because more concerns seem to be sliding into the open space. Something might be up with Wish, and now Dani seems to be extra-aggressive. He grips the steering wheel while tapping his fingers along the leather stitching. *She's got two grand for me? I'm a professor, not a pimp.* Yet her behavior thus far has seemed purely authentic. She didn't dive for the money tossed on the floor by Cherry. And she hasn't asked for anything except knowledge on how to serve others — for which she offers money in exchange. *But two grand is a lot for some advice.* His head becomes heavy with confusion. He just cleansed his RAS, a sign of gaining personal strength. But his increase in strength could mean the CS is going to attack with something stronger? He realizes that if Dani isn't as trustworthy as he hopes, then it might mean she's one of the Collective Shadow's greatest assassins.

Chapter 28

Reid completes the drive from Los Angeles to Las Vegas with ease, arriving at the park on time. He steps out of his car, feeling the hot desert sun hit his face. He quickly walks to the secluded section of the park. As he enters the tree-covered area, he sees Wish sitting with his legs crossed on top of the picnic table; he appears to be meditating with his eyes closed.

"Your drive from LA must have gone smoothly. You made good time," says Wish. He opens his eyes and turns to Reid. "You don't have to explain anything you experienced last night. We'll know if the RAS is cleared by events that occur in the future. Just remember, if more events happen that relate to you being angry at women, then you need to look further within to see what else might need to be cleared. Understood?"

"Yes, sir," says Reid. Based on the way he left Jasmine last night, he feels confident that his RAS is cleared with regards to his anger towards her. "Everything went well. So, why did you want to meet here in the park?"

"Do you remember the specifics of what happened last time we were here?"

"Yes, we got threatened by some white supremacists and you shattered a man's arm."

"I've found myself becoming judgmental of people since that day — very dangerous to have in my RAS. Those thoughts will not serve my life and will affect my ability to serve others. If I don't address the self-inflicted suffering, it will snowball into all aspects of my life and bring on more suffering. The RAS always seeks to create a reality based on the emotions that it's fed. If possible, we must step back into the scene and cleanse the emotional pain from our minds."

"I'm guessing that's why you had me go see Jasmine? Cleansing the RAS in the exact environment where a wound was created? At first I was confused, but then I felt a sense of cleansing the moment I stepped into that bedroom." Wish nods. "I made peace with the scene in that room. Then I recreated a new scene with Jasmine. I provided an ESE for her."

Wish nods, then goes to the exact position where he was kneeling when the assailant attacked. He closes his eyes and falls to his knees.

Reid steps near to Wish, then gazes at the ground. "There are still spots of his blood on the weeds."

"There are still spots of his blood on my mind." Wish places his hands in the prayer position. Reid instantly connects the comment to Wish wanting to cleanse his RAS. Wish continues: "Every single second of every single day, every single human behaves in a way that they believe will bring them happiness. The moment I judge them — which is an attempt to control their approach to seeking happiness — is the moment that I create my own suffering."

"I get what you're saying, but those men wanted to physically harm both of us."

"Those men were put on this planet with challenges they must learn to overcome, just as we were. The second those men approached us, an opportunity to improve self-love was created. Self-love can improve drastically when facing a fear. I faced the fear of dying before the mission was complete — leaving my son in a world he would struggle to understand. And those men were just as scared as we were."

"Those men didn't seem scared. They seemed filled with anger."

"The anger was a mask over their fear. They hadn't received much compassion in life, which left them afraid of compassion and creating a lifestyle that guarantees a lack of compassion."

"So how does getting threatened lead to improving self-love?" says Reid.

"Self-love can be developed through positive thought, attention to physical health, reflection, meditation — but the largest increases in self-love occur after experiencing a fear and walking right through it. This includes fears that we choose to face or fears that we are forced to face. You learned a lot about yourself in that moment. The brain needs fear-based experiences to expand with awareness. We stood our ground during a threat, and I'll soon see if they've faced their fear of receiving compassion."

Reid examines the blood-stained weeds near his shoes, feeling a tingle of the fear from that day. He realizes his entire journey has been a series of facing fears and walking through them. The outcome hasn't always been positive, but going through fear has always left him feeling uplifted, like he's growing as a man.

"Hey," a voice calls out from behind Reid and Wish.

Reid's heartrate increases. He turns and sees a man, covered in tattoos and with short brown hair, walking toward them. The man has a cast on his arm, covering the skin from his hand to his bicep. Reid connects the dots and identifies the man as the skinhead who attacked Wish.

"I got your letter," says the man. "I'm surprised that you'd actually show up on the day and time that was mentioned in the letter."

Reid glares at Wish. *You sent this man a letter with a meet-up time? Shit, he probably brought a gun.* The twigs below Reid's feet crack as he steps backwards.

"Did you come for revenge or to make peace?" says Wish.

The man lowers his chin, then slowly falls to his knees. Reid lifts his eyebrows.

The man lifts his chin as he speaks. "I came to say thank you, sir."

Thank you?

"Thank you for helping me see the light. Thank you for setting up a plea bargain for me to go to drug rehab." The man sobs. "And most importantly, thank you for convincing my ex-wife to allow my son to visit me in there."

Reid lifts his hand to his forehead, then looks at Wish. Initially he's shocked, but then he settles into not being surprised, recognizing a consistent theme in Wish's desire to unite fathers and sons — easing Wish's own guilt for having to send his son away.

Wish lifts the man off the ground so they stand face to face. "This is your first day out, correct?"

"Yes, sir."

"There were two questions in the letter," says Wish. "Are you prepared to give me your answers?"

"Yes, sir. You asked me to find a way to positively channel my anger over experiencing a lack of compassion in my life." Wish nods. "I want to be a drug rehab counselor, sir. I've stored up a lot of unused compassion over the years. I want to help people, just as you have helped me."

"That's good. And what do you have planned for your involvement with your son?"

"When my arm heals, I'm gonna teach him to play catch. Next year, I want to be his Little League baseball coach."

Wish pulls the man in for a hug. "Good man. That's all I needed to hear from you." Wish steps away from the man and walks to leave, nodding once for Reid to follow. Just before walking out of the shadows cast by the overhanging trees, Wish stops and turns back to the man. "I'll be checking to see if you're involved in Little League next summer. If not, I'll either have you killed or thrown in jail. Depends on what mood I'm in that day."

"Understood, sir."

Wish and Reid stroll back to their cars. Reid wants to question Wish, but senses it's best that this moment be reserved for silence, allowing him to review the connection between this event and the night before with Jasmine. *We just recreated positive scenes in the places where scary events occurred.* The realization serves as confirmation that he handled Jasmine correctly, cleansing his mind of the negative emotions he felt after seeing her with Daphne, leaving him with a sense of gratitude for the experience. The lightness in Wish's step signals to Reid that his mentor must be feeling the same way. *We've both done work to clean the canvas of our RAS.*

Wish and Reid stop in front of their cars in the parking lot. The relaxed muscles in Reid's shoulders stiffen as he sees Wish's expression become serious.

"Youngblood's suspension got reduced to three weeks. He becomes active again on Monday."

Reid crosses his arms. "Did you and the Sexmysts earn enough during your big push?"

"Not quite. But there's a big MMA fight going on tonight at the Largo Hotel. Fight night always fills the town with testosterone-fueled men. The Sexmysts are going to be extra-aggressive. Unfortunately, that means they'll be providing experiences for regular johns."

"But that's against what you stand for. Being with regular johns is firmly against your rules, isn't it?"

"Yes, you're correct. But there are times in life when it can be justifiable to break a rule, assuming you're fully conscious and accepting of the reasoning."

"What's your reasoning?"

"Well, we need the money. But also, the Sexmysts and I will learn more about the importance of our mission by experiencing people who don't get the mission. We'll break the rules while maintaining a growth-oriented mindset — like when Cherry uses cocaine twice a year; he always scans his brain after usage on an fMRI machine for research purposes."

Reid uncrosses his hands and stares at the gravel. He wonders if there are any rules of his own that may need to be broken. His thoughts are disrupted as Wish continues.

"I've given my investor four hundred thousand, meaning one hundred thousand remains. Since this is our last night free of Youngblood, we intend to earn two hundred thousand tonight, because of the fifty–fifty split with the Sexmysts. Much of what we earn will be in chips that you'll need to cash out tomorrow night. You won't be handling any of my chips this evening. Instead, I want you to study the scene. The Las Vegas Strip is a different animal on a fight night. The energy makes men and women act more primal. Andrew went ahead and set up a room for you — and since this is our last weekend together, he got you a suite. Pack your stuff at the Lexi Hotel and enjoy staying in the suite at the Largo this weekend."

"Really? Oh, man, thank you." Reid's grin quickly turns into a worried frown. "I don't want this to end. What am I supposed to do with the mission when you're gone?"

"You'll know after this weekend."

Chapter 29

"No freaking way," Reid says out loud to himself as he steps into his VIP suite at the Largo Hotel. He wanders along the marble hallway, entering a living room that has a long couch and a massive flat-screen TV. There is a small coffee table that rests on top of a massive white-fur rug that sparkles with newness.

Reid steps into the bedroom, snickering to himself as he studies the space. He used to enter a hotel room and wonder if the bed would be comfy. Now he scans the space, imagining how he'll maximize Erotic Sensory Experiences within the layout. He searches for where he could hide the paddles, tassels, and vibrators, and imagines the different sex positions he could place a potential partner throughout the room. He sees that the bed's headboard is designed to his liking — there are circular holes near the outer edge of the headboard, perfect for securing the bondage rope as it's wrapped around the wrists of a potential partner.

He sashays towards the floor-to-ceiling bedroom window; the view is of the Strip and the pond that has the fountain show. He looks across the pond and sees the Cleopatra Hotel, smirking as he recalls his first trip. *Lucky room, thirty-three-thirty-three.* He thinks about how he got upgraded to that suite because it was his twenty-ninth birthday and he was heartbroken. He remembers the strange combination of fear and shame he felt when crying in the parking lot of Mick's. Then he met an unlikely mentor, a pimp named Wish, who showed him the world he'd secretly yearned to be a part of. Reid laughs to himself — *but then I got seduced by a prostitute and robbed.* The fountains erupt into the opening number of their performance. *What an adventure. I can't believe this is coming to an end. Hopefully, it's just the end — for now.*

Reid slides into bed, intending to nap before leaving for the night, but his mind can't shut down. He envisions Jasmine's excited gaze if she were there with him. *Ugh, but I have to stop thinking about her.* He wonders if such a thought is a sign of more residue in his RAS that he must cleanse. *She looked so sexy the other night, though.* He shrugs, then exhales deeply, hoping to shift his thoughts away from Jasmine. Understanding the power of his RAS, he closes his eyes to picture what he wants to experience tonight and tries to add emotion to his vision. Dani is the first image to pop up. *Dani is smoking hot. And she owes me two grand.* Reid laughs. *I'm not her pimp. That's ridiculous. But I might as well check in with her.*

He grabs his phone and types a text to Dani.

I'm staying at the Largo Hotel tonight and tomorrow night. Did you book a room here too?

Dani responds: **Yes. Fight night tonight. Lots of potential business.**

Reid types: **It'd be fun to watch you work the bar scene. Meet me at the Diamond Bar, 11pm?**

Dani responds: **Yes, sir. I'll have your money then too.**

Reid cackles, then types: **Good girl. You're making Daddy proud.**

Reid manages to settle his busy mind and fall asleep for a brief nap. Then he wakes, gets ready for the night, and heads to the Diamond Bar.

He unbuttons his suit jacket and slips into the seat at bar. It's eleven and Dani hasn't arrived yet.

"Hey, Professor," says Ronald, the bartender. "Did you see the fight?"

"No, how did it go?"

"The champ, Knock-Out Jones, got knocked out in the third round. I love the irony, because the cocky bastard has a giant tattoo of his name across his chest."

"And he was lying there knocked out?" says Reid.

"Yeah, the video camera kept zooming in on his stupid tattoo," says Ronald. "You want your usual, chilled mescal?"

Reid nods and Ronald goes to fix his drink.

"Hey there, sexy." Reid hears a sensual voice from behind. He turns and receives a hug and a kiss on the cheek from Dani. She slides into the seat next to his.

"I've got something for you." Dani reaches into her purse and pulls out a neat stack of one-hundred-dollar bills.

"Whoa, whoa, whoa. Be careful. Don't be so obvious about it." Reid takes the stack and scans the bar while sliding the money into his breast pocket. He can't help but feel something is off about her generosity. "You really didn't have to pay me, but I appreciate the gesture."

"You know we'd make a good team. You even said so. Plus, nobody would believe a college professor would be involved in our business. To you it's all research, right?" Dani winks.

"Yup. It's just research." *I think.*

"What's another thing you can teach me, Professor?"

Reid takes a long sip of his mescal. The Shadow Palm Technique would be the perfect thing to teach her. But Wish stressed that it's important for the practitioner to have good intentions. Reid feels like he can trust Dani, but still he senses a slight warning poking him at the back of his head. She's almost too nice to him. But she hasn't given him any reason not to trust her. Perhaps he's just being cautious because Mia was such a hustler. He can't deny how much he lights up when around Dani; she's got to be for real.

Reid takes a deep breath. *If I can't trust her, I can't trust any woman.* "There is something called the Shadow Palm Technique. It's highly potent — effective for improving someone's life. But it can also easily be abused in order to manipulate."

"Ohhh, I'm dying to know more. Please share." Dani leans toward Reid. She edges a finger down his lapel.

"You're just a ball of sexual energy, aren't you?" says Reid.

"I can't help myself, especially when I'm around you." Dani extends her hand to lightly pet Reid's cheek.

Reid feels her fingers patter along his facial stubble, and he melts within, noticing authenticity in her touch. He still feels slightly hesitant to share, but recalls Wish's explanation that breaking a rule from time to time is understandable. The sensations Reid is experiencing from her touch certainly make Dani seem worth breaking a rule for.

Dani leans toward the side of Reid's head. His neck tingles as her lips graze his ear as she speaks. "How about you take me upstairs and show me the new technique?"

He drains the rest of his mescal. Wish said he was free to do whatever he wanted tonight, and an Erotic Sensory Experience with Dani is exactly what he wants. He slides the empty glass onto the bar, knowing to remain cool with her.

"Are you sure you want this? Your sexual experiences will never be the same," says Reid.

"I've wanted you since the moment we met. A more accurate question is — are you sure you can handle this?" Dani squeezes her breasts upward.

Reid's tongue wags inside his closed mouth. He settles himself, then gazes at her. "We go to my room. Not yours."

"You're making me break my rule of only serving men in my hotel room."

"My mentor says that it's healthy to break a rule from time to time. Plus, I'll be serving you. You're not gonna do shit to me." Reid stands and extends his open palm towards her.

"We'll see about that." Dani winks and grabs Reid's hand.

They walk towards the elevators. Reid presses the call button. Dani digs in her purse and pulls out her phone. She reads the screen, then frowns.

"I have to meet a high-roller at the Mirage. He just texted me. I have to go. Big money with this guy."

Reid tilts his head to the side. "You are such a tease."

"I'm just as horny as you. But we can do this whenever. This is his last night in town. You'll get your cut. Don't worry." Reid feels Dani's soft lips connect to his briefly, then she hurries off.

He leans on the nearby wall to gather himself, obsessing over the ESE he will someday provide for her. *We'd never leave the room.* He notes that when he does share an experience with Dani, he needs to remain fully conscious and in control like he was with Jasmine, because such an urge could distract him from the mission. He decides to move along and seek another person who needs an experience. He can't let the VIP suite go to waste.

Reid leaves the bank of elevators and returns to his seat at the Diamond Bar. He signals to Ronald for another mescal. It's quickly shaken into a glass and slid to Reid. He swallows a large amount, then swivels to scope the lively bar scene. Sitting in the back corner of the bar is a man in a dark suit with a familiar goatee. *It's Youngblood. Dammit.* He wonders how long Youngblood has been sitting there and whether he saw the interaction with Dani and the exchange of cash. He's flooded with the urge to leave, and he swivels back to face the bar, debating whether leaving is the right choice. He figures he'll stay a few more minutes so he doesn't look like he's avoiding Youngblood.

He swallows the rest of his drink, then glances to his left and catches the eye of a seductive Latina seated at the end of the bar — a potential mate to share his VIP suite with tonight. He begins to feel the effects of the booze kick in. *I'm at least going to stay to talk to this girl. I want another drink, though.* Reid signals to Ronald for another drink. The bartender quickly prepares a fresh glass of chilled mescal and hands it to him. Reid takes a swig, then stands. *I haven't done anything illegal. Screw Youngblood.* He shoots a look at the area where Youngblood was sitting, but that chair is now empty. *Good, that guy can go bask in his self-hatred somewhere else.*

Reid glides towards the Latina. He smiles and she returns the gesture. "Is this seat taken?"

"No, it's open."

"I'm Reid. I was sitting over there. And I walked over here to hit on you."

"I'm Marisol. I saw you over there too. I appreciate your forwardness."

"Did you see the fight? I heard it was interesting."

Marisol rolls her eyes. "Those fights are for boys. Please tell me you are a man."

"You've presented a tricky question, because the act of telling you that I'm a man sounds like something a boy would do."

Marisol laughs. "You're very observant. I never thought of it that way."

"I'm guessing a beautiful woman such as yourself, has someone in her life, but she's checking to see if something better exists."

"Every woman has some guy they keep around in their life."

"This might be a bit of a stretch, but I would guess that the man we're discussing takes you out to restaurants quite often?"

"All the time," she says.

"And what kind of sports car does he use to take you there?"

Her eyes expand. "Yes, sometimes we go in his Ferrari and other times in his Porsche." She smirks, then places her hand on Reid's thigh. "How did you guess that? Are you some kind of mystic?"

"Mystic?" Reid chuckles. *Interesting choice of word.* "The reason I guessed is because your question about me being a man suggests some form of sexual dissatisfaction. This can often be the result of spending time with an approval-seeking male."

"You didn't watch the fight, did you?" asks Marisol.

"I was busy with something else. Why are you in Vegas?"

"I had to be here for the fight. And now I'm at this bar because I'm — as you say — dissatisfied."

"Shall we change that?"

"What did you have in mind, Mr. Reid?"

"We can be upstairs and in my room in approximately thirty-seven seconds."

"That's slightly too far for me. I was hoping to be in a room that was only twenty-seven seconds away."

Reid hops up, then scoops her entire body off her chair. She wraps her arm around his neck.

"Ahh, *estas loco,*" she says playfully.

"To get there in twenty-seven seconds would require me carrying you. You can't walk fast enough in those heels."

Reid carries her out of the bar and continues to the bank of elevators.

"I can't believe you're carrying me," says Marisol. Reid sees her feminine glee and knows his actions are boosting her inner goddess. "I want to go to your room. But let me go to my room first and freshen up. What's your room number?"

Reid sets her down. "Forty-five-seventeen. It's on the forty-fifth floor." Reid slides his phone out of his pocket and has Marisol type in her phone number. "I'll text you the room number so you don't forget."

They both step into the elevator. Marisol presses the button for the twenty-third floor, then turns to Reid. He pulls her close for a sensual kiss. The elevator "dings" and stops on her floor. She moves her lips away.

"Give me fifteen minutes. I'll see you soon," says Marisol.

"Sounds good."

As the elevator doors begin to shut, Reid notices a shiny object on her left hand as she struts away. *Don't tell me that was a wedding ring.* The elevator takes Reid to his floor. He leans on the wall, feeling a heavy buzz. *Whatever. I don't care. Her lips tasted like juicy berries. I can't wait for more. I bet her peach tastes even better.*

Reid steps out of the elevator, then stumbles down the hallway. He enters the suite, then slides out his phone to text Marisol.

Remember, I'm in room 4517. I can't wait to taste those juicy lips again.

Reid sets his phone on the counter, his mind dancing uncontrollably. *Can I be selfish tonight? Can I just kiss her and go right into sex like Andrew probably does? All this massaging, tying women up, spanking, and teasing can be exhausting.*

Minutes pass, then Reid hears a light knock on the door. He opens it to see Marisol.

"You clean up well," says Reid.

Reid yanks her into his arms and immediately presses his lips to hers. She peels her dress off and Reid strips down naked. *Screw all that ESE stuff. Tonight will just be raw sex.* He carries her naked body to the bedroom, lays her on the bed, slides on a condom, and penetrates her fold. He applies tender kisses to her neck and breasts while thrusting in rhythm with her moans. He switches her from missionary to thrusting from the side. She then crawls on top of Reid and grinds herself to orgasm. Reid flips her back to missionary and pounds away, paying minimal attention to her sensations. He soon experiences an orgasm and rests on top of her for a few minutes. Reid then rises, cleans himself in the bathroom, and returns to see Marisol finishing getting dressed.

"That was fun," she says.

He finds his boxer briefs and slides them on, surprised by the awkwardness and lack of connection between them — the opposite of how he feels after providing an ESE. He realizes that escapism sex has very little value.

Marisol zips up her dress and heads to the door. Reid follows behind her and looks at her left hand, seeing the ring again.

"You're married?" asks Reid, hoping the ring is a fake.

"Yes. I figured you saw the ring. My husband is up in the room, fast asleep."

"Oh, shit. He's here? Why the heck is he asleep? This is Las Vegas."

"He took a bunch of pain meds. He got his ass kicked in the ring tonight."

"What? Your husband is —"

"Knock-Out Jones. Yes."

They stop just before the door. She pulls Reid down for another passionate kiss. He enjoys her lips for a few more seconds, then pulls away.

"You have your phone with you, right?" Reid reaches for the door handle.

Marisol pops open her purse. "No phone. I must have left it in the room."

As Reid pulls the door open, he remembers he sent her a text with the room number. *Oh, shit.*

He sees a shirtless man standing before him with a large tattoo across his chest that reads "KNOCK-OUT JONES." Marisol screams. The man throws a punch that connects to Reid's temple, knocking him to the floor. The man jumps on top of Reid and punch after punch smashes into his head and body. Reid manages to get both forearms up to cover his face. His consciousness begins to fade away. He senses the attacker being lifted off him by another man in a suit. *Andrew?*

Reid's mind goes blank.

Chapter 30

Reid's eyes slowly open. The bright sunlight signals to him that it must be the following morning. His body and head throb with sharp jolts of pain as his nervous system awakens. His arms are spread to the edges of the bed. He tries to move his left hand and can't. He does the same with his right hand, then realizes they are bound by straps that are attached to the headboard.

"It's about time you woke up," says a voice that could only be Wish's. Reid turns his head to see his mentor standing with his arms crossed. Andrew is next to Wish, holding a laptop.

"Why am I tied to the bed? I don't remember that woman doing this to me last night."

"Do you remember getting your ass kicked by her husband?" says Wish. Reid drops his head back onto the pillow. "You fucking child. You're lucky Andrew was monitoring the hallways last night. He saved your life."

"I thought that was you who saved me," Reid says to Andrew. "Thanks, man. Seriously, thanks."

"No prob, bro," says Andrew.

"Why am I tied here? My head is killing me," says Reid.

"You're out of control. Until you can prove to me that you'll be in control, you'll stay in this bed," Wish says.

"I'm fine, I promise. I just got a little drunk last night and lost focus."

"You seduced a married woman. I warned you to never use these skills for evil."

"But you said it's okay to break rules every now and then."

"It can be okay to break a rule for an emergency or a premeditated, well-thought-out decision. Not for instant gratification. You got lost in escapism. So the question is, what does your soul want to escape? I thought you addressed that in LA, but it seems there's more."

"Can you untie my hands?" Reid winces through another breath. "I need some pain meds."

"Your physical pain was caused by emotional pain you haven't yet healed."

"What do you mean?"

"You're not out to serve women; you're still out to prove to them that you are worthy. There's another wound you haven't healed from your ex. It was too easy for you to move past the fact you caught her with another woman. But your soul knows there is something else that happened."

"What are you talking about? I don't have any feelings for Jasmine anymore."

Wish turns to Andrew. "Play the song."

Andrew opens the laptop and presses play. A slow melody begins to pulse through a Bluetooth speaker next to the bed. It's the song that Reid and Jasmine used to share.

I would do anything for you…

I would do anything for you…

I would do anything and everything for you…

"Please turn it off. I don't need to hear that right now."

"Why are you trying to escape this pain? Allow it to come to the surface."

"She's dead to me. There's nothing there." Reid's eyes start to tear up. *Damn you. Why are you making me go here? I don't want to feel this.* "Please turn it off."

"The night we met, you told me you did everything for this woman, and you believe she ripped your heart out," says Wish. "Dive into the pain. It wants to come up. You cannot repress it anymore."

The song continues to play. Tears crawl down Reid's face. His shoulders begin to burn as he continues to try to free his wrists. The emotional pain doubles the physical pain pulsing in his head. The song soon comes to an end.

"Why are you putting me through this?"

"You either choose to take control of your life, to cleanse your canvas, or you avoid that challenge and become a victim of the

Collective Shadow. I'm not going to let you be less than the best version of yourself."

"But I've been doing everything you've asked of me. I've learned so much."

"You've done well. But there is something deeply repressed in you that you can't even recognize as being there anymore. Until you face this truth and accept it, you'll work on yourself, only to fall back into the trap of escapism."

Wish signals to Andrew to set the laptop on Reid's stomach. Andrew then stuffs a second pillow under Reid's head, supporting him to sit up straight.

Reid looks at the computer screen, then furrows his eyebrows. "So you want me to watch a video on the laptop? Do I really have to be tied to the bed for this?"

"A scene took place in this room. I wasn't aware of this when you and I met, but Andrew shared it with me recently. This occurred on the bed you are in, a week before you and I met."

Reid struggles to swallow his next gulp. Andrew touches the mouse pad on the laptop to start the video clip. The sound plays out of the Bluetooth speaker on the nightstand. Reid watches the video. The screen portrays Andrew lying naked on the bed with a brunette riding his member. Her back is to the camera.

"Ugh. I don't want to watch Andrew banging some chick. What kind of sick joke is this?"

Andrew darts a concerned look at Wish, who stands with his legs apart and arms crossed.

Reid returns his attention to the video clip. The sex stops. The girl reaches to the side of Andrew and picks up her phone.

"I have to call my boyfriend," she says. "He'll freak out if he doesn't hear from me. He's annoyingly high maintenance."

Her back remains facing the camera as she slowly grinds on Andrew, while holding the phone to her ear. "Hi, honey. My flight is on time."

I know that voice.

"Yes, hun, pick me up at the airport at two o'clock." She pauses as Andrew's stiffness slips out of her. She slides it back in, rolling her hips, while continuing to talk on the phone. "I miss you more ... I love you more ... I can't wait to see you." She increases the speed of her thrust. "I love you more ... I miss you sooooooo much ... Mmmm, big kiss! Byeeeeee." She tosses the phone across the room and falls forward onto Andrews's chest.

Andrew rises and flips her over. Her head remains down as she sets herself up in the doggy-style position. Andrew looks directly into the camera, then pulls the hair on the back of her head so she faces the camera. It's Jasmine.

"You fuck!" Reid's hips jerk upward, launching the laptop across the bed. He moves his arms to break the binds, but Wish has them tightly secured.

"Unhook this shit. Fuck you, Andrew." Reid twists his body to break free, but he remains stuck. "Wish, you're insane. Is this some kind of torture game you like to play?"

"I'm sorry, bro." Andrew places his hands in the prayer position.

"Andrew, don't speak anymore," says Wish. "You have nothing to do with Reid making the choice to suffer right now."

"I'm choosing to suffer?" Reid shifts his threatening stare away from Andrew to look up at the ceiling. *This whole thing is insane.*

"If you want to heal, you need to calm down." Wish places the laptop back on Reid's stomach. "We have your greatest fear caught on film. That's a blessing. You are blessed to be able to make peace with it."

Reid continues to stare up at the ceiling. His voice cracks. "I can't take any more of this. Please take it away. You don't understand how powerful the imagination is. My brain will torture me with these images for the rest of my life."

Wish crosses his arms. "Look at the screen."

Reid closes his water-filled eyes. "You don't understand what this will do to me. I've worked my entire life to make sure this never happens. I studied my ass off to become a god-damned professor of relationships. It's all to avoid experiencing this. You are creating a scar on my brain that will torture me forever."

"Every action you've chosen to make in your life has been done to protect you from facing the thing you fear the most — it's your RAS working to keep you in a constant state of suffering. That's exactly what the Collective Shadow wants you to do. With this mindset, nothing you do will be authentic. You will never know who you really are. Now, look at the fucking screen."

Reid slowly peels his eyes open. He clenches his teeth and glares at Wish. "I guess I'm joining the Collective Shadow then. I quit your stupid mission. You are supposed to be the Mr. Neuroscience superstar. You have no idea who I am. You don't know the powers of my imagination. My brain will never stop torturing me with this scene until I die."

Wish carefully picks up the laptop and hands it to Andrew. Then Wish turns and explodes towards the bed. He grips Reid's neck and squeezes. Reid gasps as he feels his esophagus close.

"I know exactly who you are, you little shit," says Wish as he releases his grip. "You are ... exactly who I was twenty years ago. I'm giving you the gift of not having to spend your adult life searching for what I've already discovered. You're supposed to take my research and expand it, then save the fucking world. We can't wait another twenty years for you to figure this out."

Reid coughs several times, then catches his breath. "You're just a lowly street pimp who teaches love secrets to his bitches."

Wish grabs Reid's throat again, this time with a ferocious grip. He lifts Reid's head off the pillow. "Don't you dare refer to any woman as anything less than a goddess." Wish's free hand reaches back and forms a fist, then launches towards Reid's temple. But Wish stops the punch just before it connects. He releases Reid's neck and steps away.

"A video clip won't do any damage to your brain. But two concussions within twelve hours will create brain trauma that you may never recover from."

Reid coughs, clearing his frazzled throat. Then he speaks. "There you go with more neuroscience bullshit."

Wish turns to Andrew. "Give me the laptop and wait for me outside the suite." Andrew hands over the laptop and exits. Wish sets the computer on the side of the bed, then reaches into his back pocket and pulls out his wallet. He takes out a faded business card and holds it in front of Reid's face.

"Only Dalia and Henry know this," says Wish. "Don't tell another soul."

Reid examines the faded business card. *Dr. Aloyiscious Grimm, Professor of Psychological Neuroscience. Emmott University, Washington, D.C.*

"Why are you showing me some professor's business card? How do you say his first name? Aloe-wish-scious?"

"You said it correctly. That's my first name. I've been called Wish since as early as I can remember."

"You used to be a professor of psychological neuroscience?" Reid widens his eyes. "My goodness. That explains so much."

Wish nods. "Yes. And like you, I walked in on my first fiancée with someone. Except she chose a male prostitute. Around the same time, I was approved for a grant to conduct research on the sex industry in Las Vegas. It was the early nineties. And many bigwigs in politics wanted to impeach our president because they knew he was messing around on his wife. They sent me to Las Vegas to come up with proof that erotic experiences can make someone unfit for such a powerful position. I was determined to prove that my fiancée and our president were psychologically unhealthy. But all my research ended up proving things to be different. My college didn't want me to publish my results. They didn't want me back, and I didn't want to go back. I've been here ever since."

Reid shifts his gaze to the ceiling. His brain works to unify the pieces of the puzzle. Wish first taught all of the erotic stuff by explaining the brain's response to sensations; he tutors students at UNLV for fun; he calls his work "research." Reid realizes that Wish still has that calling to be a professor, a teacher, inside him. And Cherry was his old friend who also worked in neuroscience. *Maybe Wish really does know where I'm coming from.*

Reid glances back at Wish, lowering his chin. "I'm sorry for calling you a lowlife pimp. I'm sorry for everything I just said."

"The only reason I shared all that is because you need to face this, son. You have to clean the canvas of your RAS." Wish opens the laptop and sets it on Reid's stomach. "The world desperately needs you to be who you are. But you'll only discover your truth by walking through the fears that create limitations in your life."

The opening of the laptop activates the scene to continue playing.

This is still going to be really hard. Reid takes a deep breath. "Okay, I'll do it."

"Good," says Wish. "The reward for your courage will be the freedom to live the life that is waiting for you. The real you. Andrew and I are going to leave you to make peace with what you see. Andrew set it to play on repeat. We'll be back in a few hours."

"Can you at least untie me?"

"Nope." Wish exits the suite.

Reid looks at the screen. His head throbs and his ribs feel like they are on fire, but this is nothing compared to how he feels watching the entire act of Jasmine cheating. *She told me she loved me while another man was inside her. Who in their right mind could forgive that?*

Two hours pass. Reid feels his emotional pain lessen each time the video clip circulates through. His brain reflects on all that he has learned since the scene took place, and he uses his newfound knowledge to turn the pain of viewing the clip into gratitude and acceptance. His body starts to fill with a cleansing sensation — the RAS is being cleansed, and this time it's going to be completely free of Jasmine. His head becomes lighter as the feeling of acceptance takes over his body. *Every single second of every single day, every single person behaves in a way that they hope will lead them to happiness. I don't have to agree with her style of seeking happiness. I just have to remember it has nothing to do with me.*

Images of each person he met on this journey and the circumstances that followed flash through his brain. He begins to silently express gratitude towards Jasmine, Daphne, and Andrew, whose choices in their quest for happiness created a domino effect that launched him into his new, fascinating life.

He thinks about Amber and her boyfriend robbing him and how that made Wish sense a deeper connection with him. Reid silently thanks his mom for having the courage to be honest with him, which allowed him to meet his father — and that led to Henry. Reid reflects on the potency of being touched by Tasha and learning from Dalia, and the sexy courage of Molly in allowing him to explore his developing erotic expression. He recalls the uniqueness of Cherry, showing that a man can't focus on being good all the time, but must explore his dark side from time to time while maintaining a commitment to being service-oriented. Then, of course, there is Wish. *Words cannot express what you have done for me.*

He glances up at the ceiling, suddenly hit with an epiphany. The thing that he has developed more than his physique, sexual expression, social skills, and fear-conquering mindset is self-love. He realizes that the happiness quest is ultimately about developing self-love — about asking the question "Who am I, and what do I desire?", and then having the courage to seek answers, to explore things within himself that he's afraid to admit are true. He's learned that no matter the external result, having the courage to step into a fear and seek answers will always result in an expansion of self-love.

Reid hears the front door click open, then shut. Wish and Andrew lope towards him. Andrew has a duffle bag in his hand. He sets it on the couch near the bed.

Reid smiles at Andrew. "Thank you, Andrew. This scene had to happen for me to become the man I am today. I think it's creepy as hell that you film your sexual experiences with women, but I'll work on not judging you. How did you know it was her?"

Andrew looks at Wish and points at Reid's bound wrists. Wish signals his approval for the ties to be undone.

Andrew frees Reid while speaking. "Wish had mentioned that your ex was named Jasmine. I remembered she said she was with a professor. It was random that you met Wish, but once you joined, I found pictures of you and her on Facebook to confirm it. I'm so sorry, bro."

"Don't apologize. I'm forever grateful. And I don't believe it was completely random that it happened this way."

"Nor do I," says Wish. He hands Reid some ibuprofen and a bottle of water. "You have a handsome bruise on your temple, but the rest of your face looks okay. You'll need some rest because you have your biggest assignment tonight. Youngblood becomes active at midnight. I wouldn't be surprised if he takes a big charge at us."

"I'll be ready to go by tonight. What's the assignment?"

"Ninety thousand dollars in chips need to be exchanged."

Reid struggles to swallow his gulp. "But that's too much. The casinos will want me to fill out a tax form."

"You are correct. The tax forms are for anything over ten grand. That's why the ninety grand is set to be split up. Nine grand at ten different casinos."

"Are you sure I'll be safe?" The talk of cash reminds Reid of the two grand Dani gave him last night. He wonders if it is still in his breast pocket.

"Just keep an eye out for Youngblood," says Wish. "The casino chips are in the duffle bag. Cash out everything, then go to the Essex nightclub. My personal banker will meet you in the outdoor restroom of the nightclub. At midnight, go to that outdoor restroom and enter the last stall on the left. My banker will be in the neighboring stall. He'll signal to you from underneath the divider by showing three fingers. Hand him the cash under the stall."

"Got it. Why does it have to be done that way?"

"There is a lot of heat on me, and possibly now on you. Nobody has seen me with my banker, and it's best we keep it that way. The nightclub will be crowded, so it'll be hard to get noticed. I need you to be on top form tonight. If everything goes as planned, I will be off to retirement tomorrow."

"I give you my word. I'll be on point."

"Don't be surprised if Detective Youngblood tries to pull something. Once you complete the cash handover, you should start working on a woman for the night. That way you'll have an alibi to prove you were just at the club to meet women. Don't worry about providing an ESE tonight. Use any of your skills to protect our mission — seduce her pants off if need be — knowing you are breaking the rules to support the mission."

"So I can try to create a threesome with two women then?"

Wish smirks. "You think you have that kind of game, boy?"

"I learned from the best."

Wish and Andrew leave. Reid steps out of bed and locates his suit jacket on the floor. It still contains the two grand from Dani. Again he feels slight discomfort over her giving him the money. *But she was so sweet about it. Maybe she would be open to a threesome tonight?*

Chapter 31

Reid hears his phone chime with a text, causing him to rise from a long nap. He lifts his eyebrows, surprised to see the text is from his boss in Los Angeles, Dean Anderson, the head of his college's Psychology Department.

Sorry to bother you on a Sunday. We had an instructor back out of his commitment to teach a summer school class that begins tomorrow. I know you are scheduled to be off this summer, but I figured I'd check in, just in case you'd be free to work. The class is Advanced Social Psychology 201. It starts tomorrow at 6pm. Any interest?

Reid sits on the edge of the bed, debating whether he wants to go back to work. It seems that his work with Wish will be done after tonight, and he needs the money. *But I'd rather stay in Vegas.* He wonders if there's more Wish may want him to do in Vegas once he leaves. He knows he's supposed to continue the research, but how? If he took the teaching job, would that compromise his work in Vegas?

Reid steps towards the full-length mirror, seeing that he's different now. He's a different man, and he will certainly be a different professor. *I'd have to redo all of my lectures. There is no way I'm teaching that old junk anymore. Perhaps tomorrow will be the start of the next phase in my commitment to Wish — to share the man's research with the world.*

Reid sends a text back to the dean stating that he accepts the invitation to teach that course. He showers and puts on his uniform — a navy-blue suit, crisp white dress shirt, white pocket square, and polished brown wingtip dress shoes. Like an athlete prepping himself in the locker room before a championship game, Reid studies himself in the mirror to make sure his mind, body, and spirit are in sync for the task ahead. *No booze tonight. Gotta stay focused.*

Reid goes through the duffle bag of casino chips, organizing them into piles based on their casino. He puts the small stacks of five to six chips into each of his pockets, then leaves the room. Once in the lobby, he strolls past the Diamond Bar, noticing a beautiful blond sitting by herself. It's Dani.

"Hey, superstar," says Reid. "Everything go well for you last night?"

"Yes," she replies. "I'm sorry for leaving you so abruptly, but the high-roller certainly appreciated the experience."

"No worries. I've learned recently that it's important to support everyone's quest for happiness, even if it doesn't coincide with my desires."

"I wish more people would think the way you do," says Dani. "I have your commission here with me."

"Why do you keep wanting to give me money? With the Texas guy, I understood because we worked that together. But I had nothing to do with your connection to the high-roller from last night."

"You've taught me things about people, sex, and the power of sensory experiences that I didn't know existed. I even learned from our little escapade last night. I want you to know I appreciate and value your intellect."

"But we're friends. Friends don't pay each other." Reid can't help but secretly question if he's being naïve or if she's really this genuine.

"I don't know how else to describe it, but a voice inside keeps urging me to keep you around." Dani places her hand on Reid's back and inches her fingernail down his spine. The sensation sends tingles of pleasure throughout his back, freezing his thoughts.

"You're the only man I've met in this town who I feel I can trust," says Dani. "You're aware that a woman can make a lot more money in this profession than a man. But we women also have the threat of danger. If I was in any danger, I know I could reach out to you and you'd come help — right?"

"Absolutely." The tingle works its way up to his head. *What is it about her that has me so enamored?*

"Please, take your cut of the money I earn."

Reid studies Dani's perfect curves as she reaches into her purse. He can't resist; it's as if staring at her gives his eyeballs a sensual massage. He adjusts his jacket, feeling the chips clink together — a reminder that he needs to focus on the night's mission.

He places his hand on top of hers. "Not now. I don't have room in my pockets for that." He stands to leave. "I've got a bunch of stuff to handle tonight. I need to go. Perhaps we'll connect later to finish what we started last night."

"You've got a bunch of stuff to handle? Meaning you need to check on the other women who work for you." Dani winks. "I think I've figured you out, Reid. Well, for what it's worth, I guarantee I can earn more than all of your women combined."

Reid is taken aback by her comment. *She thinks I'm a secret pimp?* He smiles, seeing how this is all starting to make sense now, feeling less worried that she's a member of the Collective Shadow.

"I'll connect with you later." Reid kisses Dani on the forehead and exits the Largo Hotel. He walks fast, focusing his mind on the mission at hand. He's determined to not fail the final assignment from Wish.

While walking along the Strip, he glances at his watch, then tightens his shoulders. He realizes he's not going to have enough time to play blackjack at ten different casinos. He's only got three hours to complete the task before meeting the banker in the Essex nightclub restroom at midnight. He reviews his mental list of the ten casinos and creates a plan. Since he hasn't been in seven of the ten casinos, he'll hit those first. And instead of playing blackjack, he'll go straight to the cashier cage — since he's never been there, there shouldn't be any trouble.

As he enters each casino, his heart beats like a bassline in his ears. He walks straight to the cashier cage and exchanges the chips for cash. The intensity of his nervousness increases as the stacks of cash fill each pocket in his jacket and pants. Yet everything seems to go smoothly. After the seventh casino, he runs out of pockets. Now three casinos are left, and that means three stacks need to fit in his clothes. *Good thing I wore long socks, because that's the only place left on me where I can store the cash.*

An hour remains. He plays a few hands of blackjack at Treasure Island and cashes out. Then he hurries to the Palazzo and does the same. *One last stop remains, the Essex Hotel and Casino. I'll handle this last spot, go to the club, hand the guy the cash. Then I'll be home free.*

Reid exits the Palazzo with his chest tilted forward as he strides across the road and enters the Essex Casino, eager to complete final tasks of the assignment. *All the other stops went so smoothly, almost too smoothly.* Reid sits at the blackjack table, reaches into his pocket, and pulls out the remaining nine thousand dollars in casino chips. He instructs the dealer to change up his one-thousand-dollar chips into smaller denominations. Another man is sitting at the table. Reid nods to say hello and the man returns a slight grin. The dealer finishes with Reid's chips, then shuffles the cards.

"I'm Reid. Where are you from?" says Reid, hoping friendly banter will help deflect his nerves.

"I'm Chuck, from Minnesota. You?"

"Los Angeles. What brings you to Las Vegas?" *Maybe this guy is interested in an experience from Dani. I could text her to come here before I go into the nightclub.*

"A conference," says Chuck, seeming uninterested in taking the banter any further.

Reid eyes the tall stacks of chips in front of Chuck. "It appears Lady Luck has been good to you." Chuck doesn't respond, leaving Reid to dismiss his thought of Chuck being a potential client for Dani. Something about this guy's cold behavior tells Reid he isn't worthy of an ESE.

Reid and Chuck place their bets in the betting circle. The dealer flips the cards to each player. Reid loses but Chuck wins. The men place another round of bets. Again, Reid loses but Chuck wins. *This guy is on a hot streak. And I need to slow down.* Reid signals to the dealer that he would like to sit out the next hand. The dealer proceeds to deal Chuck another winning hand. *I don't even need to play. I'm just gonna sit here and watch this guy for a few minutes, then cash out.*

Out of the corner of his eye, Reid sees four security guards quickly converse near a slot machine about fifty feet away. Their facial expressions suggest this is more than a casual gathering. Reid stands and gathers his chips. *They may or may not be talking about me, but I'm not gonna take the chance to find out.*

The dealer extends a finger towards Reid. "Sir, allow me to color those chips up into a larger denomination."

Reid huffs a short breath, then shoves his chips to the center of table and returns to sitting. The dealer slides the chips back towards Reid, then wags his index finger, signaling that Reid has to wait for Chuck to finish the hand that's already been dealt. Reid's back becomes slick with sweat. He wonders if the dealer is in on his capture.

Chuck has a pair of twos and is debating whether to split them against the dealer's up-card, a four. Reid stares at the dealer, but sees the security guards approaching in his peripheral vision. He tries to remember which exit would be the fastest for him to find, should he decide to sprint away. He looks to his left and sees the security guards less than ten feet away. *I'm screwed.* He lowers his chin and settles into his seat. *I cashed out nine grand at nine casinos tonight, and it's the freaking last one that busts me. How the heck am I gonna explain the cash that's spread throughout my body?*

The security guards approach the table. Reid turns to acknowledge their presence, but pauses as he hears a guard speak.

"That's a heck of a disguise, Stanley."

Stanley? Reid notices that all of the guards are looking at Chuck.

"Leave your chips on the table and never set foot in this casino again. This is your last warning," says the security guard to Chuck. "You're too talented to play here."

Oh, man. They're busting Chuck. "He's too talented" must mean he was card-counting.

Chuck and the security guards walk away. Reid turns back to the table, exhaling a sigh of relief. He sees the pit boss standing behind the dealer.

"I'm sorry about that, sir. You're free to continue your play. Let me know if we can accommodate you in any way for the disruption."

"No problem," says Reid. His body goes limp.

The pit boss nods and walks away. Reid wants to melt into the floor, but realizes he needs to appear unfazed. He slides a hundred-dollar bet into the circle, figuring he'll play a few hands and then leave. The dealer tosses him two cards that total eleven. Reid places an additional hundred-dollar chip next to his bet, signaling that he'd like to double down and take one more card.

The hairs on the back of his neck rise. Someone is watching over his shoulder. He assumes it's a casual onlooker, but then suddenly he feels a chubby hand grip his shoulder. *Shit.* Reid turns his head and sees a man in a gray suit who sports a familiar salt-and-pepper goatee. *Detective Youngblood.*

"Let's have a conversation, off the record," says Youngblood as he slides into the chair next to him. Reid keeps his gaze on the cards, intending to appear calm. The dealer tosses Reid a nine, for a total of twenty. The dealer then flips his hand, showing an eighteen. Reid wins, but expresses no emotion. He must keep cool, knowing he's so close to finishing the assignment. Perhaps Youngblood is just trying a scare tactic.

Youngblood watches the dealer pay Reid's bet. "Lucky you. Perhaps you can win enough to retire tonight."

Retire tonight? Does he know Wish's plans? Reid tightens his face to maintain the appearance of minimal emotion. He collects his winnings and leaves a hundred-dollar chip to bet on the next hand.

"I just want to give you a heads-up," says Youngblood. "I'll be having a conversation with your employer about your lifestyle choices out here in Las Vegas. Dean Anderson is his name, correct?"

"My choices? I'm just playing blackjack," says Reid. He gets dealt two cards totaling sixteen. He hits and busts out.

"Don't con me," says Youngblood. "We both know what you're doing here. I could have casino security take you down within seconds."

Reid feels a dryness in his throat. He remains quiet while focusing on the blackjack, sliding out another bet. He figures if Youngblood wanted to take him down, he would have done it already, without wanting to talk off the record. Plus, according to Wish, Youngblood doesn't return to active duty until midnight.

"I've looked into your background. You seem to be a worthwhile professor," says Youngblood. "All of your students write positive reviews about you online. I'd hate to see all of that go away because you got hooked on getting your jollies off in Vegas. You gotta understand, kid, I'm doing you a favor. You just gotta do me a favor in return."

Hooked on getting my jollies off? The comment sparks Reid to wonder if maybe Youngblood doesn't know the full story of what's going on.

"Tell me where Wish will be tonight and you'll never hear from me again. You'll be free to go back to Los Angeles tomorrow without anyone knowing of your escapades this summer."

I don't even know where Wish is supposed to be tonight. Reid glares at Youngblood. "I'm just here to play blackjack. If you want a wish, go throw a coin in that giant pond across the street and state your wish there."

Youngblood slaps the table with his hand. "You've become quite the talker." He rises and leaves.

Reid releases a long breath. He plays one more hand while analyzing the worst-case scenarios. *Well, if Youngblood does call my boss and I get fired, I could just move to Las Vegas and follow in Wish's footsteps. I'd train Sexmysts in Las Vegas. Dani is already paying me for that anyway.* He loses the hand, then sneaks a peek at his phone, noticing he has thirty minutes until midnight. He's got to hurry up and get into the club. He slides all of his chips to the dealer, who then exchanges them for larger denominations.

Reid goes to the cashier cage and swaps the nine grand of casino chips into cash. The cashier places the cash in an envelope. Reid heads to the nearest bathroom, where there aren't any security cameras. He pulls a hundred-dollar bill out of the stack, figuring a hundred-dollar handshake will get him into the club, then stuffs the envelope into his sock.

He strides over to the Essex nightclub. The line for entry looks to be a block long. He struts up to the front, where a bouncer is standing with a clipboard. Reid folds the hundred-dollar bill to fit nicely in his right palm. Then he approaches the bouncer and extends his hand out to shake. The bouncer grips Reid's open hand and shoots him a look that says, *How much cash is in this handshake?*

Reid points to his clipboard. "I'm Reid Bradley. I'm number one hundred on the list."

The bouncer nods, then unhooks the velvet rope. Reid enters a large ballroom with laser lights flashing and music blaring. Taking long strides, he walks through the crowded nightclub, en route to the back patio. He scans the scene for Youngblood — no sign. However, he can't shake off the feeling that he's being watched.

Reid enters the restroom located at the far end of the large outdoor patio. He receives a suspicious look from the attendant, which causes his chest to tighten. He forgot that nightclubs hire bathroom attendants, probably to keep an eye out for anything suspicious. He wonders if he should give him a hundred in hush money, but figures the gesture might make him look even more suspicious.

Reid passes the attendant and enters the furthest stall on the left — just as Wish instructed. He pulls his pants down slightly and sits on the toilet, appearing to be handling normal business. He peels a wad of toilet paper and wipes the perspiration off his forehead. Then he pulls out his phone in time to see the clock display that it's midnight. He focuses on slow breathing, hoping to calm his racing heart. With the sounds of drunks clamoring in and out of the restroom, it's hard to hear if someone has entered the stall next to his. *Good thing Wish set up the three-finger signal instead of something audible.* Reid fixes his gaze on the area where he figures the banker's hand will display the signal, just under the divider between the stalls.

A few minutes pass, then he notices the three-finger signal from below — time to do the exchange. As he reaches into his pocket for the first stack of cash, he glances downward and notices that one of the fingers has a gold wedding band encrusted with three small diamonds. *That's a nice wedding ring.* Reid proceeds to hand the banker the ten stacks of cash. After the last stack, the man reaches under the stall and extends an index finger, a signal to wait a minute. The man's hand disappears momentarily, then reappears with a stack that has a note attached. Reid examines the note.

This is your cut. I'm leaving now. You must wait five minutes, then leave.

Reid thumbs through the cash, smiling as he counts to fifteen grand. Then he suddenly stiffens. He pictures Youngblood waiting outside the club to catch him. He figures it would be tricky to explain having this much cash to hand. He recalls Youngblood mentioning his awareness that professors don't walk around with this kind of cash. *Regardless, fifteen grand is fifteen grand.*

Reid waits five minutes then comes out of the stall. He washes his hands and leaves a twenty-dollar bill in the tip-jar. The bathroom attendant smiles and offers him some mints, but shows no sign of suspicion. Reid steps out into the warm desert air that flows through the patio, feeling a sense of accomplishment as he glides towards the patio bar. He has the bartender shake him up a chilled mescal. He sips the drink, savoring the mesquite flavor as it hits his tongue. *Now it's time to find an alibi and have some fun.*

Reid observes the scene around the bar with a slight squint. The club is loaded with beautiful women. His gaze locks onto a woman with an exotic look. She's wearing a white cocktail dress and standing at the other end of the bar. She doesn't notice Reid because she's with another guy. Reid studies them for several minutes. Even though Reid is surrounded by plenty of viable women, he wants her the most. His mind flashes to the night Henry had him observe couples at the restaurant, studying the men who reeked of approval-seeking. The gentleman who's with the woman in white reeks of the same. They never touch, but the man continues to prod her into drinking. A few minutes pass, then Reid watches the man leave the woman in white and head towards the restroom.

Without hesitation, Reid moves directly to the woman. As he nears her, he gazes into her eyes. "Hello, I'm Reid." Such a move used to make him buckle with nervousness, but now he stands there completely comfortable with the situation — because he's completely comfortable with himself. "Are you single?"

"I'm Layla. Yes, I am single, but sort of ..."

"On a date," says Reid. "It appears to not be going so well."

She looks towards the men's restroom. "How'd you know?"

"I've been hiding behind the bushes, staring at you and your exciting date."

"You're Mr. Creepy." She playfully punches Reid's shoulder. He nods and winks.

"I'm honored to play the role of the creep for you." Reid steps back and takes a formal bow. "As your official creep for the evening, I have a few observations that I'd like to share."

"Please do." She steps closer to Reid and tilts her head upward.

"You look like you are trying to make the best of an uncomfortable situation. The man you're with is buying your drinks." Reid grins. "But he's not fulfilling your wishes for the night."

"Yeah, I just met that guy," Layla says. "My wishes? How do you know what I wish for tonight?"

"You'll be more comfortable knowing it was a lucky guess on my end," says Reid. "Why did you come to Vegas?"

"It's my first time. I've always wanted to experience it. It looked so amazing on TV."

"Do you feel like you have had your Vegas experience?"

"I've only seen a bunch of flashy lights so far."

"Have you had the experience of a man hitting on you at a club in Vegas?"

"Not really. That guy scares the men away."

Reid raises his right hand. "I've volunteered to provide that experience. In case you haven't noticed, this is what it's like when a man hits on you in Vegas."

She licks her lips, then tilts her head to the side. "You're something different."

Reid purposefully remains silent, savoring the tension. He looks down at her shoes, then slowly shifts his gaze upward, along the curves of her white dress, appreciating how it highlights her figure.

"Where are you from? What do you do for work?" he says.

"Vancouver. I'm a nurse. Where are you from and what do you do?"

"Los Angeles. I'm a professor."

"I can tell you're from LA. You're the best-dressed man here. And I love your hairstyle; it's debonair." She grabs the lapels of his suit. "It's hot that you are a professor. What do you profess?"

Gotta move this along faster. Her date will return any second. Reid gently grabs both of her hands. "I will tell you more about my job later. Come over here for a second. Our time is limited."

Like a special agent programmed to handle potential danger, Reid shifts into action, rescuing his dame from a potential male intruder who'll deny her an Erotic Sensory Experience. He leads her around a corner that has a wall which will keep her hidden from the view of her date. Reid pulls her close and draws his fingers across her exposed shoulder blades, feeling her head rest on his chest.

"I'm liking how you are hitting on me so far," says Layla.

He leans forward and begins kissing her neck while gliding his hands across her back, varying the tempo and intensity of his touch to activate her sexual sensory response system.

Layla breathes heavily into his ear. "I can't believe this is actually happening."

His lips make their way up her neck. He then returns his gaze to hers. "You ooze an irresistible sexiness." Reid kisses her plump lips. "Thank you for being you." He kisses her slowly and gently, ensuring he appreciates the taste and texture of her mouth.

Reid pulls his lips away from the kiss and notices Layla gawking at an attractive bikini-wearing cocktail server who speeds past.

"You're into women also, aren't you?" says Reid.

She nods to say yes. Reid continues: "I'm guessing you leave tomorrow?"

"Yes, my flight is at seven in the morning. I'm going to try to stay up all night and then take a cab to the airport at five o'clock."

"Who are you in Vegas with?"

"That guy is my new co-worker. He's trying to get me drunk and is crazy overprotective. He thinks we're going to have sex. But we're staying in separate rooms."

Reid takes out his phone. "We don't have much time because that guy is most likely looking for you. I want you to finish the drink he's probably buying for you right now. He at least deserves that much. Type in your phone number, Layla."

Layla types in her number, then hands the phone back to Reid.

"I want to see you again tonight. I'll be in contact."

"I feel like I'm in a movie." She smiles and pulls Reid in for a juicy kiss. She then pulls away. "Is this some kind of move that you do on desperate women? Don't you feel bad, taking me away from him?"

"First, let me say that I'm not perfect. Far from it. But each male has the power to make himself into a desirable being. Some men will do whatever it takes. Unfortunately, most settle for living a life of mediocrity. Most of their actions occur from a state of avoiding fears and begging for validation. They buy women drinks, dinners, flowers, and gifts to make up for the work they're afraid or unwilling to do on themselves. Then they settle for marrying the first woman who falls for that shit. The man suffers, and unfortunately the woman suffers even more, because she's married to a boy hidden within a grown man's body. I love women, and I hate to see them suffer."

Dammit, I went into professor mode on her. Wish would slap the shit out of me for getting philosophical with a woman who might be seeking an experience.

Layla bats her eyelashes, then smiles. *Oh good, she gets it.*

Reid's phone vibrates in his pants. He slides it out of his pocket and reads a text from Wish.

Well done. Mission accomplished. However, it's best you not stay at that club any longer tonight.

Uh oh, why would he say that? Is Youngblood here? Reid looks around. *I better get outta here quickly.*

"Are you okay, Professor?" Layla pulls Reid in for a quick kiss.

"I have to leave the club now. I'll explain later. I'll text you with instructions for where to meet me. I recommend that you tell your friend that you are going back to your hotel room to sleep. This way he won't bother you when we hang later."

Reid sees her pupils dance with a look of awe.

"Why did I only just meet you right now?" she says.

"I have to go. You'll get a text with further instructions in a bit."

"I'll be staring at my phone until then," she says.

Reid laughs. "Now it seems that you should be the one who's called a creep." He kisses her on the forehead and exits the club.

Chapter 32

No sign of Youngblood, but Reid speed-walks through the casino just to be safe. He takes the rear exit out the casino and heads towards Koval Road, the backroad that connects the rear parts of the casinos. He continuously looks back, but sees no threat.

Reid eventually flags down a cab and has it take him to the Planet Hollywood Hotel. He figures it's best to walk to the Largo while blending in with the hordes of people entering from the Strip, instead of being dropped off at the Largo valet at the rear of the casino.

Thirty minutes have passed. Reid types a text to Layla.

We don't grow as humans unless we take risks. I hope you are the type who chooses growth. Reply 'Yes' within five minutes if you still want to explore more with me tonight.

Reid chuckles to himself; this all seems so easy. But five months ago, he was a lost, heartbroken, and scared boy. Wish showed him how what seemed like the worst moment of his life was actually the greatest thing to happen to him.

Reid cruises through the Planet Hollywood casino. He walks past two women holding hands and is struck with an insight. *Layla is attracted to women. Dani and I are supposed to hang as well. I wonder if Dani would be open to a threesome?* Reid sits at a slot machine. He sends a text to Dani, inviting her to his room and explaining that another woman may also be there.

Dani responds: **I'll like any woman you like. I'll come to your room in twenty minutes. What's the room number?**

Before Reid can respond to Dani, his phone vibrates with a text from Layla.

YES! Where are you staying? I'm getting in a cab to go there right now.

Oh my. Is this really happening? Reid responds to each woman individually but with the same text.

Largo Hotel, room 4517.

Reid rises and scans his surroundings. He can't help but feel the hairs on his neck rise. Youngblood is like a bothersome fly that has stuck around all day, and even when it's not there, it still feels like it's there. He looks back and sees a man in a gray suit walk away in the opposite direction. *That might have been him.* Nerves crawl up his spine and into his brain. He realizes that this fear is different to the fear of rejection; this is fear of jail time and of losing the life he has worked so hard to have. He'd feel a lot more comfortable if he didn't have fifteen grand in his pocket; then he'd just be another tourist.

Reid walks to a nearby roulette table that has a small sign explaining that the maximum table bet is ten thousand dollars. He takes out his fifteen grand and plops it onto the table.

"A ten grand and a five grand, please — two chips only," says Reid.

He places the ten grand on black and pockets the five-grand chip. He figures walking around with five grand is much more feasible, and safer. *If the ball falls on any black number, it will double the bet. But I kind of hope I'll lose.*

The dealer spins the ball along the wheel. Reid avoids looking at the table, instead looking for any potential dangers nearby.

"Black eight," yells the dealer.

I won! Shit. He won double his bet, and now his problem has doubled — he has twenty-five grand. He pockets the chips, three in total, a five-grand and two ten-grand chips. *If Youngblood messes with me, I can just say I got hot and made crazy ten-thousand-dollar roulette bets. And now the Planet Hollywood security camera can prove it.*

Reid exits the Planet Hollywood casino, then crosses the bridge to the other side of the Strip, heading towards the Largo Hotel. He takes another quick look behind and doesn't see Youngblood anywhere, but the discomfort continues to weigh heavily on him.

Reid enters the Largo Hotel and spots two attractive women sitting on a bench. One is wearing a blue dress and another is in a sundress. Their faces are buried in their phones and they appear to be rapid-fire texting. Reid is tempted to walk away, but Wish teasing his ability to create a threesome has ignited his competitive side. *Why not invite more women to the suite, and make it a foursome or even a fivesome?* He recalls how Henry mentioned that a man's attractiveness increases when he already has a date for the night. *I might as well be bold.*

"Are you ladies texting for a booty call?" says Reid.

They giggle. The one in the blue dress glances up at Reid. "Maybe."

Reid studies how her blue dress highlights her blue eyes. *Stunning.* He peers into her eyes. "You and I are a match." *Just a guess, but I'm sensing that I might be correct.*

"Why do you think that?" she responds while rising to stand. Her friend leans her head on the wall behind the bench and closes her eyes.

Reid views her willingness to step away from her friend as a positive sign. "Because you're the kind of woman who courageously explores life. You aren't the type who says no to fun. Unlike most women, you don't go through your life fearing the judgment of others. What's your name?"

"It's like you've known me forever. My name is Avina."

"I don't understand why people choose to deny themselves pleasure," says Reid.

"Me too. Some people just don't like fun. I'm trying to stay up until my flight at seven."

She's trying to stay up, just like Layla. "I know of a good distraction to keep you awake."

Avina tilts her head and grins, as if to say, *Naughty boy.*

Reid smiles and straightens his spine. "Are you staying here at the Largo?"

"Yes. She's ready to go to bed."

Perfect. "Let's take her back to the room, then you and I will hang a bit more." Avina nods approvingly, then helps her friend rise from the bench.

They enter the casino, walking arm in arm. Something about their presence makes the threat of Youngblood disappear. Reid smiles with a business-as-usual expression, but actually he feels the buzz of excitement pulse through his body. *Avina, Layla, Dani, and me. A foursome?* Wish and Reid never covered the logistics of a foursome, or a threesome, but he will be happy to make mistakes and learn.

They enter the elevator. Avina's friend steps out on her floor, the twenty-second. And Avina stays arm and arm with Reid as the elevator moves up the shaft to his floor. *One participant is secured, two more to go.*

He turns her in his arms for a kiss. Then he wonders if she's open to multiple women being in the room. He pulls away and calmly looks into her eyes.

"Are you the type who enjoys an adventure?" says Reid.

"That's exactly why I'm here with you," she says.

"I want you to know that your comfort and safety are most important. The moment you want this to end, just say so, and I'll make sure you get back to your room safely."

"Thank you for saying that. There is something about you that naturally makes me feel safe."

"I care about your experience." *And the experiences of the two women who are about to get here soon.* He decides not to tell her just yet, hoping she'll flow into it once they arrive.

No further words are exchanged as Reid opens the door to his suite. As soon she enters, he caresses Avina from behind, then pins her to the nearest wall and they engage in tender kisses. He soon breaks the kiss, then turns her around to face the wall. He places her hands up on the wall, high and apart, as if she were getting arrested.

"This experience might be different than what you're used to. I must remind you that you are safe and you can say no anytime." Reid reaches towards her nape and grabs a handful of hair, then turns her neck so their eyes can meet. "Deal?"

"Oh my God, yes! Deal."

Reid peels her dress off her body. Then he carefully slides her underwear downward, stopping at various pressure points along her thighs to stimulate them along the way. He kisses a trail up her naked legs, back, and neck. He then takes her hands off the wall and leads her to the bedroom window, which overlooks the fountain show.

"Hands on the window. Spread your legs and don't look back at me. This experience is going to involve a lot of your senses. It's best you ignore pleasing me." Reid massages her temples. "Consciously slow your brain down right now. You are safe – give your mind permission to fully relax and take in the view."

"The view is amazing," says Avina. She starts to sway her hips slightly.

Reid takes a few steps away from her, appreciating the courage of the feminine goddess who stands naked before him. But he struggles to be fully engaged in the moment — one ear is listening for a knock that will announce the arrival of the next participant.

He returns to Avina and glides his hands all across her body, studying it like it was created by a master sculptor. "This moment is about me touching you. All you do is focus on feeling, receiving my touch. No thoughts of pleasing me. Understood?"

"Okay... mmmmmmm ... yes." She looks back. "Why aren't you naked?"

"It's not time for that yet." Reid playfully slaps her bare bottom, then follows up with a feather-light touch. "Just feel."

Reid takes his hands off her body. He goes to the drawer and grabs a blindfold, then returns.

"Take one last look at those fountains." Reid waits a few seconds, then slides the blindfold over her eyes. Avina gasps, then smiles once see recognizes what is occurring. Reid whispers in her ear, "I love how open-minded you are."

"I've always wanted to experience this," says Avina. "Did you fall from the sky to answer my wish?"

Reid steps away from her, amused by her choice of words. He feels his phone vibrate in his pants pocket. He steps away and reads a text from Dani.

I just met a potential client downstairs. He looks to be in need of my services. Hope it won't take too long. Keep your phone close. I'll touch base with you soon.

Damn. One girl tapped out. But Layla should be here any second. Reid hears a knock on the door. Avina lifts her chin.

He leans towards Avina's ear. "I have a female friend who I met minutes before you. She wants to play with us. Is that okay with you?"

She pauses for a moment, and then nods. *Yes!*

His pulse skyrockets as he walks down the hallway. He opens the door and sees Layla in her perfect white dress. He draws her in for a sensual kiss, then grabs her hand and leads her to the naked Avina, whose hands are pressed against the window. Reid places both of

Layla's hands on Avina's buttery, smooth skin.

"Layla, meet Avina," says Reid. He whispers into Layla's ear, "She knows not to move and to only focus on receiving touch." Reid moves Layla's hands slowly up and down Avina's body.

As Layla continues the touching pattern, Reid steps behind her and peels off her white dress, bra, and underwear. Reid and Layla kiss while fondling Avina's perky breasts. *Avina probably needs to see how stunning Layla is.* Reid carefully removes Avina's blindfold. She turns to face Layla. Reid notices both women moisten their lips as they take in each other's presence. Layla places her hands behind Avina's head and guides her close. Their glossy lips meet in an erotic kiss.

Reid quietly steps away from them to observe the entire scene. Two women lip-locked in front of him with the fountain show blasting away in the background ... *I can't believe this is happening.* His feeling of awe continues as he observes the women exploring each other's bodies, fondling, pinching, and caressing, while high-pitched moaning rings in his ears. He slides off his suit jacket, unbuttons his shirt, and proceeds to get naked. He sets his pants on top of the dresser and carefully rests his cell phone on top of the pants, ensuring the screen is in plain sight so he'll notice if Dani texts.

Reid feels a hint of hesitancy about joining the women. He takes a deep breath. His mind flashes to the experience with Dalia and Molly. *I've done this before. It's time to channel that guy who isn't afraid to take charge. The world needs me to be myself, and these two women definitely need me to be me right now.*

He steps towards the women, chest lifted like an experienced performer owning his presence to the point that the audience is eager to follow his every move. He grabs a handful of hair on the rear of each woman's head and gently pulls, moving their lips apart. He then leads Avina to the edge of the bed, and has her lie on her back and spread her legs. Reid curls his index finger at Layla, signaling to her to come near him. He then instructs Layla to stand near the bed's edge, between Avina's legs.

"Pay attention to what I do, then do that exact movement until I say to stop," Reid says to Layla. She agrees. He stands to the side of them, then draws his finger along the insides of Avina's thighs. "She has sexual energy stored all over her body. Your job will be to channel the energy of her lower extremities towards her fold."

Reid shows Layla how to kiss the tender zones of her calves, shins, knees, and inner and upper thighs. "But don't touch her jewel until I say."

Reid observes Layla as she dives into her assignment. Avina moans with pleasure as Layla teases her lower body with precision. Reid goes to work on Avina's upper body, kissing her soft lips, neck, and ears. Avina reaches for Reid's blood-gorged stiffness. She strokes his member once, then Reid quickly grabs her hand and places it on her side.

"Only focus on receiving," says Reid. He lowers his head, then dances his tongue around her erect nipples for several minutes.

Avina's moaning gradually intensifies.

Layla's hand slides up Avina's inner thigh and gently pets her vulva. Reid notices and moves the hand while mouthing the words, "Not yet."

"I'm amazed at how patient you are," says Layla. Reid smiles and continues to channel the sexual energy of Avina's upper body to her navel. He proceeds to work his way into the Shadow Palm Technique. Avina's pelvis begins to shake with excitement. Reid looks at Layla.

"Now is the time. But only kiss the lower part of her peach," says Reid. "I'll handle the rest."

Layla leaves a trail of saliva as she kisses Avina's inner thigh once more. She eventually lands on Avina's vulva.

"Ahhhhhh, yes!" Avina moans get louder as each second passes.

Reid continues the Shadow Palm Technique. His fingers then work their way down to the upper part of Avina's vulva. Like a jeweler setting a diamond into a ring, Reid gently touches her swollen clitoral head, knowing it will culminate in a sensory explosion.

Avina's hips lift upward. She gasps with erotic elation. His free hand pinches her nipple firmly, to provide contrast. Avina continues to moan while breathing heavily through her climax, then eventually melts into the mattress.

"My goodness. What did you do to me?" Avina's hands crawl up and down her body. Reid smiles at her, feeling honored to have served her as a Sexmyst.

Reid guides Layla to kneel on to the bed. "You've been an excellent student. I'll be giving you extra credit."

"You've been an amazing professor. Please, I'm begging for extra credit. I'll do whatever it takes to get an A."

Reid sets Layla up in the doggy-style position next to Avina, then he goes to the dresser to take a condom out of the drawer. He rips the wrapper open, then slides the condom into place. He starts to turn back to the women, but sees his phone flash with a text from Dani. He quickly grabs his phone.

I need you right now.

What the hell are you talking about? You know I'm busy. Reid sets his phone down and looks at the bed. Layla remains in the doggy-style position and Avina is now kneeling near Layla's head. She's carefully stroking Layla's back.

"I want my extra credit, Professor."

"Patience, young lady," says Reid. He sets his phone back on the dresser. *Dani knows where we are. She'll come if she's interested. I'm not gonna move these girls to her room.*

He returns to Layla and shows Avina how to properly stimulate Layla's back by paying attention to specific pressure points. Avina quickly proves that she's also an excellent student. Reid uses his hands and lips to work on Layla's lower extremities, while feeling a sense of wonderment that he was nervous about a threesome. *I've been trained to do this.* He glides his hands up her legs, then applies pressure to the erogenous zones around the exterior of the vulva.

"I want you in me so bad, Professor."

You have no idea how badly I want it in there as well. But Dani's text has occupied his mind.

Reid removes his right hand from the pressure point below her vulva. He reaches around towards her stomach and strokes her clitoris. Reid whispers for Avina to caress Layla's nipples while applying soft kisses to her spine.

"Ohhhhhhhhh. Yes!" cries Layla.

Reid backs off, licks his palm, and applies the moisture to his erection. He then slides his member into her fold and returns his hand to stroke her clit. The sensation quickly distracts his mind from thoughts of Dani. He thrusts slowly, knowing that her vulva and the inner wall just past the opening are the most sensitive during the first stage of penetration. Gradually, his thrusts become rapid and deep, causing Layla to scream louder as his speed increases. Soon, Reid sees Layla's head fall into Avina's thighs. He feels her soft insides flood with gooey bliss. He slows down his thrusting and strokes her lower back, feeling it ripple with goosebumps as she melts into post-orgasmic euphoria.

Reid pulls out, not letting himself climax; he's plenty satisfied with serving the women. He quietly steps away, feeling almost as if this isn't his reality. He takes a moment to let it sink in. He observes the women crawl under the white blanket. They snuggle up and proceed to playfully kiss each other's lips and touch each other's breasts. *Yup, this is for real.*

Reid returns to the window to take another glance at the fountain show. Except his view is slightly distorted by small palm prints smudged on the window from Avina's hands. He chuckles internally as he comes to a realization. *Some people need to meditate on top of a mountain for enlightenment. I found it in Sin City with the unlikely guidance of a pimp.* He looks back at his bed and sees two sleeping goddesses with long hair sprawled in a mess of white blankets. *I'm honored to serve. A fucking mountain couldn't teach me that.*

He sees his phone light up. *Probably Dani. Alright, fine, I guess I'd better see what she's going on about.* He shuffles to the phone and reads several texts from Dani.

I can't get rid of this guy. Come to my room, 2314, ASAP.

Where are you? I'm so scared. Please hurry!

He's in the bathroom. He says if I leave he will report me to the cops. I cracked the door open for you.

Oh, shit. What the hell am I gonna do for her? I can't fight. I don't have a gun.

Reid responds: **I'll be there in three minutes.**

I should text Andrew. I can't just leave her alone. I promised I'd be there for her. Maybe I can channel Wish's logic to avoid violence.

Reid hurries to the bathroom, removes the condom, and rinses himself. He returns to the bedroom and sees the women passed out in each other's arms. *My goodness, they are sexy. Dammit, Dani.* He quietly puts his underwear and pants back on. He feels the chips in his pockets, the twenty-five grand. Reid opens the dresser drawer and hides the casino chips in a sock. *Wait, maybe I can pay this guy to go away?* He grabs a five-thousand-dollar chip and stuffs it into his pocket. He puts on his white dress shirt and shoes, then quietly slides out the front door.

Reid texts Andrew to let him know there might be trouble in Dani's room. He takes the elevator to the twenty-third floor and hurries down the hall towards the room. He looks at his phone one more time, hoping to see a response from Andrew. Nothing. *You always respond within seconds. Come on, man, of all the nights to be off work?*

As Reid stands in front of room 2314, he's hit with a familiar feeling. It's the same one he experienced just before he walked in on Jasmine and Daphne on his birthday. The feeling suggests that if he walks through this door, his life may never be the same. He huffs a short breath, knowing he's a man of his word — he promised to protect Dani. His hand presses on the loose door. It creaks open and he enters, shocked by what he sees.

Chapter 33

Reid steps along the entryway of the standard-sized room. Dani is sitting on the couch, naked, appearing distraught. Her knees are folded up to her chest and her head is down. As he nears her, he sees that her hands appear to be tied behind her back.

"Dani, are you okay? Is he still here?"

Before Reid can console her further, he feels the back of his knees get whacked by a thick metal bar. He groans loudly and falls to the floor. The assailant quickly cuffs Reid's hands behind his back.

"You never listened to my warnings, you little twerp," says a familiar voice. Reid twists his head and sees Youngblood.

Youngblood goes through Reid's pockets. He finds the five-thousand-dollar chip. "Oh, look what you must have lost in the hallway while walking here."

Reid sees Youngblood pocket the casino chip. Youngblood then lifts Reid to stand and shoves him onto the couch next to Dani. She keeps her head down on her knees.

Reid turns to Dani. "You set me up, didn't you?" She doesn't say a word. Reid can tell by her breathing pattern that she's crying.

"Don't talk to her," says Youngblood. "I wasn't able to find your partner, Wish, but catching you will certainly lead me to him. I doubt you want to be locked up."

Reid glares at Dani. "I can't believe you set me up. Our mission was to serve others. I thought you were committed to positively changing the world. Was all that a lie?"

Dani sobs and buries her head further between her legs. Reid can't help but notice something strange on the crown of her head, bits of brown hair sticking out amongst the blond strands. It appears she's wearing a wig.

"You think prostitution actually serves others?" says Youngblood. "Sex should be reserved for marriage and kept behind closed doors. You disgust me. God is gonna send you to hell for not following His rules. You people make me sick."

"I'm gonna go to hell?" says Reid. "If going to heaven means I'd have to be around people like you, then I'd much rather go to hell."

"Well, for now you're going to jail. I have backup officers coming to take you in."

Reid scowls silently. *I've finally discovered who I am and now it's going to go to waste while I rot in jail.*

Youngblood's cell phone rings. Reid watches Youngblood step away as he answers. "Yeah, we're in room twenty-three-fourteen. The professor and his whore."

His whore? Reid looks at Dani. "Aren't you working for him?"

Dani slowly lifts her head to face Reid, then shakes her head to say no. She opens her mouth, but she's too emotional to put together a sentence. Her emotion suggests that she's telling the truth. He sees mascara run down her face and notices more strands of brown hair seeping out from under the wig. *What the hell is going on?*

Youngblood continues to talk on the phone. Reid ponders an escape as he studies Youngblood, who's pacing from side to side. He can't think of a way to escape, but he observes something peculiar. There are bloodstains around the crotch of Youngblood's pants. Reid looks at Dani. *I doubt Dani would have been working if she was on her period. If this asshole did anything to hurt her, I swear I'll ...*

Youngblood ends his call and looks down at his blood-spotted pants. He struts towards Reid with an intense expression.

"You think you're a tough guy, huh?" says Youngblood. "Your girl injured me. She's going down for assaulting a police officer." Youngblood reaches back and slaps Dani across the face. "Stupid bitch."

Dani screams and falls off the couch onto the floor. Reid swells with rage. *I'd fucking kill you right now if I could.*

Before he can act on his thought, he hears a loud knock on the door.

"Enjoy your last few seconds of freedom, Professor." Youngblood walks towards the entrance.

Reid leans forward to help Dani crawl back onto the couch, but then realizes he can't help her with his wrists cuffed.

Youngblood opens the door. "Welcome, Detective Jones. The two pieces of garbage on the couch will be your last arrests before retirement. Congratulations."

Detective Jones? I thought he was on our side?

Reid watches Detective Jones step into the room and glare at him with an empty expression. Then Jones turns towards Youngblood and shoves him up against the wall. Jones quickly pulls out handcuffs and locks Youngblood's wrists behind his back.

"What the hell?" says Youngblood.

"You're under arrest," says Detective Jones. Reid widens his eyes. Then he sees two uniformed police officers standing guard in the doorway. *Youngblood is getting busted? Are we all in deep trouble?*

"What? What for?" says Youngblood.

"Well, let's start with the attempted rape of that young lady over there," says Jones.

Attempted rape? Reid glances at Dani, who is sobbing. *Is that why she can't stop crying?*

Jones continues speaking to Youngblood as he leads him out of the room. "And you just robbed that young man of his casino chips."

Reid rocks his head back. He questions how Jones knew of Youngblood's theft. Reid looks around the room, studying the edges of the ceiling. There aren't any cameras in sight. He scans the room again, then centers his gaze on the TV stand. He sees a familiar-looking candle flickering with an illuminant flame. A chill rolls up his neck. It's the candle from Goddess Mindy's office — the one with the live-stream video camera hidden within.

Reid glances back down at Dani, who is now lying sideways on the floor with her knees towards her chest. Dani's wig has almost completely fallen off her head. Her authentic short brown hair now covers her face. Reid recognizes the short brown hair. He's seen the haircut on someone, but can't place who.

Reid sits up and examines Dani's back. There's a tattoo that reads, "Acceptance."

Is Dani actually Molly? He falls to the floor and curls up closer to Dani. He sees the stab-wound scar just below her belly button. They both gaze into each other's eyes.

"Should I call you Dani or Molly? Either way, I'm excited to meet you." Reid glances back to confirm that Jones and the officers are still out of the room. Then he returns his attention to her.

"My real name is Dani." She cracks a smile. "It looks like Wish's plan worked."

Reid stares at her intently, studying her to jog his memory. His mind flashes to when they reconnected at the Diamond Bar after the meeting at Vixen Gentleman's Club. He sensed he knew her, and his mind had the hardest time with the memory. He huffs a short breath while grinning. *Wish probably knew how to scramble my brain.* But he's also surprised that he didn't recognize her physical attributes.

"How did I not notice? I remember your lips being fuller in the cage. And your hair was different. But did you have any other disguises?"

"The lips were full from temporary lip injections. Dalia added prosthetics to make my nose and chin look slightly pointier. Wish's understanding of neuroscience helped us make minor adjustments to my face to throw off your brain's human-recognition system. And I've been gradually losing weight since we first met."

"I had no clue. But with Wish being involved, it all makes sense." Reid sees her grin, but then she sobs again. "Did Youngblood really try to rape you?"

Dani struggles to speak. She squeezes her eyes shut. "He said he was going to fuck me and then throw me in jail. Wish knew he'd try to do that."

"I'm sorry," says Reid. "I'll never mention it again. But Wish was right all along about Youngblood. The man was too focused on chasing the things he secretly didn't accept about himself."

Dani's eyes open and release a few tears. "Wish always told me that I'll be able to accept myself when I figure out how to channel the sexual energy for the betterment of society." Reid looks concerned. "It's okay, these are happy tears. I'm grateful the candle-camera worked when he forced his way onto me. Goddess Mindy is a genius."

Dani snuggles closer to Reid and wipes her eyes on his shirt. "Youngblood screamed like a little bitch and it was all on camera."

"What?" says Reid. "What do you mean he screamed? Did you

punch him?"

"I got in a few good whacks. But the thing that did the trick was a gift from Goddess Mindy — his penis got shredded by the Ghost Piranha insert."

Reid laughs. "An absolutely brilliant plan. That explains all the blood around his crotch. But I'm sorry he slapped you."

"He slapped me because his penis was on fire. I also dosed my vagina with jalapeño lube before he inserted."

"You are amazing."

Detective Jones returns to the room, comes over to Reid, and removes the handcuffs. Reid stands and watches Jones uncuff Dani. Reid's eyes are drawn to Jones's ring finger. He notices a gold band encrusted with three small diamonds — the same ring that was on the banker in the restroom. *Jones is the banker. He was helping Wish out all along. Man, Wish has some pull.*

Jones walks to the candle, blows out the flame, and checks the bottom of it to make sure it's turned off. He then hands Reid back his five-thousand-dollar chip. "We're going to take Youngblood down to the station. The department will be in contact with you when his trial comes up. For now, get some rest. You are both free to go." He winks and exits the room with the other officers and Youngblood.

Dani steps into the bathroom to freshen up. Reid sits on the couch and runs his hands through his hair. *This was all part of a plan. What now? Where is Wish? And what is taking Andrew so long?* He sits for a few more minutes. He wonders if he should go back to his room and check on the girls. Last he saw, they were asleep, but their flights leave soon.

Dani steps out of the bathroom wearing a fluffy white bathrobe, looking refreshed. Reid hears a knock on the door. Dani checks the peep hole, then tugs the door open. She throws her arms wide and wraps them around a familiar friend. *Goddess Mindy.* Reid sees Andrew standing behind Goddess Mindy, who's holding a small purple box. She wanders towards Reid, and Andrew follows. They all exchange hugs. Goddess Mindy hands the box to Reid. Once it hits his hands, he remembers seeing this box in Goddess Mindy's office.

"Where's Wish?" says Reid.

"He and Dalia left yesterday. He didn't say where they were going. But he instructed me to give you the box," says Goddess Mindy. "It contains all of his research."

Reid opens the box and sees hundreds of three-by-five index cards. Each card is filled with various handwritten notes and diagrams. Reid smiles like a kid in a candy store, eager to dive in. On top of the cards is a piece of paper rolled up like a scroll with a ribbon securing it in place. He opens the scroll.

If you are reading this then I'm happy to say, "Well done, Reid."

This box contains all that I have discovered during my research over the past 20 years in Las Vegas. Please use it to serve others and, ultimately, to serve the world. I trust that you will build on the research, then communicate it to the younger generation. I consider you to be a son, and I would be honored if you'd continue this research to someday teach my son and your future children (as I still fear that I may not be able to connect with him, but I'll be at peace if you can).

As I mentioned previously when we discussed the purpose of the mission, the common characteristic of violent criminals is that they haven't been touched enough by humans – or they haven't touched enough humans. As technology is forever increasing, tactile interactions will become less and less prominent, potentially resulting in a highly violent society.

I greatly fear a future with a violent society in which we are surrounded by slaves who have given in to the Collective Shadow. Humans will treat each other without compassion, then go home to their sex-robots and computers, which offer false affection, never touching them with actual human desire. Life will be an endless cycle of feeling unfulfilled within a system that promises fulfillment.

Years ago, our ancestors saved the world by courageously leaving their villages, despite the cries of the villagers who felt exploring the unknown was too dangerous. Yet they were driven by their sexual energy, regardless of the threat of death. They formed an Erotic Army who instinctively knew to educate the world about the power of sexual energy, and essentially saved the human race from extinction.

Read carefully, my son. The Erotic Army must be called upon to save the world again. I believe you are the one who is destined to reunite our

Erotic Army. Find our people and teach them how to provide selfless, growth-oriented Erotic Sensory Experiences. Seek to reconnect humans with the powers of touch. There are millions of people out there who are desperate to discover what you now know. Show them the way.

On your quest, you will encounter many who do not agree with your mission. And that is okay; naysayers need to exist. Our brains cannot recognize the value in seeking self-mastery unless it also recognizes those who avoid self-mastery. The Collective Shadow must exist to provide the challenges that ultimately develop your self-knowledge and self-love. So, when you encounter a naysayer, smile and nod with gratitude.

Dalia and I are no longer in Las Vegas and the other Sexmysts have retired. I can't say if you and I will meet again. Dani had been updating me on your ability to teach the ESE. You've proven to be a better teacher than even myself. I'm impressed.

The biggest regret of my life is that I couldn't remain as a professor while continuing the research in Las Vegas. But I believe you are capable of handling both.

My offer to you is as follows:

You will continue working as a professor in Los Angeles, expressing your knowledge with the goal of inspiring others to join the Erotic Army, teaching the power of sharing Erotic Sensory Experiences.

You will also take over my business in Las Vegas. Dani will remain in Vegas and handle the basic tasks, but you will be the CEO. You will train a new group of Sexmysts and gather the research from everyone's experiences. Goddess Mindy is eager to design more products for your research. Henry owns the penthouse and he has agreed to allow you to stay there, along with the brain-cage. Andrew has agreed to be your private security. And Xavier, though he is unique, will always be available for guidance; I highly encourage you to connect with him.

I'll expect nothing in return, except a commitment to improve the world that my son will soon have to experience as an adult.

I trust you'll make the decision that best suits your quest for happiness. No pressure. Just let Dani know your final decision.

— Wish

Reid puts the letter in the box and sits on the couch. His mind races. He's unsure if he can handle all this. Wish had Jones for protection; he'd be going up against law enforcement by himself. He could focus all his energy on teaching as a professor, but people won't fully grasp these concepts until they experience them in real life. He glances up at Goddess Mindy, Andrew, and Dani. Each of them appears eager to hear his decision.

Dani sits next to Reid and wraps her arms around him. "What's it gonna be, Professor? I hope you choose to work with us."

"The world wants us to be who we are," says Reid. "We must accept our light side and our dark side. Thank you to each of you for supporting me while I discovered who I truly am."

"Who would you say that you are?" says Goddess Mindy.

Reid glances at Andrew, then Goddess Mindy, then Dani. "I'm a Professor … and a Sexmyst."

Epilogue

Four weeks later — Los Angeles

Reid stands before his classroom full of students. "This is our last week. We've covered many topics during this summer semester and I'm honored that you all have accepted my new approach to teaching these materials. If there is one thing I want you to take away from this class, it's this ..."

Reid turns, steps to the whiteboard, grabs the erasable marker, and writes:

#Allow

Reid turns to face the class. "Let people be who they are. Support them on their own unique quest for happiness." He sees the students quickly scribble his quote in their notebooks.

"I'd like to propose the following question to you. This may be a bit of a shock, but I promise it serves a purpose."

The students set their pens down and give Reid their full attention.

"Let's say that you are madly in love with the person you are dating, and one day he or she comes up to you and says, 'Tonight is Gang-Bang Tuesday at an underground sex club. I'd like to participate in the group-sex activity and you can't be there. It's all healthy and done with respect.' How would you respond?"

Reid observes students shuffling in their seats. "Hang in there with me," he urges. "Assuming your partner is psychologically healthy, which is possible, what would your response be?"

"That's gross," says a female student.

"I'd tell her to F-off," says a male student in the back row.

The class erupts into heated comments. Reid lifts his hands above his head to signal for calmness.

"I'm glad you all have opinions. This is good." The class soon settles. "Please raise your hand to share your thoughts so we can explore this with some structure."

Katie, who sits in the front row, was enrolled in Reid's lecture classes in the spring. She raises her hand and Reid nods at her.

"You said last semester that cheating means one person is a lost soul with low self-esteem who can't appreciate their partner."

Reid smiles. "I was incorrect."

"So what would your response be to your question?" asks Katie.

"I'm glad you asked." Reid shifts his gaze to address the class. "You have a few options. The unhealthy option would be to freak out and tell her no."

"That's what I'd do," says a male voice from the back.

Reid grins and speaks slowly. "It's the most common response. However, in that moment you are choosing to control your partner's happiness. Are you her god? Did you create her? Have you been given the power to dictate her happiness, selecting what will or will not make her happy? She wants to participate in a group-sex activity and you tell her she can't."

"So what should I do?" says the male voice from the back.

"Accept all that she is," says Reid.

The class erupts with conflicting emotions. Reid understands their reaction from his statements, but he can't deny his new point of view.

"But I don't want to be with someone who wants to go to a sex club," says Katie.

"That's an excellent point to recognize," says Reid. "The person you are currently with enjoys group-sex activities and you do not. You cannot take the stripes off a zebra, and nor can you take a person who is not wired for monogamy and force them to be monogamous. Luckily, there are seven billion people on the planet — lots of potential to find a better match."

"But then that means we'd have to break up?" says a woman in the back.

"There are two healthy choices. The first choice is to stay with the person and support them on their quest for happiness. The second is to respectfully end the relationship while supporting them on their quest for happiness. Perhaps you could even offer them a ride to Gang-Bang Tuesday."

The class laughs. Reid takes that as a sign that their minds are opening to the concept.

"But the way you talked about your girlfriend last semester, you seemed like you'd never behave the way you are advising us to," says Katie.

"Funny you mention her. I've learned a lot since last semester. That's why I presented the question to the class." Reid straightens his spine. "I chose option two. I respectfully broke up with her. However, we've remained friends. In fact, last night I drove her to a gang-bang at an underground sex club. I dropped her off and picked her up when it was done."

Several students lean back in their desks. The class hums with befuddlement.

Reid continues to speak in a casual tone. "It was her first time. She said she enjoyed the power trip of being dominant. Men stood in line to take a chance at her, and she turned them into love slaves." Reid sees several jaws drop. "It's not something I'm wired to participate in, but I respect her courage in exploring her sexual curiosity."

Reid moves to stand behind the tall desk at the side of the stage. "Let people be who they are. Don't attempt to change anyone. You've been brought up in a society that thrives on people not living up to their full potential — it makes a person easy to control. The only way a person can access their full self is by exploring their light and dark sides. Pay attention to the moments where you freak out when someone chooses a path towards happiness that differs greatly from yours. Assuming physical harm is not caused to another human, accept their happiness quest and use your shock as a trigger point to explore further within."

Reid can't help but notice an erotic picture pop up on the screen of his cell phone, which is resting on the elevated desk. *Dammit. I told you not to text me during class.* The message is from Dani. It's a picture of a woman posing in a sexual manner. The woman is a ten-out-of-ten, knockout beauty. *I can't deal with that right now. There are sixty students staring at me.* Dani has been working hard to service clients on her own, but she's also eager to send Reid any potential employee she meets while out at night in Vegas. Dani and Reid agreed a few weeks back that it's best they not become involved romantically. They do share an ESE from time to time, but it's research based. They ask questions such as "How does this feel?" while exploring new techniques.

Reid looks at the wall clock, noticing it's time for class to end. The students begin to pack their things.

"Tomorrow is your final exam. Please arrive on time because I have a flight to catch as soon as the class session is complete." *I've gotta get back to Vegas to check on things.*

The students shuffle out of the classroom. Reid notices a female student in the back take longer to pack her things — Micah, the secret crush he had in class last semester. They haven't officially spoken to each other yet. And now she's walking towards him.

"Hi, Professor. My name is Micah. I really enjoyed today's lecture."

A warm sensation fills his body. Professor Reid Bradley is feeling Sexmyst Reid Bradley want to creep out. *Stay cool, man. You'll be in Vegas tomorrow, free to find plenty of women who won't get you in trouble. Just be sure to keep the desk between you and her.*

"Thank you. I appreciate any kind of feedback," says Reid. Micah looks toward the floor. He studies her nervous expression. "Is there something I can help you with?"

Reid hears the door slam in the rear section of the room. All of the students have left. He and Micah are now alone. He considers walking her to the hallway, where people are around, sensing that the two of them being alone could lead to trouble.

"There's something I want to talk about, but it's ..." Micah shifts the position of her feet. "It's kind of embarrassing. But your lecture today means that you'd be accepting of my questions, right?"

"I do my best to practice what I preach."

"How did you become so accepting of your scar?" asks Micah. "I have a scar too, but I'm embarrassed to let it show. I try to have my hair cover it."

"Scars are amazing. They're a beautiful part of the story of who we are. Where's your scar exactly?"

She steps around the desk so that she's now standing inches from Reid. He smells her sweet scent. *Uh oh, she's getting too close.* She carefully moves her hair to expose her neckline. Reid sees a scar that trails from the back of her ear down to her collarbone. Reid leans in to examine it. He suddenly feels her hand grab his fingers and lead them to her scar.

"Please feel it," she says. "Tell me that I'm not wrong for having this."

He feels Micah's petite fingers wrap around his index finger, then guide his fingertip along the scar. *No, no, no, this needs to stop.* She clearly needs something from him and he's a man of service. But this is too risky. He's not allowed to touch a student.

Micah doesn't let go; instead she guides his finger down the cleavage of her chest. "I can't stop thinking about you, Professor. You've made me see the world in a whole new way. And I think there is more inside you that you haven't shared with the class."

She releases his hand, grabs the back of his neck, and quickly pulls him down for a kiss. He can't help but absorb the magnificence of her soft lips. *This is so wrong, but the wrongness is irresistible.*

His newly polished animalistic instincts activate. With both of his hands, he grips her bottom tightly, lifts her, and places her on the desk. They lock lips for another passionate kiss. *This mission. The quest. My commitment to Wish. I can't lose my job. Get ahold of yourself, Reid.*

He pulls his lips away. His chest expands up and down with his heavy breathing. He sees Micah stare at him with adoring eyes.

"You're incredibly attractive," says Reid. "But this can't happen. It's too risky for both of us."

She lowers her head. "I'm sorry. I was out of line. I didn't expect that to happen. But as I got closer to you, I felt myself get sucked in. I really do just want to ask some questions."

"I understand. Please step behind the desk. That barrier will serve us well." Micah slides off the desk and saunters around as instructed. *I should ask her to leave. But she's so vulnerable right now. I need to make sure this ends respectfully, or she could easily use this against me.* "What is it that you would like to ask?"

"I love your class, but I hate school. In fact, I'm taking two other classes and failing those. I stopped going. But I can't wait to come to your class every day. I'm sad it's ending. I feel like there's so much more that I need to learn from you."

"What is it that you feel you need to learn more about?"

"This is so embarrassing. I can't believe I'm about to say this to you …"

"Please feel comfortable. I have no judgment and only look to serve as a guide," says Reid.

"I came back to school this semester because I want to get out of my current job. I've heard that education is the path to a great career. But none of the careers seem interesting to me. I used to love my job, but it requires me being around a lot of messed-up people. And I'm slowly not liking it anymore."

"What is it that you do for work right now?"

She takes a breath, lifts her head to glare at the ceiling, then returns her eyes to Reid. "I'm an adult-film actress. It was fun at first, but now they are making me do extreme scenes that are awkward, difficult, and quite painful. Last week, the director made me have sex on top of a grocery cart."

Reid swallows his gulp. "I'm honored you feel comfortable sharing such private information. What it is that you feel I can help you with?"

"Ever since I was thirteen, I've been fascinated by sex. The only thing that really interests me is sex. I can't really see myself working in a field that doesn't involve sex, but I know I can't stay in porn much longer. This class has helped me to see that I'm not a bad person for having the urges that I have, but I don't know what to do with my life." Micah's eyes begin to water.

Reid feels the need to touch her as a way to provide comfort, but resists the urge due to the potent sexual tension that's present. However, this resistance brings him to a realization. *Micah is one of us. She has the gene and doesn't understand why she struggles to fit in. She's a solider looking for the Erotic Army and doesn't know it exists.* But he can't recruit her just yet; that's a violation of school policy. Once her grade is officially turned in after tomorrow, though, he'll be legally free to interact with her.

"There are many paths you can take," says Reid. "I'm glad you have the physical and psychological awareness of how you're wired. The key for you will be to use that energy in a manner that serves others and, ultimately, serves the world."

"Serve the world with sex?"

"Yes, there is a way to do that. In fact, it may be part of your destiny. There's someone I recommend you contact. Her name is Dani, and she's figured out how to do what I've described to you. She was once in your shoes. She lives in Las Vegas." Reid writes Dani's number on a piece of paper. "Call her next week." *By then, Micah's grade will be officially posted.*

"Thank you, Professor. I'll definitely call her." Micah slides her bag over her shoulder and glides towards the door, then stops and turns back to Reid. "Will I lose points for what I did to you just now?"

"In this class, and in life, you will never lose points for taking courageous action. When you step into a fear, regardless of whether the outcome is positive or negative, you always walk away with an increase in self-knowledge and, ultimately, self-love. The people who never take courageous action are the people who remain stuck in the same place for their entire life."

She stands in awe of Reid's words. He notices her eyes squint as she appears to analyze him.

"You're so fucking hot, Professor." She giggles. "Is that another courageous act? Do I get more points?"

"You are quite the charmer." Reid shakes his head while smiling. "Just remember, the world desperately needs you to discover who you fully are. Acts of courage, often against societal norms, are the exact acts required for you to get to know your personal truth. Good luck on your exam tomorrow."

Reid watches as she leaves, and he smiles, realizing this meeting with Micah is about more than him simply helping one of his students. Somehow, just as last term when he fretted in this classroom while sensing that something was horribly wrong at home with Jasmine, he just knows that when Micah connects with Dani, something big will be the result.

Somehow he knows it's the first step in gathering the Erotic Army.

JOIN THE EROTIC ARMY TODAY!!

SUBSCRIBE TO THE EMAIL LIST

FOR SPECIAL GIVEAWAYS

AND ANNOUNCEMENTS

ON FUTURE BOOKS IN THIS SERIES

www.brandonwadebooks.com

Made in the USA
San Bernardino, CA
11 May 2020